FROM HEADLINES
TO HARD TIMES

ED MITCHELL
FROM HEADLINES TO HARD TIMES

I WENT FROM PRESENTING THE NEWS TO SLEEPING
ROUGH. THIS IS THE TRUE STORY OF MY RISE TO THE
TOP, MY DEMISE AND MY SALVATION.

JOHN BLAKE

Published by John Blake Publishing Ltd,
3 Bramber Court, 2 Bramber Road,
London W14 9PB, England

www.johnblakepublishing.co.uk

First published in hardback in 2009

ISBN: 978 1 84454 684 8

British Library Cataloguing-in-Publication Data:

A catalogue record for this book is available from the British Library.

Design by www.envydesign.co.uk

Printed in the UK by CPI William Clowes Beccles NR34 7TL

1 3 5 7 9 10 8 6 4 2

Papers used by John Blake Publishing are natural, recyclable products made from
wood grown in sustainable forests. The manufacturing processes conform to the
environmental regulations of the country of origin.

Every attempt has been made to contact the relevant copyright-holders, but some were
unobtainable. We would be grateful if the appropriate people could contact us.

To Alex and Freddie
Carpe diem, quam minimum credula postero.

ACKNOWLEDGMENTS

L uck, timing and coincidence refracted through many people made this book possible. I'd like to thank them here.

I'm grateful to Merv, Phil, Steve and Andy at Off the Fence for creating the chance to get me off the bench. Jessica at the *Brighton Argus* for setting the media ball rolling. Sian and Nick at *The Mail on Sunday* for their balanced and sustained coverage. Emma, David, Irene and Mel at Twofour productions whose two documentaries made several things possible. Amanda at Exclusive PR for her constant support and understanding. Diane for opening doors. John Blake for saying yes and Michelle for seeing it through. Dan for arranging the vital 28 days at the Priory Roehampton.

On a more personal level, I'd like to thank Ian in Puerto Duquesa for his encouragement and Neil for being there at an important moment. Mandy's love and support kept me going for the last year; without her I would have stumbled. Ann and Bernie for their warmth and sustenance.

Alex and Freddie who never gave up on me. Judy for doing so much – maybe it wasn't my time. And to my Mother for her constant selflessness.

CONTENTS

PREFACE

I wrote this book sober. A year ago that would not have been possible. It felt good. I didn't need alcohol to enjoy it or to inspire me. Having spent 40 years drinking, the last 10 heavily, and having lost absolutely everything as a result, for me it was nothing short of a miracle.

Through addiction to alcohol, I'd unconsciously built a cramped and gloomy prison whose stones were made of self-delusion, whose fetters were wrought from blindness and whose jailer was me. I constructed it brick by brick despite warnings from others, but eventually I needed help to make my escape.

My break for freedom was the outcome of a remarkable stroke of luck. Without the intervention of fate I would still be incarcerated – perhaps for eternity. I grabbed at the chance to get out. I had nothing left to lose.

I am still sober and I am filled with gratitude to those who threw me that lifeline. Today I am no longer a slave to alcohol but enjoying freedom outside the prison and in the glorious sunshine.

But I shall never forget the dark hell I was in, or those who still suffer in that bleak place now.

Though my soul may set in darkness
It will rise in perfect light.
I have loved the stars too fondly
To be fearful of the night.

Sarah Williams, 'THE OLD ASTRONOMER TO HIS PUPIL'

PROLOGUE
A WET AND SMELLY ROCK BOTTOM

The freezing rain was blasting out of the night hard into my face; needles driven by the gale-force wind, glinting orange in the promenade lights. Shoes squelching and eyes blinded, I desperately needed shelter.

The storm was powering in from the south-west. My bolt-hole would have to be east-facing. Half a mile ahead was the Babylon Lounge, its neon sign flickering in the distance a blurry and malfunctioning blue – Bablo Louge. Behind its battered seafront exterior was a courtyard garden surrounded by a wall and a dozen covered benches.

After slogging along bent at 45 degrees to the headwind for about a mile, it was a huge relief to turn into the garden. The howling wind dropped immediately and all I could hear was the roar of the sea. A couple of rusted lights barely illuminated huddled black shapes lying on two of the benches.

I was drenched, worn out by endlessly pounding the streets and just glad to get my rucksack off. Earlier in the day, somehow I'd managed to take my eye off my sleeping bag and it was now keeping someone else warm. Tonight I had two borrowed and well-used blankets – better than nothing.

Stretched out on the wooden seat, rucksack as a pillow, I took a long slug of Chekov vodka from a quarter-bottle. Almost immediately the liquid sunshine hit my brain and limbs – the world seemed bearable again. The wet, wind-whipped palm trees thrashed wildly in the garden. The rain swirled in every direction just beyond my shelter. I was beginning to drift off into an alcohol-induced sleep.

Feverish and fitful dreams of the usual missed trains, planes and broadcasting deadlines led to the inevitable search-for-a-toilet dream. My straining bladder was telling me to wake up. So was the weather. The storm had subsided, the skies had cleared and the temperature had plummeted. My body was shaking with the cold, my vodka breath condensing. But there was something else – something even more unpleasant.

During the night, my two borrowed blankets had slipped off me and on to the concrete floor, disturbing a large pile of dog's excrement – at least I think it was a dog's. I leaned over to pull the blankets out of the pungent mess, which neatly allowed the bottle of vodka to slide out of my pocket and smash – my life-saving medicine mingling with the shit and glass.

Was this rock bottom? How much rockier can it get? Anything lower and I'd be six feet under. I was 'street homeless', recently divorced, jobless, bankrupt, had lost my car, licence, passport and had just £1.42 in my pocket. I had no one to blame, nor did I want to. No complaints, no whinging and only suppressed regrets. I just felt sick, tired and frustrated.

How could an apparently intelligent, physically able, 54-year-old family man, a business journalist for 30 years, someone softened by 25 years of marriage, the comforts of a family home and frequent foreign holidays, end up as a near-penniless alcoholic dossing down on a park bench?

All too easily and thoughtlessly.

All it took was many thousands of subconscious, self-sabotaging, drink-clouded life choices. It was the inevitable result of a million, tiny, unnoticed, easy options, rather than a few, tough right decisions. I'd always pulled the warm, comfortable duvet of drink over my head.

How do you get out of the ever-tightening circles of a downward spiral? People would say, 'Get a grip, get your arse in gear, get a job, get somewhere to live, pull your socks up, stop whining (even if you're not), snap out of it, just stop drinking.' And I would answer, 'Yup, you're absolutely right.' But then think to myself, But how? It just isn't as easy as that. I've unintentionally made my own prison and now every escape route is blocked.

Facing up to the numbing cold, the nauseating smell of dog's faeces, the aching joints, the shame and the gnawing craving for alcohol, I could feel my reserves of strength running out. Was all this really happening to me? I felt like the same me, but I was helplessly watching the relentless decline of a dosser who just happened to be me.

How do I pull myself out of this mess?

It was mid-December; it could only get colder. All my attempts at getting a job, or a roof over my head had failed. It was a few days before I could get any money and less than a fortnight to Christmas. If I was going to get out of this hole, I needed a huge stroke of luck. Where's your Higher Power when you need it most?

1

STREET HOMELESS

The bench was not the place to dwell on my problems. I had to get on with another day on the streets. The rank smell of dog's muck was a big incentive to move. I consoled myself with the thought, 'This too Shall Pass'. Surely this life would not go on for ever.

I shouldered my rucksack, cleared the broken vodka bottle and ditched the pink, blue and now partially brown blankets. I tiptoed past two snoring bundles, anonymous bodies buried under many layers. It was always a relief to be back on the move. I had survived another night.

My bench was just a few yards from the beach. It was good to get a lung full of bracing Channel air. I pulled my woolly hat down tightly on my head, adjusted my backpack and headed off east.

After the night's storm the sea was brown, still with a powerful swell and full tide. The screeching seagulls were enjoying a free ride on the chilly breeze, looking for whatever had been churned up by the water. The air was crystal clear and smelled of salt, fish and something oily. In the east the horizon was turquoise above a thin layer of pink and orange. An icy Venus twinkled brightly in the south-east.

I'd been without a permanent roof over my head for a year and street homeless for about three months. I'm not a complete softie, but getting through long days and even longer freezing nights was certainly a challenge. There's a lot to learn about the basics of urban survival. Food, water, warm clothing, safe shelter and eking out a few quid are obviously basic essentials, but just as important was keeping hope alive. Not all drunks have to be 'hopeless' drunks.

Perhaps in the same way that I had unintentionally slipped into destitution, I held on to the belief that something would turn up, even if I couldn't think what 'it' could possibly be. All I had to do was to be sufficiently in possession of my faculties to spot 'it' when it did.

There were personal standards that I wanted to maintain. I never wanted to smell. I was never going to wallow in self-pity. I was never going to beg and the last thing I wanted was for anyone to know how bad things had got. I was also keen to avoid being seen drinking alcohol in public. It was illegal anyway.

I was definitely a tramp, but I was determined not to look like one. Although it's *de rigueur* in vagrant society to eschew washing, shaving and the barber's, I was not going to take on the prevailing grunge look. Missing teeth, facial tattoos, body-piercing, a dog on a rope and the repetitive use of the word 'fuck' were out of my league.

It was an hour before the off-licence along the seafront opened, so the first stop was the public lavatory about 200 yards east of the Babylon Lounge. It's a prize-winning toilet with hot water, an air dryer and mirrors, and it opened early. It was kept clean by a dedicated woman known to her homeless clientele as Ma Mop. As her name suggests, she maintained a spotless floor and sparkling porcelain. The plastic flowers over the store cupboard were a particularly thoughtful touch.

Washed, shaved and aromatic, I headed to the nearest Londis convenience shop near to the soon-to-be demolished King Alfred Leisure Centre. Thank goodness for cheap, powerful cider. White Ice, White Star and Frosty Jack are about a quid a litre and 7.5 per cent alcohol; they are quenching, mood-improving and have a subtle hint of apples. Consumed with a lump of strong cheese at bedtime, this robust aviation fuel could produce wild and highly detailed hallucinations. It had the added benefit of being a reliable laxative.

Self-medicated and with a lingering after-taste, I set out further east along the promenade. Red-faced joggers struggled past in various stages of pain, constantly glancing at their watches to suggest their seriousness. Jogging rarely looks fun. Cyclists flashed arrogantly by down the no-cycling prom apparently oblivious to pedestrians. Dog walkers were out in force, occasionally stopping to scoop poop. One of them – the dogs, that is – may have left my malodorous bedside gift last night.

I felt invisible to all these normal people. I'd slipped through the cracks of society. After 25 years of marriage and fatherhood, 30 years of tax-paying and pension-contributing work, a quarter-century of house and car ownership and a wallet formerly packed with gold and platinum credit cards, I now owned a rucksack and a pocket full of mostly copper coins.

As a new bankrupt and of no fixed abode, I had no bank or savings account, no council tax or utility bills. Eighteen months previously I'd lost my driving licence and more recently my passport had gone astray. I had also effectively slipped below the Inland Revenue's radar. My only official connection to the state was my National Insurance number and, to the outside world, my near-dormant mobile phone.

I was a promenade ghost, a seaside spectre. But, perhaps I was more *spectator* than spectre – a detached observer of my own condition.

Big Brother was also watching over me though. I glanced up at an ugly, intimidating 35ft-high CCTV camera that stared down the length of the promenade. Maybe someone somewhere was observing me (or through me). Maybe I was on television again. I gave a cheery and professional wave just in case.

Hope, a residue of pride and alcohol kept me going. But there were more practical matters. As well as staying clean, healthy and safe, it was also about keeping active and desperately trying to find a way out of the homeless trap. An extremely limited budget meant doing things that didn't cost money. Days were filled with walking to Hove or Brighton libraries, visits to the JobCentrePlus, Brighton Council's accommodation department, the Christian charity Off the Fence, Brighton Housing Trust's First Base and the regular soup runs. I was covering about 20 miles a day by foot and despite the alcohol intake – or perhaps because of it – I was about two stone lighter than when I had a home. My only luxury was reading – I was nearing the end of the whole Ian Rankin series. Thank goodness for charity shops.

That morning I headed straight for First Base. It's an organisation that, among other things, acts as a safety net for the street homeless offering various advice services and help, plus food, showers and computer access. They've got a hell of a workload in Brighton. Officially, at the time, it was said there were 12 street homeless in the city, but that figure was just ridiculous. Even the most conservative estimate from those on the street was ten times that figure. Even I personally knew 12 by name.

The early session, from 8am to 11am four days a week, was for genuine rough sleepers. To qualify officially as a 'rough sleeper' you not only had to be sleeping rough, but it was also necessary to be *found* sleeping rough by, yes, the rough sleepers' team. This could sometimes be a bit rough. They tended to do their inspection tours in a limited area and mostly after most street sleepers had packed their kit and moved on for the day. Intriguingly you would not be classed as a 'rough sleeper' if you were found sitting upright. You had to be horizontal and preferably unconscious. That second bit was easy.

When I was first faced with no alternative but to sleep out, I went to places that I had lived near, away from the city centre, where I felt slightly safer. In Portslade village, about three or four miles north-west of the centre, there was a very neat, well-kept and secluded walled garden which was rarely visited in the day. Its wrought-iron gate was locked at dusk but was easily climbed.

That's where I bedded down for a few weeks – under the Chusan palm or the eucalyptus tree. But it was well beyond the visits of the rough sleepers' team. Once I got to know the system, I moved to the area behind the seafront nightclub called the Babylon Lounge, or 'the hotel' as rough sleepers knew it. Even then it took a while for me to be found officially asleep and prone.

But, having become a fully fledged rough sleeper myself, I was grateful for what First Base provided. It was always important to get to their premises on Montpelier Place, behind Waitrose, as near to opening time as possible. That way the porridge was still hot and most of the bread, jam and Marmite hadn't been wolfed. The showers were also relatively hair-free.

It's a two-mile hike from the Babylon to First Base, but that day, with a little help from my bottle of jet fuel, which had the same effect on my joints as WD40, there was a relative smoothness in my step. My back, painful from another night on the bench, had eased up, a brilliant sun was silhouetting what was left of the West Pier and I felt at one with my Maker.

My universe had been distilled down to the simple business of staying alive and making sure I could afford a bottle or can of cider – all other worries and stresses had been stripped away. It's not a sustainable way of life – indeed, if pursued during the winter it will only lead to increasing ill-health – but at that moment it felt OK. There's a lot to be said for focus and purpose, however limited. For me it was about survival, a full stomach, peace of mind and the hope that something better would come along, despite all the frustrated efforts so far.

No alcohol is allowed on the premises at First Base, so I hid what was left of my morning supplies in my stomach. Outside there was a small gathering of rough sleepers looking pretty bedraggled and, well, rough. It seemed they couldn't get in because they hadn't been judged to be rough sleepers. Maybe they had no local connections or they slept upright.

I rang the bell and after a short delay a friendly face – Claire – appeared at a small window in the door. Thoughts of a Prohibition-era speakeasy went through my mind.

'Morning, Ed. How was your night?'

'Wet and breezy with an unwelcome deposit left by my bed, but I woke up breathing. It's a beautiful morning,' I replied.

I was always just glad to get in. Street homelessness is street homelessness, however you judge it, but I always lived in fear that they would say I didn't look rough enough to qualify, and turn me away. 'You're too tidy to be a tramp – there's no room at the inn.' They never did, but maybe alcohol-induced paranoia was setting in.

Once inside I recognised a few familiar faces – most of them looking pretty knackered. There was an all-pervading smell of old, wet clothes. A big tureen of porridge bubbled away and there was a large tray full of white and brown bread. Top priority, though, was a big mug of coffee. About ten early birds were dotted around a dozen round tables spaced out in the chapel hall. An industrial-sized fan heater noisily blew hot air across the room. Most people kept themselves to themselves, lost in their own private thoughts. There was a low murmur of conversation, quite a bit of it in various East European tongues.

Even at that time of day there was an old chap playing on an upright piano in the corner. He was actually pretty good. I'd recently found out his name was Ray Saxby. Ray was in his early eighties and had been a music-hall star in the 1950s. He was the model for the part played by Will Young in the film *Mrs Henderson Presents*, set in the Windmill Theatre in Soho.

Busying herself around the wastepaper baskets and bins was an elderly lady who I'd been told was Olive. She had spent a large part of her life recycling various materials, some of which she was able to sell. Over the decades she had apparently made £40,000 which she then gave to charity. Everyone knew her as 'Green Olive'.

I'd fixed an interview that day with Debbie, one of the advisers at the Housing Trust. I had pretty well come to the end of the line in terms of getting some sort of accommodation. Over the previous nine months I'd talked to various members of Brighton Council's housing team, but it always produced the same brick wall. In that time I'd seen at least eight different individuals.

The Council's accommodation drop-in centre was in Bartholomew Square, right next to the Town Hall. It seemed that, however early I got there, it was already full. There was always a baby crying, even if there wasn't actually one to be seen. All colours, creeds and religions were represented in the queue. Occasionally, a drunk would wander in, utter a few words of abuse at the 'system' and wander out snarling. I spent many fruitless hours there, but got through a lot of books.

The system at Brighton Housing Trust, up Queens Road towards the station, was not much better. The office opened at 9.15am on certain days of the week. I was advised to get there early. Given I had no other pressing engagements, I got there more than an hour before it opened. There was already one person sitting by the entrance. A notice on the window said that 'due to staff shortages' only four people could be dealt with that day. 'Please collect your ticket as you enter.' Within half an hour there were about 20 restless people in the queue. A youngish man, heavily tattooed (cobweb motif), unsteady on his feet, placed himself at the head of the line. Pushing, shoving and shouting developed and he decided to totter off, probably unaware of where he was, what he wanted or what had happened.

As a male aged between 18 and 65 and not disabled or mentally ill, I was quite simply 'non-priority'. Week after week I was not getting anywhere. But what might make me slightly more of a priority? At 54, pregnancy was beyond me. Alcoholism may be classed in some quarters as a disease, but to Brighton Council it was simply a 'lifestyle choice'. So that wasn't going to work as a tactic, and anyway every homeless person I knew was heavily reliant on alcohol. Given the insecurity and difficulty of sleeping and the increasing cold, alcohol wasn't really a choice, it was a necessity.

For a number of years I'd been suffering from acid reflux as a result of a hiatus hernia. The outcome was that the cells in my oesophagus, or gullet, had changed in nature and were increasingly narrowing my food channel; that made swallowing difficult and painful – particularly meat. It can be a precursor to cancer, and that was worrying. There was no doubt in my mind that the stress of being on the streets was making it worse. To be honest, gulping neat vodka and aviation cider probably didn't help, but it certainly dulled the pain.

Anyway I tried to make the case that this condition made me more of a priority because sleeping rough was making the illness worse and could make it life-threatening. Well, it was worth a try. Previously the Council had argued that it didn't make me a priority because I could easily get soup or baby food.

That morning Debbie thought it was worth having another go with the Council. The Housing Trust were in constant legal battles with them – fights that the Trust seemed more often than not to win. She did say, though, that the chances were slim. It was, she said, 'a complete jungle out there'. Recent changes in legislation had meant that the whole system was far more complicated. There were dozens of agencies operating, no one would move without a referral from someone else, but you needed a referral to get a referral. The entire byzantine edifice was being strangled by red tape and lack of funding. I had to do something, though, given that the last thing the Council had said to me was 'buy a tent'.

Debbie said she would ring around and send some emails, but she did admit it would take some time, particularly with the holidays coming up. It really was looking like Christmas on the bench.

First Base also provided a wholesome basic lunch for about 50 pence, although you could get free vouchers from a church in the centre of Brighton. An agitated and expectant queue generally formed a few minutes before noon, stretching to about 30–40 hungry homeless. They were not all street homeless – many were in temporary shelters, which, from my attempts to get in, I knew were all full in Brighton. Those who managed to get a place in the shelters generally stayed for the winter.

The hall was now almost full. Meals were shovelled down. The urgency of filling empty bellies was reflected in the style of eating – hurried, possessive and slightly furtive as if someone was going to steal the food. There was a great deal of coughing, sniffing and a fair amount of good-natured banter mostly in a gruff, earthy and repetitive way. There seemed to be a need to show how tough you were, how hard things were and what bum cards life had dealt you.

There is a form of camaraderie among the dispossessed of society – the shared sense there's nothing left to lose. Although we looked out for one another, there was also an element of the survival of the fittest. Well, maybe not the fittest, more the most ruthless and crafty. Everyone kept their meagre possessions very close by.

It was good to talk to people there, because street homelessness can be a lonely business. Sometimes I could go several days without speaking to anyone. For a relative newcomer like me, it was also vital to pick up any information and experience from the old hands. In my case that meant where to get a replacement sleeping bag and the location and timing of the next soup run.

My next port of call was Hove Library, opposite St Andrew's Church, about a mile and a half back in Hove.

I stopped off in the churchyard for a chat with several vagrants who regularly gathered among the gravestones. It's a relatively secluded spot, squeezed between Church Road and a big Tesco and within stumbling distance of a competitively priced off-licence, Mulhollands. The cemetery used to be a relaxing place to sit and contemplate the proximity of mortality, but all the benches had been removed and the gravestones were now observed by two CCTV cameras and regularly visited by the police. It was good to know that, if the dead should ever be resurrected, it would be caught on videotape.

It also used to adjoin the playing field of my children's primary school, St Andrew's C of E, before it was sold and became Tesco's car park. In those days kids would go to the bottom of the field and tease the tramps in the cemetery, who would reply with a hail of empty beer cans. Interestingly, the school field covered what was a much larger graveyard, so the tarmac now seals in the remains of many hundreds of Hove's forefathers. People in Hove now say when they shiver, 'A shopping trolley just passed over me.'

There were two rough sleepers that I knew there – Dave, a chap in his late twenties who was beginning to look more than 40. His hair was long and lank and his face had the appearance of 'peat-bog man'. Each time I met him he had more teeth missing and a few more bruises. He had teamed up with an older woman, Gloria. She had long grey hair roughly pulled back into a pony tail and had a weather-beaten face. Like all the female street homeless I'd met, she had a front tooth missing. Today she also had an impressive black eye.

The two of them were sharing a three-litre plastic bottle of Frosty Jack and were fairly drunk, but pleasant. They seemed to be educated and quite well-spoken. They offered a swig from the bottle and I happily accepted. Long gone were the days when I cared who I shared a drink with. I reckoned this strength of cider killed all known germs.

'What's your name again?' said Dave. He asked the same question every time we met.

'Hi, Dave. I know it's a difficult one to remember, but my name's Ed.'

'Yeah, sorry. You got any spare coins?' Again the same question every time.

'No, you're out of luck, I've just got enough for one can to get me through the night.'

'Gloria and me are getting out of here. We're heading to the West Country. Can't stand it here any more. The police are giving us a bad time. Bastards.'

Gloria and Dave had been leaving for the West Country for as long as I'd known them. I wished them well, but I knew they'd always be around as long as their health didn't deteriorate any further. Just before I went, Gloria caught my arm and looked me in the eye as well as she could and said, 'Someone like you who's got an education should tell people about what it's like to live rough. Go on, Ed, why don't you write something in the papers? You could write a bloody book about it!'

I crossed Church Road to the library. I liked to read *The Times* every day if possible and, at 70 pence, it was too expensive to buy.

Without any doubt the very worst aspect of being homeless and on Job Seekers Allowance of less than £60 per week was simply not having any money to do even the simplest things. Once money is taken out for the mobile phone – the last link to civilisation – bus fares, train fares, food, basic toiletries, occasional repairs and replacements and of course the cheapest booze (fortunately, I don't smoke), it's pretty near impossible to get through the fortnight without facing several days with absolutely nothing in your pocket. Money by itself may not buy happiness, but the complete absence of it does make life extremely difficult and frustrating.

There is a facility called a 'crisis loan' which can get you through a crisis, but it has to be paid back out of your Job Seekers Allowance, and anyway there's always a crisis. Totally skint, I'd got into the habit of walking along the street looking in the gutters, around benches and bus stops in case anyone had dropped some coins. I was getting a permanent 'gutter-crick' in my neck. People only ever seemed to drop copper coins – perhaps they thought they weren't worth bending down for.

The library was nearly full and someone already had the one copy of *The Times*. I made do with Ian Rankin's novel *Set in Darkness* until the newspaper became available. It was the same old faces in there – mostly retired or unemployed. They all seemed to sniff constantly and obliviously, turning the pages of the newspapers aggressively while muttering about the state of the country. Were they actually taking anything in or just going through the motions?

The low murmur of reading, breathing and sniffing was frequently interrupted by the screech of a heavy oak chair as someone got up. The big advantage of the library, apart from the free reading material, was that it was warm and dry and had a huge, lockable toilet and hot water. The top of the cistern always seemed to be oddly covered with a thin layer of white dust.

My joints were beginning to stiffen up and the afternoon was wearing on. I began to think about another night on the bench. I had to get a sleeping bag from somewhere. I'd heard that morning that Off the Fence were giving them away free.

Their anonymous-looking office was in Portland Road, Hove, about a mile west of the library. Net curtains hid the interior from the outside world and made it look like a solicitor's or maybe a chiropodist's. Inside there was just room for about six or seven people to sit. In the back was a small office and kitchen. There was a fridge, hot drinks, free sandwiches and three computers for anyone's use.

The place was run by some kindly souls, Merv, Phil and Steve, among others, who were always very welcoming and generous. The idea was to offer the dispossessed and homeless some comfort and companionship and perhaps an introduction to the Christian faith. Once I even saw Steve washing the feet of one particularly elderly and footsore tramp. (Perhaps it was a chiropodist's.) Seeing that sort of pure altruism in action brought a lump to my throat.

They took a fair bit of flak from my fellow vagrants with admirable stoicism. It struck me that almost all of those who went there regularly were non-believers, and some were pretty hard-nosed, if inarticulate, atheists.

I enjoyed a good-natured religious debate, however futile it might be. The end result would always be the same: 'Well, it's a matter of faith, and if you don't have faith you will never understand.'

Fair enough. I certainly didn't expect any Damascene experiences after half a century of scepticism. Given the overwhelming evidence of everyday life and history, it has always been difficult for me to believe in a personal God who intervenes in human life on the side of good and responds to individual prayer. An all-powerful, all-knowing and all-loving God surely would never permit evil. I do have a deep-seated awareness of some sort of Universal Divine that sustains existence and that our rather elementary human consciousness gives us only a hint of something larger than ourselves, some sort of Higher Power.

That day my Higher Power did appear to intervene on the side of good – in the form of a brand-new, top-of-the-range sleeping bag. Having virtually nothing, I found a gift like that just wonderful. It would also be a life-saver. Not only that, I was given a new pair of gloves and a hat – both Thinsulate, no less.

Before I left, Merv, who knew I had been a journalist and broadcaster in a previous life, casually mentioned that an Off the Fence team would be coming round that night to the well-known seafront benches with coffee and sandwiches – something they did fairly regularly. One of the volunteers, he said, happened to work for Brighton's local paper, the *Argus*, and would I be willing to have a chat about how things were for me? Since I only slept fitfully and enjoyed a midnight natter, I agreed willingly.

That evening I returned to Hove seafront and watched the sun go down at about half past four. The sky was clear and the temperature was falling rapidly, but I now had a good-quality hat, gloves and a sleeping bag. My luck seemed to be in – I'd found a pound coin in the gutter, and that went towards a nightcap.

Around 8pm I was tucked up on my usual (but now, thankfully cleaned-up) bench behind the Baylo Lunge and had drifted off into some sort of sleep, when I was woken by flashing torches. It was the Off the Fence team. They were always very friendly and whoever was on the benches – that night there was only one other – took the opportunity to down several hot drinks and stock up on sandwiches and chocolate. You never knew where the next supply might come from.

The conversation ranged over the usual philosophical and religious subjects and then after a prayer for our safety and souls – which, even as an agnostic, I was willing to say 'Amen' to – one of the team, Andy, said, 'I hear you used to work for the BBC and ITN. Merv told me you had big debt problems and had fallen on hard times. I was thinking it might make a good story... You know, a couple of weeks to Christmas, people running up debts, no room at the inn, "riches-to-rags", all that sort of thing. Is it OK if I take your mobile number and pass it on to one of my colleagues at the *Argus*?'

Why not? As a journalist I could see it might make a brief seasonal story. I had nothing left to lose. I'd ceased to care what people thought. Maybe some good might come out of it. Maybe nothing at all.

'Sure, no problem. I'd be glad to.'

My night visitors left me to the darkness. In the east Sirius glinted crisply. The roar of the seafront traffic began to fade. The Bbylo Loune was shut for the night, and all I could hear was the rhythmic sound of the sea raking the pebbles and the buzz of snoring coming from two benches away. I soon joined in.

2

NON-PRIORITY

For months now I had been desperately trying to avoid being homeless. I'd pushed the awful possibility to the back of my mind in the hope that something would turn up. But as time went by nothing did. I just kept thinking, or perhaps deluding myself, that it couldn't happen to me.

The house I owned with my family in Portslade sold within three days of going on the market – an easy £4,000 fee for the estate agent. Because I had buried my head in the sand and alcohol for so long, I hadn't much idea what I was going to do next. My wife, Judy, and I had recently divorced and she was moving into a place of her own with our son, Freddie, while my daughter, Alex, had been living independently for some time.

At that stage I had about £200,000 of credit-card and bank debt in my name, which, even at minimum monthly payments, was difficult to sustain on a reasonable salary and impossible on Job Seekers Allowance. Just to tread water, it was costing more than £2,500 per month in interest alone. The ultimate outcome of that simple arithmetic was obvious even to someone whose brain was dulled by alcohol. No amount of twisting and turning or fancy financial footwork could dig me out of that hole. It would be a monetary albatross round my neck until the grave.

What I needed to do was keep the cards and bank account going as long as possible by using the 40 per cent share I would get of the net equity from the house. It was about six months' worth of minimum payments on the credit cards. That would make sure that Judy was completely distanced from my financial black hole.

More pressing was the question of what on earth could I do with my clothes and books, the only possessions I wanted to keep from a quarter of a century of marriage. I've never particularly liked owning things (must be something to do with being a Piscean) and it felt like a breath of fresh air to be free of years of clutter.

My mother's mostly empty garage in Lancing was the only possible temporary option. It might have had a serious roof leak and was certainly not a place for anyone with arachnophobia, but the alternative was expensive storage. So I hired a van to shift what stuff I had to Lancing, plus what the professional removal people weren't able to take to Judy's in Portslade.

It was a long and hot day that went on till the evening. I thought a few beers would be my reward. Unfortunately, driving a white van after dark in certain areas attracted the attention of the police.

I was pulled over, breathalysed and failed the roadside test. Drinking and driving is, of course, inexcusable under any circumstances, so it was a fair cop, but I thought the over-tight handcuffs behind my back and a night in the police cells in

Hollingbury security station were a tad unnecessary. I was a perfectly compliant and lucid prisoner, but it didn't prevent me going through 17 very long hours of solitary. The endless screaming and shouting of my fellow prisoners was unsettling.

The case came up within a few days and I was banned for 18 months and given the same time on probation. Mercifully there was no fine, but I was ordered to attend an evening course to learn more about alcohol and the impact it has on one's ability to drive. It was a 15-week course in Lewes, about six miles from Brighton, with each weekly session lasting two hours. However important it was to drum in the lesson that no one should drink and drive, even the most slow-witted pupil probably doesn't need 30 hours to grasp the point.

I wasn't alone among the group of 12 offenders attending the course to find it a bit repetitive and wearing. It certainly got off to a poor start when we were divided into two teams and set the task of putting together a structure out of newspapers and sellotape. Whoever built the tallest paper tower won. It was apparently all about bonding and teamwork, but I had the nagging feeling the contest wasn't that relevant to drinking and driving.

After a couple of weeks of this, a few of us chose to have a few pre-lecture beers in the many pubs of Lewes. One evening I lingered a little too long in the White Hart and arrived late for the lesson, almost certainly smelling of Harvey's Special. The result was that I was removed from the course, which I would have to retake at a later date.

It also meant another court appearance. The magistrate imposed the penalty of 40 hours of community service, which I chose to serve in one go – eight hours a day for five days. I thoroughly enjoyed it. Each day began with an early-morning meeting at the offices of the Probation Service at the Steine in Brighton. There were about eight or ten of us on community service, some doing several hundred hours. We'd all be transported by minibus to a different venue around Sussex. Each day involved a different job. We never knew whether it would be painting, weeding, landscape gardening or mucking out animals at a wildlife centre.

One of the days was devoted to cleaning rabbit hutches. It was useful activity, although by the tenth hutch I was losing a bit of enthusiasm for repaying the community. But, by the end of the week, I did have a real sense of worth and achievement.

Those in charge of the community service programme ran it in a disciplined but friendly way and the mostly young offenders put real effort into the tasks. I wasn't convinced that wearing a chain-gang-type high-visibility bib increased awareness of paying back society given that almost all the jobs were not in the public eye. Anyway, since every public-sector worker seems to wear high-vis clothing in the streets, we offenders would have just merged into the background.

As it turned out, I never did go back to the drink-driving lectures in Lewes, because no other courses could be organised before my 18-month probation was over. I'm certain I don't know any less about the dangers and irresponsibility of drink-driving. I do know a lot more about rabbits.

Weekly probation attendance was just something that had to be done. The probation officer was pleasant enough, but, as soon it was clear that I was not a problem, it all became routine. Actually it turned out to be rather useful, because she put me in touch with a financial adviser at the Citizens' Advice Bureau. The CAB suggested the only realistic way I could deal with my disastrous financial state was to petition for personal bankruptcy. Ironically, it costs nearly £500 to go bankrupt, which at that stage I certainly didn't have.

Thankfully, they gave me the details of the Newspaper Press Fund, a journalists' charity based in Dorking which exists to help those in the profession who have fallen on hard times. They very generously provided the money.

The actual bankruptcy process was surprisingly straightforward. When the judge looked at the forms detailing the size of my debt, my recent divorce and the fact that I was unemployed, on probation and homeless, he said, 'My dear chap! I wish you luck,' and quickly stamped them. There was absolutely nothing the Official Receiver could take from me except the contents of my rucksack and some damp suits and a few hundred paperbacks in a leaking garage. It was a massive burden lifted from my shoulders – a burden that sadly has led many in a similar position to take their own lives.

All this was a distraction from working out where I was going to live. Initially and briefly, I went to my mother's place, but it was clear very early on that it was not a sustainable option. At 82, she deserved to enjoy her own company in her twilight years, and anyway what man in his mid-fifties wants to be back at his childhood home?

But I had to have my kit somewhere, I had to have a 'care of' address and, being a complete novice at this homelessness business, I was quite simply scared of sleeping rough. I just never really believed that was what it would come to.

Over the previous few months I'd been getting on very well with a girl called Mandy, who was helpful and good company. There's no doubt that we shared an interest in drinking. She was living in a flat in Hove with her parents, Ann and Bernie, and, knowing the difficult position I was in, offered to put me up for a while.

It worked well for some time, but it's fair to say that my

increasingly heavy drinking was not going down a storm in the household and it was made pretty clear to me that I should leave. I made a couple of further 'undercover' returns. At that time the outside of the three-storey building was being refurbished and so was covered in scaffolding. Late one night alcohol suggested it would be a good idea to climb the scaffolding and say hello to Mandy through her top-floor window. Somehow I made it, even though the ladders had been removed.

The next night, convinced I was now an experienced climber, I decided to do the same thing. Once again I made it, despite the fact that the topmost layer of scaffolding had been removed. How I scaled the last ten feet through thin air I will never know. In the cold, sober light of the morning, I gazed down at the 60ft drop and reminded myself that I was in my mid-fifties and scared of heights.

During that time I was making frequent visits to Brighton Council's Housing Department but was making no headway. There was just simply no way I could get out of the category of 'non-priority'. The Council did not have a 'duty of care' to house me because I was not classed as being sufficiently vulnerable.

Out of the blue I received a call saying that I could have temporary accommodation at an address in Hove if I got there by five o'clock, before the caretaker left. At the time I was ten miles away and it was four o'clock, so my only choice was to spend my last £15 on a taxi.

I arrived just as the caretaker, an Iranian, was hurrying to leave the building. He explained he was late for his flight to Tehran, but he just had time to show me up the almost one hundred steps to the top-floor room. It was extremely small with just a bed, a desk, a chair and a sink. Previous residents had clearly not been house-proud, but I wasn't expecting much for a weekly service charge of ten quid. There was quite a good view over the Hove rooftops towards the west, where the sun was beginning to set. The caretaker thrust a wad of electricity meter cards in my hand and left for the airport. I never saw him again.

The room was one of about 20 in a Regency terrace at the top of Brunswick Place, an area known for students, immigrants and the temporarily housed – DSS-land. It was a surprisingly warm evening, so everyone had their windows wide open. The air was filled with the smell of exotic cooking and the sounds of music, loud conversations, arguments in a variety of languages and the revving of cars. Someone in the block was screaming for his mother.

I made myself as comfortable as I could but, because of the rush to get there, I had very little with me. I had no bedclothes or pillow, but fortunately I did have a quarter-bottle of Chekov and a good book.

Despite the continuing noise outside and the fact I was lying on a bare, plastic-covered mattress, I drifted off to sleep, dreaming I was lost drunkenly in Cairo.

I woke suddenly with my heart pounding to the sound of thumping, crashing and the full-volume rendition of a tuneless Irish song, followed by the slurred words, 'You're all focking conts. All of youse.' There was then a noise that resembled a huge sack of potatoes being dropped. A brief silence followed and then snoring. I didn't feel confident enough to open the door and complain.

In the shared bathroom in the morning I met last night's crooner. He was a big Irishman with a deeply lined face, teeth that pointed in several directions and misaligned eyes. 'Marnin'. The name's Seamus. Who the fock are you?'

Guessing which eye to concentrate on, I answered, 'I'm Ed. I'm your new neighbour. Good to meet you, Seamus.' We shook hands. There was a sound of cracking.

Over the next few days we bumped into each other regularly. Seamus turned out to be one of the most helpful, honest and genuine blokes I'd met. He regularly came back late at night pissed, cursing and singing. Occasionally he made it into his room.

One morning he told me he'd received a letter that informed him he had to leave by the end of the week. There was no explanation except to say that he was considered 'non-priority'. He had no idea where he was going to go. A couple of days later I found his room door open. I peered in. The place had been trashed; the fridge was full of smashed eggs and there was rubbish everywhere.

I got used to my little room, even began to feel vaguely at home there. Mandy brought around bedding, a kettle and saucepan and, most importantly, a small television which drowned out the multi-lingual babbling outside.

Brunswick Place did have a secured front door that needed a swipe key-card, but the lock was faulty and frequently didn't close properly and the caretaker was absent. Anyone could get in or out as they liked and I often came home at night to find slumped bodies in the hallway. Drug dealers were regular visitors to the block.

I had been there a couple of weeks when I came across a letter addressed to me that had been left on a shelf downstairs in the entrance hall along with dozens of other letters to people who had long gone. It contained the words 'non-priority'. I had to be out in two days.

I hadn't a clue where to go. But, by a pure stroke of luck, I happened to be walking along Church Road with my worldly possessions and was called over by two people I knew who were drinking at a table outside a pub. One of them was going on holiday for a couple of weeks the next day and he wanted someone to look after his flat. Could I move in straight away? Well, that takes care of the next 14 days, I thought.

After Brunswick Place it was absolute luxury – spotlessly, if not obsessively, clean and completely quiet. It also had a waterbed, something I would never buy even if I had the money. It was a relief to be there, but I was only putting off a longer-term solution to my housing problem.

During the time there I made several more, mostly fruitless, visits to Brighton Council and Brighton Housing Trust, but something did eventually turn up. I was offered temporary accommodation in Olympus House on the seafront along Marine Parade in Kemp Town. It's a form of hostel with 24-hour security which provides people with a room and shared bathroom and kitchen.

After a short interview to determine whether I would fit in or not – or perhaps if I posed any sort of risk to the other residents – I was accepted. I was given a room at the front of the property on the first floor which, despite the scaffolding outside, had magnificent views of the sea and Brighton Pier.

A couple of the other residents seemed barking mad, but it was generally a friendly, safe place and surprisingly quiet. The room above me was empty. There were brief moments when I felt quite happy there, particularly if I had enough money to buy a bottle of wine.

While I was there I had a bicycle, which was a real lifeline. There's a very good cycle path on the seafront that runs westward from Seaford, going under the cliffs, past the Marina, along Brighton and Hove seafront, then along by

Shoreham harbour and beach, through Lancing and all the way to Worthing. For various reasons I was easily covering 150 miles a week despite three punctures, a buckled wheel and a drunken crash that landed me in A&E. My bike was eventually stolen.

After I'd been at Olympus House for three weeks, a letter arrived containing the words 'non-priority'. Once again I had to be out in two days.

I hadn't a clue where to go. My only option at that stage was to sleep in my mother's garage without letting her know. The first night I stayed there I went over to Lancing late in the day and sat nursing a pint of beer in the Crabtree pub until it got dark. I had a key to the garage so that I could get to what remained of my possessions.

Each night after that I'd sneak into the garage around 10.30 with a bottle of cider, hoping the next-door neighbour's dog wouldn't start barking. I'd make up some sort of bed on the floor among the mildewed cardboard boxes, suitcases, rusting gardening tools and cobwebs. Going to the toilet in the pitch blackness was a complicated manoeuvre, particularly because the garage was not plumbed in. I'd leave early in the morning, hopefully unnoticed, with a fair amount of recycled cider to dispose of.

My time in the garage coincided with a particularly wet period and the roof let in water freely. I slept surrounded by gradually filling buckets. It was safe, though.

That era came to an end with the news that I had been offered a place in an Emmaus community in Portslade. I'd put my application, or referral, in quite some time ago, but only now was there a vacancy. I was due in the next day.

The name Emmaus comes from a village in Palestine where, according to the Bible, Jesus appeared resurrected to his disciples on Easter Monday. It's a Christian organisation founded by a former member of the French Resistance, Abbe Pierre, after the Second World War to look after the poor and destitute. The aim is to help the casualties of society to regain their self-respect through work and responsibility in a self-supporting community. The work was not intended to give a person something to live on, but a reason to live. It is now a big international operation.

The Emmaus in Portslade is one of the largest of the 14 in the UK. It's set in beautiful grounds next to the Norman church of St Nicolas and a ruined 12th-century manor house. The building itself was a nunnery and now houses about 40 mostly male 'companions' as they're called. Quite a few of the nuns are buried in the gardens, but as far as I knew none of the companions.

The community runs two shops selling bric-a-brac, clothes, books, furniture and electrical goods which come from donations. A lot of the donations are repaired and renovated on the premises. There's also a popular cafe open to the public. I used to go there when I owned the last house I had, just round the corner. I certainly didn't think at the time that a year later I would be a member of that community. I remember feeling rather sorry for the inmates and briefly wondering what had gone wrong in their lives for them to end up like that.

I arrived on a Friday morning and was shown around by the community's leader, Matt, a large genial character, who explained the rules, two of which were no alcohol on the premises and you can't be pissed in a community area.

The room I was given, number 42, was at the back of the building. It was small and functional, with a single iron bed, a chair, wardrobe and sink, and overlooked an industrial-sized skip filled with the donations that couldn't be sold. All the companions were out working so the building was quiet except for a dog barking across the hallway. 'No pets' was another one of the rules of the community.

As I had some time on my hands, I thought I'd go for a stroll around the area where just a matter of months earlier I'd lived with my family. I felt rather isolated and disorientated despite it being such a familiar place. I walked past the old church to Easthill Park via the village off-licence and sat in the sunshine with a half-bottle of vodka, listening to the blackbirds and escaped parakeets, watching the squirrels chase the magpies and one another.

Feeling no pain, I walked back to Emmaus for the evening meal. The food, simple and hearty and dished out from vast tureens, was served at 6pm in the companions' dining room. The queue had formed by about one minute before that and the whole meal was consumed and the room emptied by 6.30.

I found an unoccupied seat at a table of five. One of them, a man I'll call Peter (not his real name), was in his mid-thirties, slightly red-faced with watery eyes and spoke with an upper-class drawl. He welcomed me to Emmaus.

'It's not a bad life,' he said. 'It's a great opportunity to get some order back into your life. You've got meals, a bed and some sort of structure. I've never really had a proper job, so for me it's been a good chance to work at something from nine to five.'

It turned out that Peter was a recovering drug addict who had recently returned from Spain, where he'd been in prison for drug dealing and attempted bank robbery. 'It was quite an enjoyable three months, actually. I'm fluent in Spanish, there was a swimming pool, plenty of time to sunbathe and we were able to visit the bar across the road.' His ageing father had said that he would not inherit anything of his apparently sizeable estate unless he got himself clean.

Across the table was Mike from Manchester, a former physical training instructor with the Grenadier Guards who once, he said, had made a great deal of money selling fire extinguishers before the demon drink and a bad divorce had resulted in his losing everything. There is no real 'look' for an alcoholic – many, if not most, are very keen to look after themselves to hide their addiction – but Mike looked as if he had come out of central casting: large purple nose, unshaven, a darting tongue and swivelling eyes.

But he talked good sense, and explained how the system worked at Emmaus. He outlined which were the best and worst jobs to have and how we got our 'allowance', a form of pocket money rather than pay, so as to avoid any tax issues. Going into Emmaus meant signing off Job Seekers Allowance. The rooms were financed by Housing Benefits paid directly to Emmaus, which amounted to a considerable income for the community.

I remained in the dining area alone for a while contemplating the next stage of my life. Was this going to be home for the next few months, or years? Was this going to be where I would grow old? I made my way up several flights of echoing stairs and along the long corridors. Each room was emitting the sounds of what seemed to me then rather sad lives. I settled down in bed for my first night as a companion. From outside came the sounds of an owl, foxes screeching and someone playing a solitary game of late-night pool. I looked out of the window across the half-filled skip towards the games room, but could see no one at the table.

I woke to Radio 4's *Shipping Forecast* (which I used to sub–

edit when I was at the BBC), which was surprising because I didn't have a radio. The walls were so thin that I could make out every word. I was pleased to hear that barometric pressure was rising, the wind was a force four from the south-west, visibility 'good' and the sea 'slight' in the Wight coastal waters.

The bathroom was at the end of the long corridor. I thought I'd get in there before the other residents got up. It had a bath that you could lie full length in. If you sat up and looked through the open window, you could see the sea, Southwick power station, along the coast to Worthing Pier and beyond to the Isle of Wight. Just across the courtyard, painted brightly on the side of a warehouse, were the words: 'Serve first those who suffer most.'

A self-service breakfast was available from 7am and I aimed to get in the dining room before all the others. The huge catering-sized fridges were well stocked with donated food and the walk-in larder was packed with dry goods. No one ever went hungry at Emmaus – in fact, there were quite a number of impressive paunches.

With half an hour before the first commitment of the day and feeling a bit wobbly, I strolled down to Patel's for a quarter of Chekov, some mints as camouflage and a copy of *The Times*. I sat in the quiet of the walled garden under the eucalyptus tree, drank the vodka, read the obituaries and letters to the editor and listened to the rustling trees. I recalled the idea that *it is through trees that we see and hear the wind*. The vodka was doing its job. I no longer felt wobbly.

The companions, community assistants and leader all gathered at 8.45am for the morning meeting. This was the opportunity to raise various issues, make suggestions or complaints, but most importantly to allocate jobs. I was welcomed as the new boy.

Those with driving licences and who were reasonably fit got jobs on the vans that picked up and delivered old furniture, TVs, fridges and so on. Those who had some sort of kitchen experience went either to the public cafe or the companions' kitchen. There were also jobs sorting donated clothes in the two shops, or in the repair shop or the store house, as well as gardening and domestic duties around the building.

Gardening would have been my first choice, but those jobs clearly went to the 'old hands' who had served some time. I guess because I had no physical deformity, facial disfigurement or speech impediment, I was allocated a 'front of house' role as waiter and general helper in the public cafe.

In good weather the cafe was a very attractive place to come to for simple, low-priced food and teas. There were dozens of tables spaced out around the gardens and it was my job to serve and clear up. Customers were mainly the retired or young mums with toddlers. I always hoped I wouldn't have to serve someone I knew.

I also helped in the kitchen, which seemed to function very smoothly when it was quiet but tended to fall to pieces when there was a rush on. Some of the companions weren't good with stress. After a working shift the companions could do as they pleased for the rest of the day. I got into the routine of finding a quiet spot somewhere in the gardens and reading a book. Somehow the confines of our rooms felt claustrophobic. I wanted to make the most of the fresh air until the sun went down.

Pay day was on a Saturday. Just before 5pm a queue promptly built up for the cash handout at the door of the accounts office. There was a lot of good-natured complaining about the pittance we were about to be given and how short a time it would last. We talked about the Emmaus 'happy

31

hour', as that was how long it would take before all the money was spent on booze. My first week's allowance was £42. Five pounds was kept back as savings for the time you finally moved on.

Almost all the companions were drinkers, whether it was those struggling to recover from it, secret drinkers or those who were more dedicated and open about it. As the rules stipulated no alcohol on the premises, some of the newly enriched companions went via the off-licence to Easthill Park, where there is a memorial garden dedicated to those who gave their lives in two World Wars. This secluded area was known as the Emmaus Arms.

Five of us, Peter, Mike, Chas, Tony and myself, gathered there on a west-facing bench surrounded by hawthorn bushes and pine trees drinking super-strength beer and cider, discussing the meaning of the universe, swapping tales of what we'd been through and enjoying the sunset.

Mike launched into a long, detailed story about his time in Israel and the fact that he spoke fluent Hebrew. He might as well have been. By this stage we needed sub-titles to understand him. But, however slurred and repetitive the conversations became, for all of us it was a lot better than sitting alone in our dark rooms. I was heartened to see that everyone disposed of their empty cans and bottles. Dossers with standards.

Sundays and Mondays were days off and the whole community seemed to disappear, the buildings and grounds becoming like the *Mary Celeste*. With cash extremely short, there wasn't a lot to do except walk, read and think. There were no set meals but there was plenty of food available in the huge fridges, much of it donated by local supermarkets.

Emmaus had its advantages. It was safe, and hunger and exposure were not a threat. But in a way it was a trap. Five days a week you'd work nine to five with little chance to contact the real world or look for a proper job. Sundays were completely dead, which left only Mondays to look for a way out and that had to be done on a very limited budget. There was a real danger of becoming completely cut off from society and ultimately lazy and institutionalised. Some companions had been residents for years and might eventually spend their last days there. There was plenty of room in the grounds for their remains.

For me, though, this dilemma didn't go on for long. After a few weeks the feeling of being cut off and trapped had led to an increase in my drinking. Although the budget was tight, a full bottle of vodka in Tesco cost only £6.99. I'd been warned that some of the community assistants had smelled vodka on me. I had always thought that vodka was odourless, but apparently it gives off a tell-tale aroma through the skin. I must have reeked like a Russian.

There were occasional spot-checks on rooms and a bottle was found in mine. I was summoned one morning to the community leader's office. In a friendly and calm way, Matt said, 'This isn't really working, is it, Ed? You're clearly drinking too much and you've broken the rules on alcohol. I'm going to have to ask you to leave. No hard feelings. We would've liked it to work out – you would've been a valuable member of the community. If you get your drinking sorted out, maybe you could come back, if you get another referral.'

I wasn't really sure what to do next. Together my last allowance and a few weeks of held-back savings amounted to about 60 quid, which would have to last for at least two weeks. My possessions, such as they were, I left in an Emmaus store house. I headed to the off-licence and then to the Job Centre to sign back on.

That night was clear and dry but beginning to get quite cold. I was now street homeless. I thought I'd go back to Emmaus and see if I could get some shelter in the safety and familiarity of the gardens. At the back of the community there's an area where they dumped furniture awaiting repair or disposal. I pulled an old mattress under a tree and found some canvas sheeting to cover myself.

I lay there facing the starlit sky. The seven-day-old moon looked clear in the south-west. A light, cold breeze stirred the dry leaves of the tree. Some had come to the end of their lives and swirled darkly to the ground. Through the branches I could see the familiar shape of the seven stars of the Plough pointing to the Pole Star, the heavenly body that had provided direction for wayfarers for thousands of years. I had definitely lost my way.

At that moment I heard the sound of a sash window being pulled up. A light went on and someone shouted, 'What the fuck are you doing sleeping on the tip?'

I recognised the voice of one of the companions, Nick.

'Do you want a drink? You look like you could do with one. Here, catch this!'

Out of the window flew a quarter-bottle of whisky, which luckily I caught cleanly. It was two-thirds full.

The rest of the night, as far as I remember, was more comfortable.

There was a time when I felt embarrassed and ashamed to be signing on the dole. The first time I had claimed for a brief spell was years ago, during the recession of the early nineties. At that time the queue to sign on stretched out of the office and along the street. I was there for all to see, and, however many tens of thousands of pounds I had paid in National

Insurance, getting benefits made me feel uncomfortable and a failure. But I had long ceased to worry about that.

Nowadays, queues were a thing of the past. Brighton and Hove still had fairly high unemployment, but new claimants applied on the telephone, not at the office, which might sound efficient, but only if someone answered the phone. Once you'd signed on, changing even tiny details meant lengthy forms had to be sent off to various offices scattered the length and breadth of the country which didn't seem to be on the same computer system. Several times my papers, in some cases the originals, were lost. Phoning any of the offices around the country made me lose the will to live.

Almost all the staff at the Portslade Job Centre were friendly and pleasant, but I got the impression that their main concern was to reduce the numbers on the books, so as to meet targets, rather than genuinely find someone the right work. In my case I didn't blame them. There wasn't a lot of hope for a white male in his fifties, homeless and bankrupt and with a CV that tended to put people off. I was willing to apply for anything and take anything except working in an abattoir or, worse, telesales, but my particular skill profile didn't really fit much locally.

It was on the day that I returned to the Department of Work and Pensions after being expelled from Emmaus that I heard a rich, deep, baritone voice saying, 'Edward, my dear boy! I haven't seen you in ages. Hail fellow and well met. I don't suppose you could spare £2.50 for a packet of fags? I'm gasping. I'll pay you back as soon as I get my pension.'

Tony, or AK as he was usually known, was in his early sixties and was a heavy smoker and drank as much as his limited budget would allow. His face betrayed his love of liquor and his voice had a whisky-and-tobacco timbre but he never slurred. He was always genial and polite in an old-school way. Oxbridge educated, he had been among other things – some jobs might even have been real – an English-language teacher.

'Ah, AK,' I replied. 'Well, the truth is I'm pretty skint myself, but I'd hate to see a man suffer. Here's the cash, I reckon I can trust you.'

'For ever grateful, dear boy. Let's meet tomorrow for a drink and I'll pay you back. *Dictum meum pactum.*'

We did meet the next day at the Bell in Hove and his word was his bond. We lingered over two pints of strong cider and I explained my recent history, including my expulsion from the community. AK had also fallen on hard times and was living in a small council flat on the infamous Knoll Estate. It's an area where Jeremy Kyle would have had no trouble in finding an endless supply of studio guests. Apparently there were plans to rename it the Kyle Estate.

AK explained his flat was a bit cramped and rather untidy but he kindly offered me a temporary floor. 'At least it's a roof over your head,' he said.

The nights were definitely getting colder, so I gratefully accepted the offer. 'Rather untidy' was a serious understatement: it made a trashed student squat look pristine. AK had lived there for five years, but there was no carpet and only hanging material for curtains. A lifetime's collection of papers, documents and books were scattered everywhere. Several ashtrays were piled high. The shower room and kitchen needed the urgent attention of the ladies from Channel 4's *How Clean is Your House?* But even they might have baulked at this assignment. Strangely there were no insects. There were cobwebs but their residents had upped and left long ago.

My snoring was too loud, so I slept in the small entrance area just inside the front door and outside the toilet. AK made frequent visits to the loo during the night which involved stepping over my body. Given that he didn't wear much in bed, the view was unedifying.

AK was an intelligent and entertaining chap, but our relationship seemed to be based on mutual financial support: I lent him money when I had it and he let me borrow some when he had it. His pension went into his account at about 2am on a Saturday morning. He would leave the flat at that time and walk several miles to the cashpoint and then come back with bottles of cider from the all-night convenience store.

I knew that my Knoll phase had to come to an end. AK had made it clear it was a temporary arrangement. In his position I'd have felt the same way and I didn't want to outstay my welcome. Even though winter was not far off, the complete freedom of a park bench beckoned.

It was then that I knew that my options had definitely run out. It really did mean accepting life on the streets.

So began my time of living rough. As I mentioned earlier, it started in places I knew and was familiar with in the Portslade area, including the walled garden, Easthill Park and occasionally the grounds of Emmaus. Only later did I move to the Babylon Lounge and gain 'rough sleeper' status.

As time wore on and the weather got colder, sleeping on a bench was beginning to take its toll in terms of tiredness and more frequent chest infections. I was also becoming more accident-prone. On one occasion I was passing through a building site (for reasons that are now beyond me) and I fell awkwardly down a five-foot foundation hole. I ripped the cruciate ligament in my left knee, which resulted in another visit to A&E. That sort of injury can take some time to heal and rest is important, but that's not really possible for someone who's homeless. Keeping moving was the only way to stay sane and warm.

And so it was, early on 11 December 2007, that I decided to take the number 1 bus up to Portslade and seek refuge in St Nicolas's Church. It's a wonderful little church: beautiful, spiritual, quiet and smelling of incense. It is almost always open, despite the threat of vandalism from the surrounding bandit country.

I sat on a back pew. A thin, watery sun streamed through the stained-glass windows, illuminating the suspended motes of dust. A dove cooed gently outside. I was completely exhausted and my leg was throbbing, but I was warm and safe. My bottle of liquid optimism was doing its job and my mind began to drift back over the years to happier times.

It would be a good idea, I thought, to stretch out on the stone-flagged floor between the ancient wooden benches, close my eyes and dream of hot sunshine and a time when I had everything to live for. All these days that have come and gone, I did not know this was life.

3

SUN, FUN AND BEER

I can't remember choosing to be an alcoholic, but I do remember instantly loving the stuff. I can picture and feel the exact moment when the love affair began. It's a hot afternoon in the middle of June 1969. I'm 16, sitting alone in an old canvas deckchair in the back garden of my parents' bungalow in Lancing in Sussex. The sun beats down out of a clear blue sky, there's almost complete quiet except for the low, languid drone of a Tiger Moth biplane, the sound of a distant radio playing Fifth Dimension's 'Aquarius' and in the background the hum of honeybees. Countless peacock butterflies flit around the purple buddleia.

I'm in the middle of the novel *2001: A Space Odyssey*. My O Level exams are almost over and I'm confident I've done well. There's something in the air. I sense a near-perfect moment, but nearly perfect just doesn't seem good enough. I feel almost content, happy even, but something is missing – things could be even better. From apparently nowhere springs the thought – a bottle of cider will turn a near-perfect moment into the real thing.

I'd never properly tasted alcohol before, but I was aware that I loved the smell – recalled from long before – of that heady, warm cocktail of beer and cigarette smoke wafting out of the pub door as my brother and I waited for my father, usually on the steps outside the Marquis of Granby in Sompting, with our Smith's crisps and bottle of Corona lemonade. I used to hear the laughter inside and knew my father was happy, which made me feel the same way.

An eager bike ride to the off-licence of the Crabtree pub up the road produces a large bottle of Woodpecker. The cider is cold, sweet, thirst-quenching and easy to drink. The effect is magical. It electrifies my veins, a thousand ideas race through my mind. I am above the earth, in space and slowly turning in the warm sun. A swiftly empty bottle and re-entry was a let-down, but I knew then for sure that I'd discovered something that made me feel wonderful and complete.

Whatever had been missing in me had now been found. From that moment on I felt that all good times would be associated with alcohol and all bad times could be erased by it. The most reliable friend I could have. Over the next three decades alcohol would always be connected with sunshine and fun.

For as long as I could remember, there had always been that vague, underlying feeling of dissatisfaction that, whatever I was doing, there was something out there that was much better; that everyone else (whoever they were) was having a much more enjoyable time than I was. I always wanted to be somewhere other than where I was. Alongside this was the belief that, if something makes you feel good, two or three times as much will make you feel even better. What's the point of moderation?

That's a heady cocktail for someone who has a

predisposition to excess – loving the taste and effects of alcohol, believing it makes up for something that is missing, being convinced that more is better and thinking it will always take away discomfort and smooth the rough edges of emotional pain.

But, as a 16-year-old, I didn't use those words to describe whatever it was I was feeling. All I was really conscious of was that drinking was a hell of a lot of fun. I seemed to have a huge capacity for booze. I rarely, if ever, puked. I never got aggressive, just amorous, and I was certain, if no one else was, that I became far more interesting, creative, articulate and better-looking. The spinning bedroom at the end of it was well worth it every time.

Having a brother older by two and a half years was like having a pathfinder. Les seemed to take all the flak from my ex-career-soldier father. I was just as keen on going out as he was, but going through that stage a couple of years later allowed me to slip below the discipline radar. Les was born in 1950 and his first teenage experiments provoked much more of a clash with our parents. When my turn came they'd pretty well given up.

In the mid-sixties things were changing so rapidly it was like a generational change in the space of a few years. Les was a Mod, very much into Vespas and Lambrettas with all their accessories and upgrades. A parka and partially back-combed hair was the uniform. Brighton was the place to gather and watch gang fights. Greasers were the enemy. From about 1967, through black and white television, I began to become vaguely aware of wider events and trends – hippies, Woodstock, peaceniks, flower power, Maharishi and the emerging green movement. Vietnam seemed just like another war film.

Les was far more practical than I was, at one stage completely rebuilding a Triumph Roadster from a rusting heap on the back lawn. I was happy with a 50cc moped with a top speed of 28mph. No helmet required… ah, the reckless freedom. It took me 14 hours non-stop to get to the Bath pop festival.

Neither of us can remember taking our 11 Plus exams, but the different results produced fundamentally different life paths. Les went to Boundstone Lane Secondary Modern in Lancing and I went to Worthing High School for Boys, a traditional grammar school. The theory was that he was practical and I was academic – a decision taken on the basis of one day's exams and a selection made some three years before puberty. Fortunately we'd probably have headed in our different directions with or without the exam results.

Social life for me centred on Worthing. The 'in' place was the Thieves Kitchen, a multi-floored, many-roomed, wooden-beamed pub in the centre of the town that had an unspoken territorial arrangement. Groovy, cannabis-loving hippies occupied one part of the pub, senior citizens another and young beginners like me a third area. No Greasers.

We – which usually meant about six of us, Spud, Graham, Paul, Rob, Pete and myself, from the High School – would gather at the Thieves and generally down about eight pints of lager and lime during an evening for a ten-bob note, which was about half a week's wages from an early-morning paper round. During a night out we'd usually hear of a party at someone's parents' house. That would mean another outing for the trusty and increasingly rusty big tin of Watney's Red Barrel Bitter. This 'Party Seven' never actually got opened but was the entry ticket to many parties. It's probably lying sealed now in some landfill, a beery time capsule.

We rarely left the kitchen, made every effort to empty every bottle or can and danced only when pissed. Being from an all-boys' school, chatting up girls was awkward, painful and almost always futile. I was a slow learner, but it eventually became clear that girls always signal who they want. Even so, if they were signalling in my direction, it passed me by.

I can't remember any houses being trashed, but certainly most carpets needed replacing. I always chose to walk home – often five or more miles – absolutely loving the peace, solitude and what always seemed to be clear, star-filled skies. Generally I was locked out after 11.15pm but I came to love the garden shed.

In my drinking days at school the need to pay for booze was the driving force behind the part-time jobs I took. I had a paper round for five years, worked on a local farm at harvest time for three summers, swept the streets, emptied dustbins (no plastic wheelie bins or bin liners), stacked supermarket shelves, picked cabbages, was an usher and intermission ice-cream seller at the Odeon cinema, washed dishes at Joe Lyons, sorted recycled rubbish and taught English as a foreign language.

Those were golden times. I had money in my pocket, no debts (the concept of owing money was completely alien), I was healthy, I loved school, exams seemed pretty straightforward and, although there were periods of sheer boredom – Lancing, as its entire population would agree, is a soulless place – I had this vague feeling of excitement about the future and a world filled with potential.

My parents were just simply good. The house was not exactly filled with openly demonstrated love, but we never felt that we were not loved; just never thought about it or spoke about it. There were never any childhood parties or family holidays, but we never lacked for basic material things. Discipline was threatened more than implemented.

Mum always cooked wholesome 1950s food (and still does, half a century later) and worked for many years at Boots the Chemist. Dad had a sharp wit, but seemed directionless after leaving the Royal Electrical and Mechanical Engineers after 25 years. He barely drank, but smoked about 60 cigarettes a day and died of lung cancer at 69. The small bungalow was always thick with tobacco smoke, and above his armchair the ceiling was yellow. My mother often said goodnight to us by inscribing the words 'sweet dreams' with her burning cigarette in the darkness of the bedroom that Les and I shared.

For me there were absolutely no deep-seated emotional reasons or excuses for drinking. Quite simply, as a teenager, alcohol made me feel good. Not because I was feeling particularly bad – it just made 'OK' much better. Even then, I was vaguely aware that too many nights of boozing made me feel down and sluggish. I was nearly obsessive about health, weight and spots, so I'd often stop drinking for several weeks. I jogged, cycled, went for long solitary walks, took Ryvita (margarine on the flat side) to school for lunch and forced myself to eat yoghurt when Ski launched that exotic new food in 1966.

I was two people: one determined to be fit and healthy and another that kept going back to alcohol to get something that seemed missing. Naturally, at that age I had absolutely no idea what an alcoholic was.

In those days in a state grammar school, the cool guys were the intelligent ones who were in the top streams without appearing to try too hard. It was important to be seen to breeze through exams without any show of effort;

being good at sports was a bonus. But being clever, sporty and going out to pubs was a full house. Being thick, in the lower streams, athletically uncoordinated and a non-drinker spelled social isolation. Being fashionably dumb was some years off yet.

Everyone had to wear the school uniform of green blazer, black or grey trousers, white shirt and tie (cap until the sixth form), but the idea was to make minor changes to hint at awareness of fashion. If you smoked, it was seen as trying too hard – a bit obvious. A car at 17 was a huge advantage.

One of our small band of brothers was fairly well-off. His dad owned a pub, but more importantly Paul owned a flash Lotus Cortina with all the accessories. Drinking and driving just didn't seem to be an issue – no breathalysers and fairly empty roads. It was decided – naturally over a few pints in the Thieves – that we'd celebrate the end of O Levels by heading down to Torquay and Newquay to camp for a couple of weeks in late July. It was my first holiday.

It actually rained most of the time. Streams of water poured through the badly sited tents, but my memory was of sun, fun and burned skin, all fuelled by the local farm's scrumpy. Apparently this sort of selective memory is called 'euphoric recall' and my recollection was certainly one of elation and euphoria.

I had exactly that feeling when I found out my A Level results in August 1971. They were good enough to get me into my first-choice university. I'm really not sure why I chose Durham except that it's a long way from Lancing. I'd been told it was the next best after Oxford and Cambridge and that, having chosen University College, I'd be living in a Norman castle.

It was a thrilling and daunting prospect, made even more

awesome on my first journey there. The train slowly pulled noisily round the final bend before the station to reveal the mighty, grey vision of the Cathedral and Castle which dominate the city of Durham. It made my heart thud and my bottom tighten. It still does.

As a Fresher, I wasn't in the Castle but outside in a modern rabbit hutch called Bailey Court. My window was at pavement level, facing the entrance to Hatfield College – archrival to 'Castle' – and very much on the frontline. Hatfield men all seemed to be heavy-drinking rugby types and made their presence known raucously every night outside my room.

At 18 and away from home for the first time, I felt pretty provincial and unsophisticated, particularly compared with the apparently smooth, confident, well-connected and travelled students who'd attended public schools. Consumption of beer seemed to be a leveller. Freshers' week, although it was supposed to be about joining clubs, was, of course, focused on getting as much booze down as possible.

All colleges then were single-sex. Castle was essentially a continuation of a public school – formal dinners in the Great Hall, gown wearing, High Table, bedders (cleaners), sconcing (fines) and a long Latin grace. One of the biggest advantages of Castle was that it had the best bar in the university, if not in the county. The Undercroft Bar was about ten feet below the Great Hall and reached by narrow, well-worn steps. It was basic and earthy like a large, open cellar supported by vast stone arches. The bar was at one end and a pint of Newcastle Brown cost about ten old pence (4p). A cool 'Newky' is just about the easiest beer in the world to drink. Being a barman there meant extra cash, limitless opportunities to sample the stocks and, since the bar required no licence, flexible opening times.

My studies – various social sciences, including psychology, anthropology, sociology and economics – were not particularly time-consuming, but the lectures did attract the best-looking girls. This lack of pressure allowed me to throw myself single-mindedly into activities that didn't involve writing essays or going to the library – the rowing club, rugby, the university newspaper *Palatinate*, darts, clay-pigeon shooting and the organisation of the thrice-yearly Castle balls. I was also in charge of the college flag, which meant running up the 180 steps of the Castle Keep every morning and raising the standard to coincide exactly with the seventh chime of the Cathedral's huge bell. All these activities were tackled with enthusiasm and amateurism and all of them involved beer.

I never actively looked for a relationship with the opposite sex – being exclusively with a girl meant missing out on all the fun with the lads. But I just couldn't resist one particularly beautiful girl from St Aidan's College. Jane was blonde, blue-eyed, fresh, petite and always smiling, and she liked a few beers as well. I lost my virginity soon after my 19th birthday. What became a love affair felt as intensely idyllic as young innocent love can be – long summer-evening walks by the River Wear under the vast twin towers of the Cathedral, rowing up the river to the Seven Stars in the ancient village of Shincliffe or picnics on the island of Lindisfarne, drinking the local mead.

Jane was studying French, which meant she had to spend her middle year in France. Her final few weeks at Durham were bitter-sweet and, despite promises and pledges, the year away meant the relationship petered out.

Like most colleges, Castle had a Junior Common Room which ran student affairs, sports clubs and social activities.

Various elected officers ran it, but the prized position was 'Senior Man' (President). What made it sought after was that whoever was elected got a suite of rooms with an open log fire on Norman Gallery, overlooking the courtyard on one side and with a commanding view of the city on the other. Another attraction was that the job meant endless socialising and a drinks allowance.

It seemed tailor-made for me. My academic course wasn't my top priority, I was quite happy to get a 2:2 degree, along with 80 per cent of students, and being involved with the rugby club, rowing, organising the last six college dances and being increasingly generous at the bar made election victory look like a breeze – which it was.

My year of office was among the happiest of my life. I was 'King of the Castle'. Rarely has a dinner jacket got so much use (and abuse) and rarely has a young ego had so much freedom to play. I celebrated my 21st birthday while I was Senior Man. One of the perks was having a reserved and special chair at the end of one of the long dining tables in the Great Hall. On the evening of my birthday I arrived to find the table covered with bottles of whisky and champagne – all consumed democratically in the Undercroft Bar that night. Even then I knew that little could surpass this in the future.

I dreaded the end of my three years at Durham. It was time to get a real life and a proper job. I'd avoided the university's careers office for as long as possible – I just thought that something would fall into my lap.

Towards the end of my year as Senior Man, I had come across a genial but rather mysterious graduate of the college who occasionally stayed in the Bishop's suite of rooms. Rupert usually turned up in a yellow and black vintage Rolls-Royce and always stood his round in the Undercroft.

It was towards the end of one well-oiled evening that he took me to one side and suggested vaguely that I might be interested in going for an interview in London. The people I would see were looking for 'chaps like you', and he said he knew I was made of the 'right stuff' and loved my country. After about six pints of Newcastle Brown, I loved everyone in the bar and would have died for my country.

I hadn't a clue what this was all about, but some weeks later I went down to London – to Carlton Terrace – for an interview with someone from a department called, I think, the Coordination Staff of the Foreign Office. After I'd signed the Official Secrets Act, a large, red-faced man in a regimental tie chuntered on for a while about the Cold War and barely asked any questions. He explained that if I pursued this career I would be attached to one of HM's embassies or consulates abroad as a third or second secretary but would be involved in additional activities to gain intelligence that might involve turning someone into a traitor to their own country. It would mean having a secret life, several identities, living a lie and lying for a living.

As someone who blushes when I tell a fib, this didn't seem the ideal job for me, but the prospect of international travel appealed and anyway I had a very well-used dinner jacket which I guessed was vital for the job. Clay-pigeon shooting would, I thought, be useful experience for handling a Walther. On the interviewer's desk I could see a thin file marked with my name – thin, I assumed, because I had done virtually nothing in life.

Two weeks later I travelled to a second interview on my moped (but without any gadgets fitted by 'Q'). This time the interviewer's attitude and questions were a lot more direct and serious. The file in front of him was much thicker, perhaps increased in size by the fact that I had recently been for an interview for an officer's commission with the Royal Welch Fusiliers in Brecon. That position was offered, but I never followed it up.

I was asked directly to consider whether, at some future date, I might be interested in the intelligence services. At 21 I was too young to be involved now, the interviewer told me, but if I did something useful and relevant over the next few years, they would get back to me.

Well, they never did directly, but I have always wondered whether they followed what I eventually chose to do and whether it had any influence on subsequent events.

Purely by chance, I applied for a graduate trainee position with the international news agency Reuters. I knew what they did, but that was about it. Later I'd find out that the news-gathering function of a Reuters Correspondent is very close to that of HM's intelligence services, although Reuters, naturally, emphasise their complete independence and objectivity.

I completed a selection test which involved general knowledge and various writing exercises, and thought nothing more about it. Many thousands apply for the few trainee places available, so I wasn't surprised to receive a letter in the post turning me down. The real surprise came in the post two days later. Apparently Reuters had made a mistake and I was being offered an interview at their headquarters in Fleet Street. Was it really a mistake, or had someone intervened?

The interviewer, an American, spent the entire half-hour sitting in his swivel chair with his back to me looking out of the window. Only at the end did he swing round and look directly at me and say, 'You look like a regular kinda guy, I guess we can offer you a job in our Economics section.'

That year more than 4,000 graduates had applied for just

eight positions, three of them in Economics. For just a 'regular kinda guy' who'd got a very ordinary Second Class Honours degree and spoke only schoolboy French and German, I'd been uncannily lucky.

By chance I rented a room in a house in Cheyne Walk, Chelsea. I'd read somewhere that James Bond had lived just up the road. It was owned by a stern but motherly woman who could have been Clarissa Dickson Wright's sister. Her large house was filled with mysterious military types who lived quietly and kept strange hours. I travelled to work by number 11 bus each day, reading a string of John Le Carre novels.

Fleet Street in 1974 was still home to most of the big national newspapers. Number 85, Reuters' HQ, was an impressive building designed by Sir Edwin Lutyens, right opposite the *Daily Telegraph* and the *Daily Express*. Huge articulated lorries carrying massive rolls of news print thundered down the road to unload in narrow side streets. The air smelled of printers' ink, exhaust and beer. My new workplace was right next to the journalists' church, St Bride's, but, perhaps more importantly to me at the time, within a few steps of the Punch Tavern, the Bell, the City Golf Club and not far from the Cheshire Cheese and El Vino.

In those days Reuters (now Thomson Reuters) was still a trust owned by the newspapers. It was known and revered throughout the world for its objectivity, reliability and speed.

It was in my first few days there that I was told the story of a BBC Correspondent in South Africa who was also a 'stringer' for Reuters. A big political story broke and he decided to file it first for his main paymaster, the BBC. The London newsdesk refused to run the story, saying, 'Sorry, we can't use it until we've had the wire story from Reuters.'

'But I am the Reuters Correspondent.'

'Sorry, we just cannot run your story until we've seen it on Reuters.'

So he filed it with his Reuters hat on, and only then did the BBC broadcast it – showing the immense influence that the agency had.

Reuters was founded in the mid-19th century by a German, Paul Julius Reuter, in Berlin. It supplied various financial prices to a number of markets faster than anyone else, but there was a gap in the line of communication between Aachen and Brussels which was filled by using homing pigeons. That financial function, although profitable, was always seen as the poor relation to the more glamorous Reuters general news service. But at the time I joined that was all about to change with the arrival of Reuters Monitor, which provided news and prices via a desktop computer fed by the worldwide network of reporters.

It was a revolution that would make huge amounts of money and lead to Reuters becoming a quoted company in 1984 and a global communications giant – until the next revolution, the Internet, came along.

At the end of 1974 Reuters Economic Services still used ancient manual typewriters with stories written on 'sandwiches' – multi-leafed, thin booklets made up of alternating carbon paper and normal typing paper. These sheets were then separated, addressed to various subscribers, and put in a rubber belt which took them to the 'oily rags' section, the printers, who typed up the material on telex machines, producing vast quantities of ticker tape.

International markets hung on every word and statistic sent by Reuters. The aim was accuracy, but speed also mattered hugely as it was vital to get a 'beat' on the opposition – Associated Press (AP), Agence France-Presse (AFP) and United

Press International (UPI). Mistakes were occasionally made, some by trainees, which could result in multi-million-pound surges or crashes in currencies, commodities or equities.

Almost all the journalists and printers went to the surrounding pubs at lunchtime – it was just the natural thing to do. To my knowledge, gyms didn't exist then. Rolling back to work under the influence was barely noticed.

As trainees we were taught the basics of journalism, reporting, speedwriting and law. The classes were conducted at the offices of Independent Radio News in Gough Square off Fleet Street and just round the corner from Samuel Johnson's house and the Cheshire Cheese, a Dickensian pub with a labyrinth of small dark rooms with open fires, nowadays full of American and Japanese tourists.

After a few months in London it was time for the first foreign posting. Of the three trainees in the Economics section, two spoke near-fluent French and German, while I made do with English. One of the others was sent to Paris and one to Frankfurt. My assignment was Hong Kong – what luck not to be a linguist.

My first stop was the library to raise my knowledge of the colony from zero. My second stop was the colonial-style outfitters Airey & Wheeler on Piccadilly ('supplier of lightweight clothing to people who matter') to buy a sand-coloured tropical suit with short sleeves, epaulettes and innumerable pockets. I was convinced I looked the business.

At the age of 22 and heading off to the Far East as a Reuters Correspondent – albeit a 'down-desk' trainee – I was bursting with excitement which was well concealed, I thought, by a newly acquired seen-it-all-before demeanour.

On the Cathay Pacific flight to Hong Kong I was upgraded to business class. It must have been the impression created by my new tropical suit – clearly I mattered. Hours into the flight and looking out of the window over Vietnam, clouds made incandescent by lightning storms, Barry White's 'Love's Theme' blasting on my headphones and at least four large cognacs in my bloodstream, I felt exhilarated. I would remember this moment for ever.

As the 747 turned sharply into Kai Tak Airport, narrowly missing washing hanging out on bamboo poles on the surrounding blocks of flats, I felt like throwing up.

With 'doors to manual' the heat flooded in, and so did the stink of the 'Fragrant Harbour'. Through the airport terminal windows I could see skyscrapers on Hong Kong Island dwarfed by the partly clouded Peak.

My instructions were to go to the Reuters office in Des Voeux Road in the island's Central district. The ancient red and white taxi with hot leather seats and windows wide open raced through the Harbour Tunnel out past Causeway Bay and into Central via the Hong Kong Club and cricket ground. All the way the driver gabbled in raucous Cantonese. My suit probably made him think I was a local.

I dropped my bags in the Reuters office. It had no air-conditioning and so the French windows were wide open, leading on to a long balcony. In one direction was a narrow glimpse of the harbour, filled with merchant ships and criss-crossed by junks and the green and white Star Ferry. Behind, in the distance, was the Peak's towering presence.

I was introduced to the Bureau Chief, Alan Thomas, and the head of the small Economics section, Phil Wardle. Still a bit hungover from the 14-hour flight and befuddled by the humidity and heat, I was whisked off to Wanchai, the once infamous girly-bar area of Hong Kong's waterfront. I glanced out of the taxi window to see groups of white-uniformed US

Navy shore patrols carrying mean-looking truncheons and wearing facial expressions to match. For the Americans the Vietnam War was coming to a painful and ignominious end and Hong Kong was still their preferred place for R&R. In the harbour, the aircraft carrier USS *Kittyhawk* lay brooding at anchor.

I had my first of many large bottles of San Miguel beer in the 747, where the bar girls were apparently happy to supply other services for a couple of hundred HK dollars. Alan and Phil were determined to pack in as much as possible on my first day, so the next stop was further along the road at a Shanghai steam bath. It was dingy and scruffy, with vast shared tubs of boiling hot water followed by a massage during which one of the Chinese attendants walked up and down my back.

We hit the hot streets and were almost immediately sweating again. We took a clanking, windowless tram back to Central for about 20 cents and were the only *gweilos*, 'foreign devils', on board.

Needing further refreshment, the three of us went to the 'pub' opposite our office in the Swire Building. It was a kit-form bar based on an English racing and hunting theme and called the Jockey. The waitresses, young expats, were dressed in red hunting jackets and long black skirts. The temperature in the bar was sub-zero. I would have enjoyed a hot toddy.

My hotel that night was in a noisy part of the city, but then again there wasn't actually a quiet part. After a feverish, almost hallucinatory sleep, I woke to the sound of pile-drivers. As I was subsequently to hear in almost every conversation, 'Hong Kong will be marvellous when it's finished.'

A week later I inherited the flat vacated by my trainee predecessor. He had been keen to 'go native', had a Chinese girlfriend and spoke workable Cantonese. With his housing allowance he'd chosen a flat on the tenth floor of a vast block above Hong Kong's first McDonald's and the Empire cinema.

It was small, hot, almost bare, smelled of mildew and echoed to the sounds of hundreds of cramped Chinese families, all with their washing flapping on long poles extending from each window. Their noise was nearly drowned out by the clattering and scurrying of a million cockroaches in all the cupboards.

Well, I was keen to integrate with the locals, but I needed some peace.

Victoria Peak is about 1,800ft high and covered in tropical greenery, spends several months in warm, wet clouds and has a scattering of big houses and a number of apartment blocks. It's reached by a narrow sinewy road or a steep climb by funicular railway. A few decades earlier it had been exclusively for expatriate Europeans.

I came across a tiny advert in the *South China Morning Post*: 'Peak, very small house in rural surroundings, furnished, $HK2,700 pcm.' 'Rural' and 'house' are words rarely used in the Hong Kong property market.

The place was on Lugard Road, which circles the very top of the Peak along with Harlech Road and can be reached by the funicular railway. Right at the western end was a big house owned then by Chemical Bank and named Dragon's Tavern. *Yesss*, perfect, I thought. A rural tavern. My own little country pub! The house had a large lawn that projected horizontally from the side of the Peak, forming a space underneath. Through the damp undergrowth a narrow stone path led to glass doors – the garden flat. I was to be a Chinese Hobbit.

The views out over the harbour were spectacular. Dozens of ships from all over the world were anchored there. In the distance was Lantau Island and even further the mouth of the

Pearl River, Macau beyond and on the horizon the still secretive sleeping giant of China. What bliss it was to sit outside the doors of the flat or on the lawn above and watch the sun setting over the China Sea, sinking the traditional expat gin and tonic and surrounded by large, multi-coloured, wafting butterflies.

Although small, the flat had two bedrooms. To begin with I shared it with several six-inch millipedes, some geckos and a few saucer-sized spiders. Reuters paid my rent by cheque, but I worked out I could double my income by sub-letting the spare bedroom.

There was a huge response to the ad I placed in the *Morning Post*. Most applicants were put off by the flat's inaccessibility, the smell of wet vegetation and the various resident life-forms, but my final choice was David Fraser, a corporate lawyer with a big international company and an amiable chap, if slightly eccentric. But then up in the rainforest clouds it helped to be a bit other worldly.

It was a choice that would have profound implications later in my life.

At that time David had a girlfriend called Judy Mackenzie. They had a healthy relationship, as the thin bedroom wall confirmed most nights.

Social life in Hong Kong centred on the expat clubs – the Hong Kong Club, the Jockey Club, Yacht, Cricket, Tennis and Country Clubs – and, for us journalists, the Press Club and the Foreign Correspondents' Club, which was then in the Hutchison Building on the waterfront. The FCC's urinals offered a stunning view over the harbour, which, I suppose, became fractionally less fragrant each time we visited.

Coming out of the sauna heat of the street into the FCC,

it seemed as natural as drawing the next breath to have a cold San Mig or Tiger and stroke the condensation on the side of the glass like the final scene in *Ice Cold in Alex*. It was easy to slip into hard-nosed, world-weary, heavy-drinking journalistic mode, especially when wearing a sweat-stained tropical suit.

In 1975, mainland China was closed and secretive. Chairman Mao was still alive. Few journalists were given access to senior political figures, and those who had been were always interrogated over a few beers at the FCC.

Probably the most senior of the journalists and a regular drinker at the club was Richard Hughes, author from 1971 to 1983 of the 'Barefoot Reporter' column for the prestigious *Far Eastern Economic Review*. In 1968, he had published the classic *Hong Kong: Borrowed Place − Borrowed Time*, and its cover deftly summed up the position of the colony, which was to be returned to Chinese control in 1997. It showed an English cricket team playing on the well-kept green grass in the middle of the business district in front of the Bank of China, which was draped with Mao banners.

While I was there, 1997 − more than 22 years away − seemed so far off as to be irrelevant or unreal. It was just something for others to deal with. Now was the time to make money and be gone before the handover.

Weekends in Hong Kong could be oppressive in the humid heat, unless you were fortunate enough to have wangled an invitation on to a corporate junk, a Chinese-style boat specifically designed for entertaining clients − or, as in my case, hangers-on. I'd got to know several young graduate employees of the Hong Kong and Shanghai Banking Corporation who lived up on the Peak at Cloudlands, the bank's 'bachelors' mess'.

It was through them that I got an invitation to the New Year's Eve party at the Hong Kong Club and the offer of a day out on one of the bank's many junks. I rather overindulged at the party, overslept on New Year's Day and missed the sailing time.

In a hungover and nauseous state, I rushed down to one of the jetties on the waterfront and hired a *walla walla*, a small, slow, wallowing Chinese boat used for transporting a few people or cargoes. I couldn't quite manage the Cantonese for 'Follow that junk!' (and anyway there were dozens), but we set sail for Lantau Island in search of the New Year's Day floating party. It took many hours to get there and scour the coast. Sadly the junk had gone to Lamma Island, 20 miles in the opposite direction. I'd got the 'L' right.

That day I learned some interesting Cantonese which, when translated, strongly urged me to do something anatomically impossible to myself.

Most of my time was spent with my Reuters colleagues. One of them, Barry Simpson, six years older than me, had come from a posting in Brussels. He was almost a caricature of a journalist – hard-living, hard-drinking, heavy-smoking and a would-be thriller novelist. He lived slightly higher up the Peak on the other side of Lugard Road. We drank together in the Jockey, the FCC and sometimes in an ersatz English pub called the Bull and Bear. The trendiest place was the Godown, a well-established bistro/club which attracted a younger set of Europeans and local Chinese. Sadly Barry is now in the great big celestial Press Club.

Alan Thomas was the Bureau Chief of Reuters World News. He lived with his wife and children right at the top of the Peak on Mount Austin. His huge colonial house was surrounded by a long veranda that gave 360-degree views of the harbour to the north and all the many islands far out to the south. I spent Christmas 1975 with the Thomases. After quite a few hefty pre-prandial gins, I thought it would be a good idea to explore the local scrubland of Mount Austin before the late festive lunch. My sense of direction deserted me and I was lost for a couple of hours. Despite the December chill, I staggered back drenched in sweat and covered with exotic plants.

Phil Wardle was the head of the Economics team and had a beautiful waterfront house in the south of Hong Kong Island at Stanley Beach, famous for its extremely cheap market and its prison, as well as for being the site where British prisoners of war were executed by the Japanese.

One of the highlights of the year was the annual Dragon Boat race held at Stanley Beach. A dragon boat is a gaudily painted war canoe holding about two dozen paddlers coordinated by a standing drummer. The Hong Kong Press Club (sponsored by Cathay Pacific) entered a crew and several of the Reuters staff had made it into the boat, including myself. Most of Hong Kong's journalists gathered at Phil's house, which was extremely well stocked with the local beers on draught and crates of gin.

Winning a Dragon Boat race is about good coordination, a sense of rhythm and discipline rather than brute strength. The Press Club boat just had alcohol-fuelled passion. We were knocked out in the first round. That left the entire day for drinking the vast supplies of booze under heavy grey clouds that unleashed several hours of warm monsoon rain.

A huge crowd of several thousand had gathered on the beach to watch the races. Phil's house was positioned at one end of the half-mile-long sandy strip. Barry thought it would be a good idea if, for a $HK500 bet, I ran the full length of the beach naked. Many pints of San Miguel made me think it was a good idea too, and who needed drenched clothes anyway? I may have been in the communications industry, but clearly I misunderstood the bet. I had it fixed in my mind that I should run the length of the beach *and back*.

The Chinese police either found the outward run mildly amusing or missed it altogether. It was on the way back that their patience ran out. They chased after me with their gabardine raincoats, covered me up and wrestled me to the sand. Being naked and vulnerable (and pissed), I didn't resist. I was driven off in the back of a police van handcuffed – still gripping 50 green HKSB banknotes – charged and bailed to appear in court 24 hours later.

One member of the crowd was a talented photographer, and the next day a rather impressive, but suitably modest, picture appeared on the front page of both the *South China Morning Post* and the *Hong Kong Standard*.

The charge I faced at the Central Magistrates Court was 'Indecent Exposure in a Public Place, Contrary to Section 4(24) of the Summary Offences Ordinance, Chapter 228'. I was fined $HK500. So, a zero-sum streak.

Two days later and my time in Hong Kong was over. One of my colleagues, Roger Jeal, had composed a poem:

ODE TO ED
What Godiva did to Coventry,
While riding on a horse,
Young Edward did to Stanley
Beside the Dragon Boat course.

He threw convention to the wind
And all his clothes as well.

Then streaked across the crowded sands
Tanked up on San Miguel.

He turned around and made for home,
But what was this he saw?
Some gentlemen in uniform,
The long arm of the law.

His friends then reassured him
It won't stand up in court.
It's just a prank and no one
Could think ill of me, he thought.

In court next day Ed hung his head
And said, I'm sorry, Sir,
I only did it for a bet
And not to cause a stir.

He made his mark here in Hong Kong,
And gave us many a laugh.
But the final act on Stanley Beach
Will be his Epitaph.

R.J. 3 June 1976

For my return journey to London I first flew to Vancouver, from where it was five days on Canadian Pacific Railways to Montreal. Then it was another flight across the Atlantic for a week in Rome before taking the train through Italy and France to England.

4

NEWSMAN

Suntanned and still wearing my well-travelled and fraying tropical suit, I reported back to 85 Fleet Street and the hottest summer since records began. No need to change my outfit.

It was a return to the dull routine of filing stories for the Economics printer wire service and the increasingly dominant Monitor screen information set-up. After the excitement of Hong Kong, boredom was setting in and my editorial judgement was beginning to be clouded by hangovers and long lunches. I didn't see it as a problem then, but others were beginning to think it was. My adventures on Stanley Beach hadn't gone down a storm either.

After a few months I got wind of the fact that the BBC was recruiting for the Radio Newsroom at Broadcasting House in Portland Place. I reckoned the basic skills of writing for the Reuters file would serve me well in putting together radio news scripts.

I was invited for a day of writing assessments, interviews and general knowledge tests, which seemed to me to go well.

A fortnight later I received a letter with the dreaded word 'regret' in it. It was followed two days later by another letter saying there had been a mistake and there was a job on offer. Once again something odd seemed to have happened.

So, at the age of 24, on 15 June 1977 (the same day incidentally as Jennie Bond, who went on to become Royal Correspondent) I joined the BBC on £4,500 per annum. At the time I was living with a girl in Belsize Park, not far from Hampstead Heath. My route to work was a glorious walk each day through Primrose Hill and Regents Park.

Pushing through the heavy bronze doors of Broadcasting House in Portland Place, I would always feel a huge surge of pride to read the inspiring but mostly incomprehensible long Latin inscription over the reception desk. It spoke of an all-knowing and all-powerful God spreading wisdom around the world. I had joined an institution guided by the principle that 'Nation shall speak Peace unto Nation'. I was in the fields of Elysium, particularly when enjoying my canteen lunch (ambrosia) on the BBC roof 'garden'.

I felt very at home at the Beeb. To begin with I was a lowly newsroom sub-editor writing scripts for the news slots and bulletins on all four radio stations and local radio. It was before computers, so a sub would gather together bits of paper wire copy and reporters' scripts, assemble the information in his head and dictate the short news item out loud to a typist who was typically female and matronly.

When I began I tended to whisper the words and it was clear the typist knew more about how to write radio scripts than I did. The more experienced chief subs would deliver their material in an authoritative, stentorian manner as if their words had come down from a mountain and were carved in stone. They spoke 'Peace unto Nations' without needing a transmitter.

Drinking was the norm. The newsroom staff generally gathered at the Crown and Sceptre (aka the Hat and Stick) on the corner of Great Titchfield Street and Foley Street, fraternising with the ITN and Visnews people from round the corner in Wells Street. Occasionally it might be a long lunch at the nearby Montebello (now Sergio's). If the lunch was extended enough and ran on into the evening session, it became a 'full Monte'. Frequently reporters' packages for the early-evening news betrayed a certain softening and sibilation of the letter 's'. Afternoon naps in the office seemed perfectly acceptable.

Pubs closed in the afternoons in those days – all-day opening was only a distant dream. For the truly dedicated there were the private drinking 'clubs' down some of the back streets near Goodge Street or off Regent Street, the most frequented being the Marie Lloyd. They were poorly lit, furtive and full of dodgy characters, almost all of them senior policemen.

As night shifts were generally slack, this provided a good opportunity to tour the hospitality drinks cupboards around Broadcasting House, which were well stocked and rarely locked. The building was a labyrinth of corridors, stairs and hidden and disused studios – nine floors above ground level and, below these, three floors which rumbled to the sound of the Bakerloo Underground trains. At that time there had been little refurbishment and so some of the studios had the original equipment from the Second World War. It was easy to slip into Churchillian mode after a few 'liberated' brandies and cigars.

After about six months I was assigned to coverage of the debates in both Houses of Parliament for broadcast on Radio 4's *Today* and *Yesterday in Parliament*. Being junior I was sent to the House of Lords along with another newsroom sub-editor, Paul Gibbs. Although we were both dedicated and highly professional journalists determined to accurately reflect the wisdom generated in the chamber, the five bars in the Palace of Westminster were a distraction.

The debates in the Lords are far more real and interesting than the party politics of the Lower Chamber, or Commons. Even so, they were often delivered in a rather soporific way. The combination of a small, stuffy press box, the mesmerising gold decorations and acres of mostly unoccupied red leather, the long, hypnotic speeches and a couple of bottles of House of Lords finest claret led to a loss of concentration, if not coma.

The theory was to follow the arguments closely and choose recorded highlights that best illustrated the flow and direction of the debate. Often Paul and I hadn't a clue about what had been said. The only solution back at the Parliamentary newsroom across Westminster Bridge was to make a random selection of clips, held together by an inspired guess at what they had been on about. Uncannily, this often accurately reflected the way the speech had, in fact, been delivered. We were clearly on the same wavelength as our Peers of the Realm. There were never any complaints. The programme was broadcast late; maybe their Lordships were already tucked up in bed.

Increasingly, headline news was being made by business and financial news – oil prices, sterling crises, financial scandals, big takeover bids and so on. In response to this the BBC formed the Financial Unit, a small team of economic 'experts' who would provide the rest of the corporation with output and advice. There were already specialist programmes such as *Moneybox* and *The Financial World Tonight*, but the unit was more like wholesale news for any takers – a sort of money sausage factory. I joined as a chief sub in 1978.

The team – Peter Day, Simon Rose, Martin Essex, Martin Crass and Danielle Donougher – did have its own daily output in the form of Financial Report towards the end of *The Six O'Clock News* and three times a day a ten-minute round-up of international market news for the World Service. In the pre-Internet days this summary of the main stock, bond, currency and commodity markets was a vital source of information for small traders or those away from the office around the globe.

For, say, the Bolivian tin miner in the Andes, the silversmith in Delhi, the gold bullion dealer in Johannesburg or the expat pensioner on the Costas or in the Canaries, the closing prices and market reports were eagerly awaited. It had to be correct and clearly enunciated, though these high standards were very occasionally fallen short of thanks to the rival attractions of the Hat and Stick. I hope the tapes are no longer in existence.

The Financial Unit was a useful stepping stone for a number of young hopefuls who went on to greater prominence, including Middle East Editor Jeremy Bowen, James Long, Francine Stock, Shadow Minister for Immigration Damian Green, Jonathan Charles, Andrew Rawnsley and Hugh Pym.

I never knew why, but I became an 'expert' on the international crude oil markets, a role which had the bonus that I covered the regular and sometimes emergency meetings of OPEC (Organisation of Petroleum Exporting Countries) in either Geneva or Vienna. Once you knew the ropes, these were great stories to report.

The delegates would generally gather in a five-star hotel,

usually the Intercontinental, hold an opening plenary session for the cameras and then disappear for closed sessions in various meeting rooms. In the absence of any hard news, the press corps fed on rumours and counter-rumours, almost all of which were mirages.

The wire services reporters from Reuters, AP, AFP, UPI, Platts or Knight Ridder scurried around in packs sniffing for scraps of news. Whether anything happened or not, they had to file repetitive holding stories. This journalistic froth more often than not bore little resemblance to what was actually going on behind the closed doors of the hotel suites.

The different requirements of the BBC meant my tactics could be slightly less frantic. I'd sit at the corner of the bar with a direct-line view of the lifts, watching for any activity from the delegates. I'd also keep a close eye on the most experienced correspondent from the *Financial Times*, who also stayed near the bar, but the key thing was to keep tabs on the Saudi oil minister, Sheikh Ahmed Zaki Yamani. Saudi Arabia was and still is the world's largest exporter of crude oil, so any deal was pretty meaningless without his say-so. The rest was just bubbles on top of the barrel.

Having a relaxed attitude towards news gathering allowed a lot more time in the hotel pool or at a particularly beautiful restaurant along the edge of Lac Geneva which had a spectacular view of distant Mont Blanc. The fact that I could keep an eye on several of the key delegates as they ate leisurely lunches there helped my sanguine approach.

Towards the end of my coverage of OPEC, the main story was whether international crude oil prices would fall to $10 a barrel or below and Saudi Arabia would in response cut production to boost prices. It was frequently described as an oil 'crisis', but I never did understand why cheap oil was seen as a crisis. With crude prices at the time of writing having touched $147 a barrel, there were urgent meetings trying to get the Saudis to boost production to cut them. But prices are not driven by diplomacy. They're the direct result of supply and demand, self-interest and the extraordinary madness of crowds (markets). It's more hysteria than haggling.

Reporting the oil markets meant having a close relationship with BP, a company that was always generous with hospitality and trips to its facilities. One particularly memorable visit was arranged by the head of press relations, Roddy Kennedy. It involved an overnighter in Stavanger in Norway and then picking up the well-stocked BP Lear Jet to Longyearbyen in Spitzbergen, 700 miles inside the Arctic Circle.

Apart from a good 'jolly', there was a serious story involved. The aim was to show what lengths an oil major must go to in order to secure new sources of crude. In the case of Spitzbergen that meant using new technology to drill through moving glaciers and into the rock below. At the time it was technically possible but uneconomic unless oil reached about $55 a barrel, an unthinkably high price then but certainly workable now.

Despite the story's demands, there was plenty of spare time to take out the powerful skidoos miles out across the endless, creaking ice wastes. We were advised to carry a rifle as the polar bears were emerging with empty bellies after a winter of hibernation. My firearm remained holstered mainly because I never saw a single bear, hungry or not. I doubt we'd been given any ammunition anyway.

The trip was during the late Arctic spring. The 'nights' were spent consuming generous meals of reindeer meat and Norwegian schnapps, then sliding back to our wooden huts to enjoy the sight of the midnight sun still well above the horizon, completely oblivious to temperatures of -35 degrees Celsius.

My salary at the BBC had risen to the dizzying level of almost £6,000 a year, which meant I had something that I haven't had since – savings. I've never particularly lusted after, or felt defined by, cars, but an MGB Roadster seemed a good idea even if it was just for that distinctive low growl. It handled a bit like a tractor – not much acceleration but some real power eventually. I'd passed my driving test only a few months previously, so fully comprehensive insurance was out of the question.

The car was pure enjoyment and I reckoned I had the measure of it, but one night on the way from one pub in Worthing to another in Steyning with about 20 minutes of opening time left, I managed to roll it and hit a flint wall. The car remained upside down with the canvas roof offering little support. Seat belts weren't compulsory then and I wasn't wearing one, which saved my life. The car rolled clockwise, throwing me into the empty passenger seat. Held upright by a belt, I would have been decapitated. Apart from being impaled on some fashionably extended dashboard switches, I was unscathed, but trapped. My main concern was that I'd just filled the fuel tank and there were people outside smoking. What a waste of petrol.

Fortunately I hadn't been drinking and I wasn't charged with careless driving. The official version was that a tyre blew. It could have been just crap driving. The car was a write-off and a new flint wall cost a fair amount.

My next car, a few months later, was more sedate – a Morris Minor; beautiful cars with a neat trumpet sound from the exhaust on every gear change. Lift the bonnet and it's clearly an engine rather than a computer. Unfortunately I took the wrong, beer-induced decision to drive it home from a stag night.

I saw two brick walls and chose to go between them – a bad move for someone who was seeing double. This time wearing a seat belt would have been sensible. The impact launched me from the seat and my head made contact with the chisel-shaped bracket that once held a sun visor. It surgically removed a large layer of my scalp. Blood was spattered on all the windows, including the back one. It looked like a particularly messy assassination.

The police had plenty of readily available sample material and it was clear I was over the limit. The hospital sewed me up with 40 stitches, but the wound was still bleeding inside. I spent the night in hospital, but the car, obviously a write-off, was towed and left outside my parents' house. They discovered the bloody wreck the next morning and naturally feared the worst.

Returning home, I calmly assured them I just had a bump and a bit of a headache, but at that moment the pressure of the blood under my sewn-up flap burst the skin like something from a Sam Peckinpah film.

I was now reduced to a bicycle. You'd think that any intelligent person might have come to the conclusion that drinking too much was causing problems for me, as well as being a danger to others. But I just wasn't seeing it that way. My free time still revolved around friends, pubs and the belief that the only way to have fun was to be intoxicated. On two occasions I was cautioned by the police for being drunk in charge of a bicycle.

The loss of two cars and, subsequently and separately, the

fracture of both my ankle bones all happened in the same year, 1978. It should have hinted that a pattern was emerging. Maybe it wasn't all fun. Perhaps it was time to settle down a bit.

While I was at work one day in early 1980 I had a surprise call from David Fraser, who had shared my flat at Dragon's Tavern five years earlier in Hong Kong. His former girlfriend, Judy, was visiting her mother in Hove for a while. Would I like to meet up with her?

Well, I'd found her attractive in Hong Kong and she'd sounded interesting, and I was living in Hove at the time (actually in the Sussex County cricket ground), so why not?

We saw a lot of each other, had several outings in my latest Morris Minor (green, four-door, 1969, no sun visor) and I was extremely impressed with her map-reading skills and sense of direction. She lived in London and I missed her when she wasn't there. I fell in love and, at the age of 27, I proposed marriage. I was convinced she was the right one at the right time. We were married less than a year later on the Spring Equinox, 1981, at St Mary de Haura in Shoreham-by-Sea and had our reception at Shoreham Airport. The plan was to leave by helicopter but the wind speed rose to force seven, which was probably too risky a way to start a marriage, so we spent the first night of our honeymoon at nearby Gravetye Manor instead.

From there we went to Ireland, first Dublin and then three wonderful weeks in a cottage near Kenmare in the south-west.

Back at the BBC, I was sailing a bit close to the wind, but, given the prevailing drink culture at the time, I didn't stand out too much. In fact, my assessment reports suggested that I might be going places, which could be taken in more than one way.

Business and financial news was increasingly topping the news bulletins, notably stories like the Guinness affair and the increasing turbulence of international markets.

The Financial Unit was asked to supply a daily three-minute business slot on lunchtime television. It was completely up to whoever drew the short straw that day to choose the subject, and this resulted in some pretty quirky selections.

There was an autocue, but not as we now know it. The script was typed on a strip of cellophane which was wound by hand and, if it got stuck, tended to melt on the hot bulb. The words were projected on to a piece of white cardboard taped just below the level of the camera, but in the hot studio the tape's adhesive powers were unreliable. The presenter's eye-line, being below the level of the camera, produced a look that was shifty at best and, more often, swivel-eyed and insane. This was all thrown together in a makeshift studio in the basement of Broadcasting House and sent 'down the line' to Television Centre in Shepherds Bush, so there was plenty of room for technical glitches.

The likelihood of being made to look a complete tosser in front of several hundred thousand people made me edgy. My solution was to write my script very quickly, leaving enough time to nip out of Broadcasting House and round the corner to the Hat and Stick, down a swift pint of Bass and jog back to the studio. If I'd got my timing right, the beer would have done its job and I'd be oblivious to looking deranged.

Clearly the 'deranged' look was becoming fashionable at the BBC because I was invited to present the main lunchtime news over at Television Centre with Richard Whitmore and, on a couple of occasions, Moira Stuart. Live broadcasting always made me twitchy and the thought that I was looking on edge produced a sense of panic with all its visceral accompaniments – tremors, sweats, rabbit-in-the-headlights eyes, loss of control of bodily functions, etc.

Given that there were no pubs within jogging distance of Television Centre, medication for my nervous disorder lay in the BBC Club bar. Pretending I was going to make-up, I'd nip up there in the lift, order a pint and drink it on the open-air roof terrace looking out over London. The IPA made me ready for anything. Afterwards I'd need another couple of pints to soak up the adrenalin. It was a dangerous combination.

Judy and I had bought a top-floor flat in Palmeira Square, one of the Regency squares that grace Hove. Soon afterwards, in October 1982, our daughter Alexandra was born, weighing in at just under seven pounds. Mother and new arrival were happy and healthy. I was there for the birth and, having attended pre-natal classes, was highly trained in saying, 'Keep breathing' – an exhortation that clearly worked. Witnessing the arrival of our first child was a moment that little would compare with in later life. I celebrated in the pub just round the corner from the maternity ward in Brighton.

Not long before Alex was born, I had been in the Queen Victoria Hospital in East Grinstead, having a malignant melanoma removed from my foot. It involved a skin graft and two weeks in the McIndoe Unit in a wheelchair. The McIndoe is famous for its pioneering work on repairing and reconstructing the damage caused by burns, most notably those suffered by fighter and bomber pilots in the Second World War. These airmen were given the nickname 'Guinea Pigs'.

Next door to the hospital was a pub called, naturally, the Guinea Pig. My hospital bed was right by double glass doors that opened out on to large, well-tended gardens, and I was able to propel my wheelchair, under the cover of the rhododendrons, and escape to the pub. Several veteran aircrew drank there regularly and always gave me a warm and generous welcome. Later I would return to my hospital bed flying on all engines, frequently hitting turbulence over the herbaceous borders.

My two-week stay at the hospital coincided with the height of the Falklands War, and I knew where many of the burns victims, particularly from the bombing of the *Sir Galahad*, would be treated.

Living in Hove meant commuting to London, which, taking into account the time getting to the station and then from Victoria to Oxford Circus (which I walked), was about two hours each way; that's 20 hours and 600 miles a week.

I started commuting just after the era of the *Brighton Belle* Pullman service, which was far too popular and profitable to be allowed to continue. However, the commuter camaraderie generated on the *Belle* continued in the replacement trains' buffet cars, which served snacks and alcohol in a friendly, club-like atmosphere. The regulars tended to be the more outgoing and interesting travellers and usually the smokers. I'd get home reeking like a kipper. My suits were hung out on the fire escape.

The buffet car had a seating area which suited poker and bridge players and those who couldn't keep their balance standing up with a drink. The more dedicated drinkers stood at the back door of the 'galley' and played the three-coin gambling game Spoof, ate cheese on toast with Worcestershire sauce and got through several outrageously priced miniatures. As a journalist I came across some of the best contacts I ever made on the train and some of my best friends. Most of the 'buffet car boys' are now either dead or retired to Spain.

For the first few decades I drank only on the journey home, but that gradually led to having a 'heart-starter' on the train up to town with some of the other veterans.

Eventually, once again the popularity and profitability of the buffet cars came to the attention of the killjoy management and they were condemned to the great big sidings in the sky. The hard core resorted to buying take-outs and using the wooden guard's vans — freezing, noisy and full of bicycles but very popular. These eventually suffered the same fate as the buffet cars.

'In-flight' refreshment has finally been distilled down to a wildly expensive trolley that never makes any progress through the train because there are too many passengers — sorry, customers — standing up. They're not popular or profitable, so they haven't been scrapped.

My career at the BBC was still on track. Each year one individual was chosen from the BBC to join other young professionals from around Europe to attend a prestigious gathering called the Salzburg Seminar in Austria. For some reason I seemed to fit the bill at the time.

Founded in 1947 by three Harvard students amid the destruction of the Second World War, this aimed to bring young Europeans together to make sure it would never happen again — a sort of Marshall Plan of the mind. It was to be 'an institution focused on global change — a place where innovative ideas lead to practical solutions. As an independent, neutral forum, the Salzburg Seminar engages current and future leaders in candid discussion to inspire new thinking and to pioneer strategies for change.' Crikey – me a 'future leader', a 'pioneer'! More importantly, it was a week off work in the Austrian mountains. Bring on *vielen Bieren, Wienerschnitzel und Mozart!*

The Seminar holds its sessions in the Schloss Leopoldskron, a beautiful rococo palace commissioned by the Archbishop of Salzburg in 1736. It stands on the shore of the Leopoldskroner Weiher lake, which most days reflected a perfect image of the snow-capped Unterberg mountain on the far side of the water. Behind the Schloss was the imposing Hohensalzburg fortress and the ancient town itself, filled with the sound of bells.

The Schloss is best known for its appearance in the 1965 film *The Sound of Music*. Some of the lake scenes and the bit in the gazebo were filmed there, but most of it was shot in a mock-up of the Schloss terrace further along the lake. They don't tell the tourists that, though.

My seminar course focused on International Relations, the centrepiece of the week being a mock World Summit. We all had parts to play, some as Summit 'sherpas', a team of civil servants who prepared the way for the leaders of the G7 nations. My role was the then Japanese Prime Minister, Yasuhiro Nakasone, a part I took sufficiently seriously to dress in Japanese national costume.

At night all the participants slept together in a big, mosquito-infested dormitory. A few of us went into Salzburg in the evenings to sample the surprisingly active nightlife, rarely returning to the 'dorm' before 3am and rarely sober. The mosquitoes gorged on my blood, but I never felt anything. They probably didn't either.

Most of the 'delegates' took the whole role-playing thing

very seriously and out-hot-aired even the real Summiteers. The young 'future leaders', the 'pioneers' of Europe (many of whom are now real European leaders), had a wonderful chance to create a radically different Summit communiqué, or at least a mildly interesting one. But the outcome was a bland, timorous, bureaucratic piece of irrelevance which would be published, remain unread and ultimately filed in a dust-gathering box. Yup, uncannily like the real thing.

There was a fair bit of free time to wander about the fragrant gardens of the Schloss and round the lake, where occasionally lectures and meetings were held in the shade of the cherry trees beside the water. As the only journalist there, I thought it would be a good idea to publish a newspaper using the Seminar's typewriter. It was called the *Leopold Times* and was loosely modelled on *Private Eye*, though it was a form of humour that left the Germans and Scandinavians unmoved.

Back in Hove, Judy and I had sold the Palmeira Square flat for £28,000 (it's currently worth £320,000) and bought a solid, semi-detached, three-bedroomed house built in 1926 for £46,000. Our second child, Frederick, arrived in April 1985. Just under seven pounds, as Alex had been, Fred was a healthy baby but took rather longer to arrive and made a few complicated somersaults involving his umbilical cord before his entrance.

We lived in that same house in Braemore Road for the next 20 years. It was about 400 yards from the seafront (and near a nightclub called the Babylon Lounge). We were about as statistically average a family as a pollster or market researcher could possibly dream of: a married heterosexual couple, husband in full-time work, wife a full-time home-maker, 2.4 children – girl, boy and dog (Dalmatian) – three-bedroom semi in a tree-lined suburban road, one car (Peugeot estate), regular family holidays and children educated at the local state schools. On Sundays I washed the car, mowed the lawn and carved the family roast joint.

Commuting to London meant setting off early, often in the dark, and getting home after sunset. In the early years Judy and I would share a bottle of wine with the evening meal when I returned. For me sometimes the wine was more important than the meal.

In other words everything appeared to be 'normal'. I had an above-average salary, neither of us was particularly profligate, but month by month the household budget arithmetic was not really adding up. I was in charge of the domestic finances and I could see the way things were going, but credit was easy to obtain and my earnings potential looked healthy as long as I held on to my job. Anyway the future could look after itself. *Carpe diem*. Seize the day. Live for the moment, for tomorrow we die. There are no pockets in a shroud. No one on their deathbed ever wished they'd spent more time at the office. Life is not a rehearsal – and so on.

In the mid-eighties the City of London was on the verge of profound changes in its structures and regulations. It seems the Chairman of the BBC and the Governor of the Bank of England had met for lunch and, presumably over brandy and cigars, decided it would be a jolly good idea for the two institutions to get to know each other better. Why not exchange two keen chaps on six-month secondments?

Well, the BBC chose me to go to the Bank, whereas the Old Lady couldn't get anyone to come to Aunty.

Before starting at Threadneedle Street, I went with the

family on a three-week holiday to Hong Kong, staying in a flat in the New Territories. It was fascinating to be back after ten years. The colony never stops evolving and even one year can produce dramatic changes, so a decade had resulted in some breathtaking additions. It was also very different for me to be back there with Judy and the children. It was made even more memorable because it coincided with a visit by the Queen.

On my mind was the possibility that I might be leaving the BBC not just on an attachment, but for good. The world of television was changing quickly as a result of rapid developments in technology, particularly satellite technology.

ITN were setting up a new pan-European satellite sub-division called Superchannel. I'd been approached to present the business element of it and, after nearly ten years at the BBC, I was thinking it might be time to move on. My prospects there were still bright, despite my best efforts to self-sabotage, but I could tell things were changing at the Corporation.

I had joined when the staff numbered more than 33,000. That figure had been cut to about 28,000. There is no doubt that costs had to be cut, as Aunty was definitely carrying a bit of excess weight. But there was a danger that her diet might threaten all that was good about the BBC. The men in suits were coming. The era of the accountants, 'management speak' and 'Birtism' was dawning.

I went ahead with the six-month attachment to the Bank of England on 27 October 1986, my arrival coinciding exactly with Big Bang.

'Big Bang' was the expression used for the sudden deregulation of financial markets. This encapsulated a wide range of measures, including the abolition of the distinction between stockjobbers and stockbrokers on the London Stock Exchange. It changed the system of dealing from open-outcry to electronic, screen-based trading. Deregulation made London far more competitive and was aimed at securing its role as the world's leading financial centre.

It was absolutely riveting to be at the Bank at that time. I was given an office of my own just down the corridor from the Governor, Robin Leigh-Pemberton. I also had my own peg in the toilet, a hand towel with my name embroidered on it and shoe-cleaning equipment – only black polish, naturally.

The deal was that I had access to everyone, everywhere and every meeting on condition that I did not report on anything. For a journalist, this was unprecedented.

I was invited to sit in on all the Bank's committees that regulated the markets in commodities, precious metals, bonds and money. It was particularly impressive to witness the high-powered meetings involving the Executive Directors, Ian Plenderleith and Eddie George (who went on to become Governor in 1993). Both men being chain-smokers, the air in the committee room would become rapidly impenetrable, though the discussions remained clear-sighted and incisive.

It was a time of volatility in the foreign exchange markets. For a financial journalist it was pulse-quickening to watch the Bank's dealers intervene in the market, sometimes in unison with other central banks, with tens of millions of pounds to influence exchange rates. Just a whiff of the Bank in the markets was enough at that time to swing rates sharply. Six years later, of course, it failed on 'Black Wednesday', when the Bundesbank refused to help and the UK was, thankfully, forced to leave the Exchange Rate Mechanism.

I was also invited into the Holy of Holies, known as 'Books' – the 11am meeting between the Governor, the

Executive Directors and the department heads in the ornate, panelled Court Room. Here, in the centre of the ceiling, a dial is linked to a weathervane on the roof, which in days gone by was an important guide to the movements of ships that would need financing.

This meeting of the top brass was to agree, among other things, on the day's tactics in the various markets, particularly the money markets. Ultimately it was the gathering that decided interest-rate policy, which, in those days before its independence, the Bank operated very much hand in hand with the Treasury.

My time there also meant I could go down to the vaults and stare at several hundred million pounds' worth of gold bullion. It's now worth a great deal more than it was then, though a large proportion was sold off a few years ago at a low point in the price. I was particularly fascinated by the department that designed new banknotes incorporating all the latest technology to foil the forgers. It was especially interesting to me because as a teenager I'd spent a fair amount of time trying to perfect my own banknote-forging techniques. My tour included a visit to the department that destroys old notes. It's an unsettling vision seeing several million pounds' worth of used, but surely still usable, banknotes being shredded and burned in ovens. Come on, no one would miss a couple of grand, would they?

After a month or so, having toured all the departments and interviewed most of the senior staff, I began to fade into the background. It was up to me when I came and went and, the Bank being right in the centre of the City, there was a wide range of good restaurants and bars to fill the time. One of my favourites was the George and Vulture. Established in 1600, it's tucked away in one of the narrow Dickensian alleyways that link Lombard Street and Cornhill. Lunch is available each weekday and the food is simple – pretty much steak or pies and gallons of red wine, served by genial but no-nonsense waitresses. They were cockneys (or at least Essex) then, but probably Polish or Ukrainian now. Sleep would come easily in my own quiet, book-lined office – highly polished shoes up on the Queen Anne desk.

Having merged into the Bank's chintz wallpaper, I was invisible enough to take off for lunch with the editors back at ITN. The Superchannel project was going ahead and the money that was being offered was well above my BBC salary.

The team looked interesting – it included John Suchet, Bob Hunter, Sue Carpenter and Nigel Dacre, among others – and was being assembled very quickly. Given the cramped conditions at ITN in Wells Street, the only solution was to put the mini-studio in a Portakabin and lift it by crane on to the roof. It was linked to the inside of the building by a perilous metal fire escape. The arrangements put in place for the new channel aptly summed things up – it was a low-cost venture, rapidly thrown together, loosely attached to ITN itself and with a future that was rather up in the air.

It might be a risky proposition, I decided, but after nearly ten years at the BBC it was a good time to move on. For no more profound reason than 'let's go for it and see what happens', I accepted the job.

I still had a couple of months back at the BBC. At the time the Corporation was (unofficially) looking for a new presenter of the flagship *Nine O'Clock News*. There was a great deal of ill-informed speculation in the press about who it might be. As a result of a well-oiled journey on the buffet car of the Hove train with Brian Hitchen, editor of the *Daily Star*, my name was dropped into a story headlined 'The New

Nine O'Clock News Hunk'. It went on to say that I was now the 'bookies' favourite' to be the new face of the relaunched news. Apart from the fact that the 'bookies' hadn't a clue who I was, it was all fabricated nonsense. But the odd thing was, as a result of the newspaper story, I was urgently invited to do an audition for the presenter's job. I had to inform them that I was leaving the BBC. I would have been crap at it anyway.

As it turned out, the last report I did before moving on was the lead story for *The Nine O'Clock News*. There had been a surprise change in Base Rates by the Bank of England. The Economics Correspondent, James Long, was away and the Chancellor, Nigel Lawson, had unusually offered to do a last-minute interview.

I happened to be in the right place at the right time and was asked to get to the Treasury as quickly as I could. The only possible way to get from Shepherds Bush to Whitehall in time was on the back of a dispatch bike. The 600cc machine roared through the London traffic with me clinging to the pillion seat. We made it in time and the Chancellor gave all the obvious answers to all the obvious questions, oblivious to my helmet-shaped hairdo.

The report was the top item on the bulletin and I had to deliver it live. My hands were shaking, but I was sure it was just the after-effects of the ride on the Kawasaki.

5

FLYING HIGH

In the mid-eighties, ITN news was generally regarded as being more dynamic and professional than the BBC's news department. ITN was much smaller, and so more fleet of foot. And, because the chain of command was shorter, communication was swifter and riskier decisions could be taken. *News at Ten* was then well ahead in the ratings. It also appeared to attract the best and brightest and certainly paid above average.

In today's world of competing and fragmented news providers – satellite and cable TV, the Internet and mobile sources of information, ITN isn't quite so outstanding, but back then I was proud to be joining 'the opposition', even if the section I was joining was a bit of a sideshow in a hut on a roof.

Superchannel had that exciting 'start-up' atmosphere – a feeling I was going to get familiar with in the future. It's a heady cocktail of unbounded optimism (or at least temporarily concealed scepticism), mixed with small-team camaraderie, an 'anything is possible' attitude, fuelled by the adrenalin of tight deadlines which are usually rescheduled. 'It's revolutionary, it's cutting edge, it's going to be the best. What a team! What a launch (even if it was delayed)!'

It's a bubbly drink that quickly goes flat, but is great while it lasts. It soon gets watered down in the face of the realities of fewer viewers than forecast, budget constraints, cost-cutting, diminishing novelty value and the sheer grind of putting out regurgitated news from the same wholesale sources on a relentless daily basis.

I was employed to produce and present a short daily business section in the half-hour news. It was the 'must have' – business/financial/economic news was making the headlines, so Superchannel news had to have a business slot.

But here lay several contradictions. If it's big enough news, it won't be in the slot. If it's routine but worthy, it'll need 'sexing up', but if it's sexed up it often becomes distorted and laughable to a viewer who knows the subject. If it's aimed at the professional business person, they'll probably get the information from other sources. If it's aimed at the small investor, it gets bogged down in the minutiae of building society accounts, saving rates and pensions, which to me was numbingly boring and very hard to make into illustrated television.

I didn't lose any sleep over this as long as I filled the slot. It was just good to be at ITN and I didn't take the business section too seriously, which is just as well because it didn't survive that long. Nor did Superchannel.

At that time, though not now, there was a drinking culture at ITN, but there was sufficient professionalism for it not to adversely affect the output. The company had an in-house bar on the top floor that had generous opening hours. A few well-known individuals would have 'sharpeners' early on – I knew because I was there with them. It tended to be 'blue' vodkas. Most of the drinking, though, was done after *News at Ten*.

The main company watering hole was Wolsey's Wine Bar, across Wells Street and about 25 yards from our building. I had arrived at ITN just after the newsreader Reggie Bosanquet ('Beaujolais') had gone to the Green Room in the sky. He was alleged to have got the pacing just right so that he could leave Wolsey's just in time to reach the studio and get wired up for the bongs that heralded the *News at Ten*. The truth was likely to have been more prosaic – Reggie probably left a good ten minutes before the programme started.

Superchannel had its own rather cramped newsroom. My seat happened to be right at the end of the long desk, which put me directly outside the office of Sir Alastair Burnet. I had met him already through our mutual friend, Brian Hitchen. Brian and Alastair's friendship went back many years to the time when Alastair was editor of the *Economist* and then the *Daily Express*. It was also evident that both men admired Margaret Thatcher.

ITN appeared to have a particularly warm relationship with Mrs Thatcher. In the early days of Superchannel she was invited to have a look around the newsroom. She was just over halfway through her time as Prime Minister and at the height of her power. I was able to have a long chat, and a drink, with her. My impression was one of an intensely intelligent woman, but not especially domineering or overpowering. It did help that I was a good listener, though. To me she came across as almost huggable. More soft toy than Iron Lady. But then again, I didn't have to deal with her in Cabinet along with the 'vegetables'.

As a newcomer to ITN, I was in awe of Sir Alastair. Most

mornings he would invite me into his office for a chat about the day's news. He was an impressively knowledgeable man and always hospitable. Our sessions were a big incentive for me to keep up to speed with all the latest developments.

The usual routine was to have a large vodka in the morning from a bottle secreted at the bottom of Alastair's filing cabinet. An organised man, he kept it under the letter 'V'. We'd talk about a wide range of issues. His main aim was that *News at Ten* should reflect what the ordinary person on the bus or in the pub would be talking about the next day, and perhaps help them to discuss it in a more informed way.

In the afternoon he'd invite me back in to run through how the programme was shaping up. He'd pour out a hefty glass of whisky, a bottle of which was filed under 'S'. I had been advised by *News at Ten*'s editor, Nick Pollard, that it was a bad idea to try to match Alastair drink for drink and still hope to do a professional job. It was worth a try, though.

On one occasion it did go too far. Thinking it was a slack news day, I'd had the usual 'editorial consultations' with Alastair, plus a hefty and traditional City lunch, followed by some liveners in Wolsey's. Unfortunately there was a late-breaking piece of business news. The decision was taken to make it *News at Ten*'s lead story. There was no time to put together the usual graphics or do many interviews, so most of it would have to be done live to camera in the studio.

I cannot remember a thing about the broadcast. I woke the next morning wondering what the main news had been the previous night, not realising that I had been the one broadcasting it. I just hoped all the viewers had been in the same condition.

Alastair often invited me to his regular lunch spot, the

White Tower in Percy Street, about half a mile from ITN. It was a place I already knew vaguely, having very nearly fallen out of the first-floor window at a private function. Thanks to Alastair, I made some influential contacts and being known to lunch with the company's main anchor didn't do my career any harm either. It might even have saved it.

I was impressed by the way Alastair presented *News at Ten* after a day of pretty continuous drinking. His *Spitting Image* puppet was always portrayed broadcasting the news slightly slurring, a large glass of whisky in front of him. The only inaccuracy was the slurring.

Alastair's natural air of authority was backed up by the fact that he really did know what he was talking about. And his style of delivery displayed no daft affectations, unlike the 'sing-song' presentation of some of the main news broadcasters now.

The increasing amount of coverage of business stories, coupled with the wide-ranging changes following Big Bang, resulted in ITN advertising for a City Correspondent. The print industry was scoured for likely talent, but the view was that newspaper journalists weren't the right stuff for television – too ponderous. Print journalists generally took the view that television was too glib, shallow and populist.

In the end I got the job. I joined the other ITN Correspondents in the corner room of ITN overlooking the King's Head pub in Riding House Street. I had my own desk and my own agenda. Up to that point in my career I had always had regular commitments and regular deadlines. Now my time was my own as long as I produced the stories. The pressure was on. It was a dangerous combination in my case.

To begin with, I generally went for stories that involved travel – much more interesting than standing in a dealing room talking about exchange rates, or doing a piece to camera outside the Treasury.

In the news at the time was the (then) European Community's moves towards reducing the trade barriers between member countries. The plan would be to follow, over a week, the experiences of a British road haulage company as its lorries travelled through France, Belgium, the Netherlands and Germany. It would have the human element as we interviewed the drivers en route, a worthy business aspect and great pictures of the trucks thundering through the countryside of the Continent. It would also mean some good hotels and the best restaurants. As the cameraman on the trip said to me, his Michelin guidebook was his most important piece of luggage. With background music and eye-catching graphics, the week-long series went down well with ITN management but probably left the *News at Ten* audience unmoved.

In those days ITN issued correspondents with an American Express card to cover expenses. The bills went directly to the company's account and didn't need much, if any, written explanation or justification. It was a financially dangerous situation to have widely travelling journalists who enjoyed the good life carrying charge cards with virtually no limits. The system was changed, but not before ITN discovered a £10-million hole in its accounts.

International oil prices were never out of the headlines, and, with my already established contacts at BP, a facility trip was offered to see the company's drilling operation on the north coast of Alaska at Prudhoe Bay. The same offer was made to the BBC's James Long, whom I knew from my time in the Financial Unit.

I met the camera crew at Heathrow only to be told that British Airways had over-booked in economy class on the flight to Tokyo via Anchorage. Would we be prepared to accept a cash sum in compensation and get the next flight, or suffer being upgraded to first class? We dithered for a good fraction of a second before choosing to turn left and board the plane.

On taking my seat in Row 1, I discovered I was sitting next to Sir Laurens van der Post, friend of Prince Charles, godfather to Prince William, author of *The Bushmen of the Kalahari*, expert on Jungian psychology and acclaimed raconteur. Sadly he slept all the way.

Despite our best efforts there were several bottles of champagne left when we disembarked at Anchorage, but the very hospitable in-flight attendants gave us take-outs. Sir Laurens, undisturbed, went on to Tokyo.

We spent the night in Anchorage and then boarded a cargo plane going north. The flight involved a change of planes on the way. We reached the small airport, somewhere in the middle of the state, where we were going to transfer and I got talking to some oil workers in the bar, for background information purposes. They assured me they were on the same flight onwards and I only had to stick with them. Maybe I had misunderstood Alaskan humour, but they weren't flying anywhere and nor was I. I watched my connecting flight make a perfect take-off from my vantage point in the airport bar.

I caught up some time later. It was a fascinating trip which produced stunning pictures, particularly the low-level helicopter flight down a section of the Trans-Alaska pipeline. There wasn't an especially strong news peg, but it ran on all three news bulletins. I reckon BP got its money's worth.

One of the more imaginative facility trips was thought up by the newly formed Channel Tunnel company, Eurotunnel.

Construction of the tunnel had only just begun in 1987 and the company was keen to raise its profile and increase awareness of the enormity and importance of the project.

Discussion of the PR strategy must have gone something like this: 'Let's show a group of journalists how the rail-tunnel system is already working for vehicles. Where are they operating now? ... Ah, yes, let's go to Switzerland. Next, geology is important – the tunnel has to go through 50 kilometres of chalk marl. Where are there already tunnels dug through chalk? ... Ah, yes, let's go to the storage caves for millions of champagne bottles around Reims and Epernay. Hmmm, bit of a round trip. OK, we'll charter a plane.'

And so it was that a group of six journalists took off from Gatwick in a twin-engine turbo-prop for a fact-finding jaunt around Europe – first stop the Gotthard Rail Tunnel, then a big lunch and an overnight stay in a chalet in the Alps. It was absolutely riveting to see how cars are loaded on to trains and then go through a tunnel. I could have watched it all day, but we were herded off for more food and drink. Our final stop was a little private airport just outside Epernay, followed by a night in a chateau which involved a sumptuous meal and much sampling of the local produce. From a geological point of view, chalk marl was fascinating.

The flight back to Gatwick was through clear skies, but the atmosphere in the small cabin with six drunk journalists on board must have been pure alcohol. Judging by the acrobatic landing, the pilot had been breathing too deeply.

But the clouds were building up over the City and the entire international financial system. It was October 1987 and forecasters, both meteorological and financial, were unaware of the power of the storm that was about to break.

I was completely oblivious to the raging winds down on the coast in Hove during the night of 15–16 October. I slept soundly through the whole thing, having arrived home late from another long day at ITN. The worst of the force-12 winds came pounding in around 1am. Our house lost some tiles and our wooden fences. Two roads away a woman lost her life when the chimney stack crashed down through her bedroom.

I woke early, intending to set off to London for work, but it was quite clear that no one in the south-east was going anywhere. With 15 million trees uprooted, road and rail links were blocked. I spent the day at home.

The chaos also meant that very few London Stock Market traders could get to work. That week, equity and bond markets around the world had been a bit jittery in response to comments from the US Federal Reserve and movements in the dollar. London traders couldn't reach their offices to close down trading positions.

It was made worse by the fact that Wall Street was down quite heavily on that Friday night. So there was a backlog of business pent up ready for the opening after the weekend. I knew I had better make an early start at ITN on that Monday, 19 October.

The next day, Saturday, I wasn't thinking much about financial stories. I had been due to fly out to Chicago but all arrangements had been cancelled. Instead, Judy, the children and I thought we'd have a look at the storm damage on our favourite hill, Chanctonbury Ring, the highest point on the South Downs, between Steyning and Findon. Almost the entire inner section of ancient beech trees had been flattened. Only a thin outer circle of younger trees remained standing. Twenty years of subsequent growth have not really made much difference.

London traders had been expecting to do some catching up on Monday morning, but few could have predicted the tidal wave of sell-orders as they reached their computer terminals. Hong Kong and Tokyo were down dramatically and all other European markets went the same way. The London Stock Market plummeted more than 22 per cent, its headlong retreat accelerated by a massive fall on Wall Street. The New York market nose-dived more than 500 points – which may not seem that big now that the Dow Jones average is so much higher but, scaled up, it was a drop of nearly 3,000 points. The selling had been made much worse by the impact of programme trading as computers blindly took over when markets dropped to a certain level. Programme trading is a system whereby computers are programmed to trade in a certain way when specified trading levels are reached or breached. If a market falls to a certain point, a programmed trading system will intervene.

It was financial carnage – a collapse greater than the Wall Street Crash of 1929. It became known as Black Monday. For me, as the City Correspondent of ITN, it was Golden Monday. The story led all the main bulletins for weeks – not just the market story itself, but also endless speculation about the threat to the world's financial foundations, the impact on international economic growth and what it meant for the man in the street.

At the time there was a temptation to talk in terms of Doomsday, but, even at my age then, I'd already experienced two recessions and was well aware what goes down tends to come back up. The world economy was reasonably strong and so the market meltdown did not have much of a long-term impact on fundamentals. The real world recession came three years later.

I barely made it home for several weeks and pressure of work, combined with increased drinking, left me exhausted. At that time I was doing short morning-news updates, which meant very early starts in front of the camera. One morning, well into the story, I was so knackered and probably still drunk that my brain and mouth just simply would not work. Fortunately the financial storm was beginning to subside, because I was running out of different ways to describe market movements and different dealing rooms to say it from.

While I was at the BBC I had covered the Spring (now Autumn) Budgets for Radio 4, along with Dominic Harrod, Vincent Duggleby and Peter Day. It was only natural that ITN would consider me for the 1988 Budget. Alastair Burnet was stepping down from presenting it, so I joined the team with Alastair Stewart and Carol Barnes.

Covering a budget on television was far more than just reporting what the Chancellor announced. The central task was computer analysis of the impact on consumers and tax payers in various income bands. This would then be turned into colourful, spinning and flashing graphics. It was my job to help present the programme and make instant interpretations with the help of my computer. It was the sort of operation that required a very clear head – something I didn't have for the rehearsal, but did have, just, for the real thing.

ITN also wanted me to put together a book packed with useful information so that viewers would be up to speed when the Chancellor presented his Budget. The company gave me an Amstrad computer to write the book on. I'm sure it's in a museum somewhere now. As hard as I tried, I could not produce enough information to fill an entire book and so the type size had to be increased significantly to make it look like a book – very useful for the visually challenged. It didn't exactly fly off the supermarket shelves and most copies were pulped – probably along with copies of the Budget itself.

As part of the promotion for the *Budget '88* programme, the three of us (Alastair, Carol and I) had our picture taken outside 11 Downing Street with me holding my newly published, slim and ephemeral volume. The picture was published in *TV Times*, but would be reproduced several times many years later (including on the back of this book) in very different circumstances.

Alastair and I also had a pre-Budget lunch with the Shadow Chancellor, Gordon Brown, in a restaurant just round the corner from the Houses of Parliament. It was a pleasant lunch, if rather dry in every sense of the word. He came across as being rather detached and distant. Perhaps his mind was on another recent lunch in Islington. I remember little about the meeting. That probably says everything.

Gordon was, at the time, on the opposition front bench; 20 years later I was on the seafront bench. It's hard to say, at the time of writing, which one of us is now the happier.

Budget '88 went to air without any major cock-ups. I overindulged on the post-programme drinks, had more on the train home and threw up copiously when I arrived at Hove Station – fortunately on the tracks.

But at least I did get off at Hove. One of the major problems of being a commuter working long hours and drinking too much was waking up well beyond the right station or even in the sidings. I was increasingly finding myself in Eastbourne, Portsmouth, Southampton or Bournemouth. On one occasion I was tired and emotional and so took the precaution of getting a Brighton train, which cannot go any further because of the sea. However, on this journey my sleep was sufficiently sound for me to remain asleep in Brighton and still be on the train for its return journey to London. London looked very much like Brighton and so I got off. That night I slept on the floor at ITN.

Commuting, long hours and drinking were definitely putting a strain on my marriage, but the money was coming in and the mounting bills were just about getting paid with a little help from American Express, Barclaycard and a growing wallet of competing credit cards. We had a medium-sized mortgage, an average family car (a small Volvo five-door) and no school fees. Holidays were usually packaged. Commuting was expensive, and not just the cost of the season ticket, but living in Hove was cheaper than London. The thing that never existed in a quarter of a century of marriage was savings.

Competition in the pan-European satellite world was increasing with the arrival of Sky and CNN. There were plans brewing for a dedicated pan-European business channel. Common sense would suggest that it should be in a leading financial centre – London, Frankfurt or Paris. Wherever it was based, it would have to be in English, the *lingua franca* of the business world.

It gradually became clear that a group of investors were putting together a project to launch a business television channel in Zurich. It was vague at that stage but it was apparently going to be backed by Swiss banks, Thames Television, possibly Swatch and a few others that were suitably mysterious, secretive and, well, Swiss.

Zurich is a financial and banking centre, probably best known for its gold market, but it's not really in the big league when it comes to stock, commodity, bond or currency markets. It does have the advantage of being geographically central in Europe (although a television station could theoretically be anywhere), multi-lingual and, being in Switzerland, would be associated with neutrality, quality and trustworthiness. The downside was that it would be expensive, would come up against restrictive labour laws and would display a conservative attitude, even fear, towards new ideas.

It seems the Swiss don't much like foreigners or anything that threatens their safe, established lives. There is a vein of paranoia running through the national psyche, though, in my experience, they never seem to be like that when they leave Switzerland.

The driving force was a Swiss national, John Winistoerfer, who ran a television facilities company in Schlieren, an industrial area just outside Zurich. He had been sizing up potential editors-in-chief around Europe but had received a rather sceptical response. But then he made contact with Will Hutton.

At that time Will was working on the BBC's *Newsnight*, but I already knew him from his days on Radio 4's *The Financial World Tonight*. Enthusiastic, affable, intelligent, Will was an ideas man, maybe even visionary, rather than practical; some said other-worldly, which was possibly what attracted John Winistoerfer.

I had several lunches with Will, who brought along Paul Gibbs (we'd napped together a decade earlier in the House of Lords press box) and James Long, BBC TV's Economics Correspondent. I was offered the job presenting the morning (and only) programme. The project had its attractions – not least a six-figure Swiss-franc salary and a potentially comfortable lifestyle – but anyone who could add up would have had serious worries about the business plan.

I made a couple of exploratory trips to Zurich, but my first reaction was that the whole thing was suspect, weird and a bit spooky. What swung it, though, was the offer of even more Swiss francs and a memorable lunch with John and his wife at Switzerland's finest restaurant, the Kronenhalle, on Ramistrasse in the centre of the city. There I had one of the best meals I've ever had – *Zurcher Geschneltzeltes mit Rosti* plus a number of bottles of Dole, a Swiss white wine, followed by chocolate mousse – but what really made it outstanding was the dining room itself. The walls were hung with genuine masterpieces by Picasso, Miro and Monet, among many others. Our table was under *Still Life with Oysters* by Matisse.

Leaving the restaurant and walking down to the lakeside, feeling the cool, fresh air blowing off the shimmering water and seeing the sunlit, snow-covered Alps in the distance, I thought back to the dark slog of commuting to London and a future of endless pieces to camera in City dealing rooms. The decision, at that moment, was clear.

It was a risk and it could end in disaster, but it would be an adventure for the whole family. The children (five and three years old) would only gain from the experience and Judy, having been born and brought up in Hong Kong, would probably like the idea of living abroad again – which she did.

So I signed up with the European Business Channel (EBC) in the autumn of 1988, as did a large group of other UK journalists, including Will Hutton, James Long, Paul Gibbs, Jane Ellison, Dermot Murnaghan, Nigel Parsons, Ian Smith, Heather Scott, Nick Toksvig and Robin Gould.

For the first couple of months I was there without the family. As I returned to Hove most weekends, the bars of

Kloten Airport became very familiar and the children received an endless supply of Toblerone.

I couldn't possibly imagine it was intentional but Dermot and I were booked into the Zurichberg, the only *alkoholfrei* hotel in the area. This was on the edge of a forest, near the zoo and high above the city and the lake, and its brochure announced: 'Founded in 1894, the Zurichberg is considered to be a pioneer in the specific branch of temperance gastronomy'. *Wunderbar!* Dermot and I would be able to sit in the hotel gardens in the clear mountain air sipping *Apfelsaft*.

Well, if the hotel was *alkoholfrei*, the cafe right next door to the EBC studios down in Schlieren was the exact opposite. The Wagibeiz, known as the Wagi, conveniently opened at 6am and closed at a time that I was never really fully conscious of. There wasn't the concept of licensing hours in Switzerland. Alcohol could be bought and consumed at any time. Certainly the boiler-suited local workers kick-started their day with a beer, cognac or glass of red. It was easy to go native.

The EBC studios were being constructed in what looked like a disused factory – and probably was. It was part of the same building that housed the aptly named Black Box, the facilities company run by Winistoerfer. I say 'aptly named' because what applied here was the concept used in science, particularly psychology, whereby it's of no concern to the experimenter what goes on in the 'black box'; what matters is what the inputs are and what the outputs are.

Black Box seemed to consume a lot of money, there was very little output and there appeared to be nothing going on inside. It was beautifully designed in a glass and aluminium sort of way, but the clean, polished corridors were silent and the studios, filled with the latest expensive equipment, stood empty.

EBC's basic strategy was a good one: broadcast business news in English and German across Europe to high-spending, luxury-buying, decision-making professionals at a time of day when there was no real competition and on a subject that allowed viewers to gain a competitive edge at the start of the day. It would pull in advertisers wanting to attract the hard-to-reach, so-called ABC1 demographic. Putting it out in German as well as English would mean it was possible in theory to produce two programmes for the price of one. It just needed good translators.

Clever plan. Sadly, reality intervened. The huge advertising sales force of two failed to sell adverts. It was never really possible to prove the size of the audience because, being so small, it didn't really register using any known measuring techniques. A vast multi-lingual news production team, mostly from outside Switzerland, cost an absolute fortune. My pay packet alone would have broken most companies and I was some way down the salary scale. At its peak there were about 130 members of staff producing an hour of output.

We could see the flaws in the vision, but the view was, let's enjoy the experience while we can. It's not our money anyway. Let's pour resources into Big Ideas and let the Swiss banks take the strain. Big Ideas certainly gushed out of Will Hutton. The morning editorial meetings were grandiose and other-planetary. Some of the story proposals actually made it on to videotape – at least during rehearsals.

A serious flaw was the idea that the half-hour of English material could easily and cheaply be turned into a German version using the same scripts and video. But English television script-writing and reporter packages could not simply be transposed. There existed a fundamental difference in the hard-wiring of the British and German journalistic brains. Complete rewrites and recuts were always necessary and that took time and money. One wonderful example was a story that reported a poor decision by a business leader who had 'shot himself in the foot'; the German translation had him committing suicide.

Despite the fact that the business plan, as it stood, was probably doomed, despite international stylistic friction and despite the fact that several members of staff spent too much time in the Wagi, the launch in November 1988 went surprisingly well. The studio and graphics were attractive and there were no obvious howlers.

My style of presenting was informal and, I hoped, had a humorous, light touch. We were only talking about money after all – no one gets hurt except sometimes in the wallet. The 6am Feldschlosschen beer may have helped. This less formal approach was received as a breath of fresh air in Swiss broadcasting – which was actually not that hard to do. The Swiss business community was initially shocked when I talked casually to the CEO of, say, the Union Bank of Switzerland, and used his first name, but gradually they came to like it. I got a fair bit of freelance work in Zurich teaching Swiss business leaders how not to be stiff-arses.

One possibly trivial example was that I suggested that viewers send in their company's or personal favourite ties and I would wear them on air and give them a mention. A small gesture, but the ties poured in and I quickly had enough ties to wear a different one every day, however long EBC survived. In the end I had a lot left over – unworn and now circulating in the Oxfam system.

The routine was for the production staff to go straight to the Wagi at 8.30 after the broadcast and discuss the programme, gossip about the management and get stuck into the Feldschlosschens and plum spirits. Swiss clocks seemed to go faster than elsewhere and, before we knew it, it was lunchtime, which meant a meal somewhere in Zurich. This often went on through the afternoon and evening to the point where it was barely worth going to bed. The early shift began again at 1am.

Judy and the children came out to live in Switzerland a couple of months later and, to begin with, we had an apartment near the lake within consultation distance of two large houses formerly owned by Sigmund Freud and Carl Jung – the Swiss have always been significant contributors to, and consumers of, psychoanalysis.

Our landlord lived on the ground floor below us. He must have had good ears or had our apartment bugged. I used to regularly listen to the BBC World Service. One day the landlord called me downstairs and accused me of being a spy and a threat to Swiss state security. He clearly thought my short-wave radio was espionage equipment.

Maybe he was on to something. The fact that every Swiss building had a nuclear shelter and every able-bodied male between certain ages was required to serve in the army and keep a gun on the premises surely indicated that Switzerland was under imminent threat of invasion by Soviet tanks... or little green men. Since the landlord presumably had a rifle in his bunker, I wasn't going to disillusion him.

Soon after having my cover blown, we moved up the hill to Zollikon, a village said to be the richest per capita in Europe. It might well have been but I rarely met anyone who actually lived there. The 16th-century, black-beamed and white-walled houses were beautiful but mostly unoccupied. Most front entrances had several brass plaques carrying exotic-sounding company names headquartered probably in Liechtenstein. The streets were uncannily empty. I always wondered what went on behind the pretty window boxes and dainty net curtains.

Our apartment was pristinely clean and we were ordered in no uncertain terms to keep it that way. The village authorities, the Gemeinde, also spelled out the local by-laws, which included, among a long list, no hedge-cutting at certain hours, no washing the car in the road outside or the drive and no flushing the toilet during the night. Shoelaces had to be done up at all times. Leaving litter was a capital offence.

We had two cars, a Subaru estate and a leased Fiat Panda. I needed the Panda to get to work at 1am, leaving Judy the Subaru to take the children to the International School in nearby Zumikon. At that time in the morning the streets were empty, so I tended to put my foot down. I hadn't taken account of the fact that in Zurich the speed cameras were not that conspicuous. Unknown to me, I got flashed twice and so I lost my *Fuhrerausweis*, my driving licence, which meant I had to retake my driving test – theoretical and practical – and in German.

The examiner was dressed casually but would probably have preferred to wear a black uniform bearing lightning-flash insignia. I was only obeying orders and passed first time.

I went out to celebrate at the James Joyce pub in the centre of Zurich and miscalculated my consumption. I fell off the bar stool and was taken away by ambulance to A&E at the Stadtspital Triemli. I was the only one there and was treated immediately. The scrupulously polite doctors conferred at length and made their diagnosis: 'Alkoholrausch/Sturz vom Barstuhl. Therapie: nihil.'

Getting pissed and falling off a bar stool sounds so much more clinical in German.

The work at EBC wasn't exactly onerous, but the unusual hours and the excess drinking did begin to have an impact. Meanwhile, as a family we took full advantage of the generous income and being in one of the most beautiful countries in the world. It was only a 45-minute drive out of Zurich before we reached the snow-line and the first of the ski resorts. The picturesque lakeside town of Zug was less than an hour away. Food, even in the most out-of-the-way restaurants, was always of a high standard. Taking boat rides on the Zurichsee down the length of the lake to Rapperswil was just idyllic, as were the walks and picnics in the flower-covered Alpine meadows, listening to the well-washed cows tinkling their bells.

We spent a week in St Moritz, enjoying sleigh rides under fur covers, watching the horse races and polo on ice with the fabulously wealthy and eating delicious, steaming cheese fondues in the crisp mountain air. It was a world away from catching the crowded 5.57am train in the damp darkness from Hove every day.

As with all new television projects, the excitement and enthusiasm at EBC began to fade as the daily output became rather routine. A loyal band of viewers enjoyed the quirkiness of the output and, in the days before the Internet, the channel was actually a valuable source of live business data and it had very little competition.

There was a sort of 'local TV' feel to the output and Zurich was, in some ways, like a village. As a presenter I was regularly recognised as I walked down the main shopping street, Bahnhofstrasse. One day a Swiss chap – a stockbroker, I think – stopped me and said, 'Gruezi, Ed. Good to see you. Love the programme. Great sense of humour. You know, I've always wondered... what do you do with the rest of the day, when the programme's over so early in the morning?'

Jokingly I replied, 'I spend it with your wife.'

'Ach, gut, super... That's a joke, jah?'

The Swiss have never really been renowned for their sparkling wit, and I never did find any venues for stand-up comedians in Zurich. A viewer did actually send me what he claimed was the entire collection of Swiss jokes but the one sheet of paper just had the usual international jokes with 'Swiss' used instead of 'Irish' or 'Polish'.

There was a certain amount of friction between the German expats and the Swiss. The Germans tended to look down on the locals as country bumpkins, because Swiss-German comes across to them as agricultural, rather like someone from Somerset sounds to a speaker of RP English. The Swiss had a distinct work ethic – make sure you look like you're working; get in as early as possible, shuffle a lot of papers, attend frequent meetings and always leave your jacket on the back of your chair. All this was particularly true of EBC's 'marketing department'.

As time passed, anxiety grew among the staff, British, German and Swiss alike, about the continued lack of advertising on both the German- and English-language programmes, but we were constantly assured that once EBC had broken into the lucrative German cable networks the revenue would start pouring in. It wasn't enough to convince Will Hutton to stay with the project. He resigned about a year into the project for a job on the *Guardian* and went on to write the best-selling book *The State We're In*. Back at EBC we were gradually realising the state we were in.

John Winistoerfer had all along stated that television start-ups were risky. Almost everyone understood those risks, especially the employees who had brought their families over from another country, but it was thought that solid, safe, Swiss backing from some big institutions would mean that we were in for the long haul.

Cracks began to appear when existing investors started to back away and potential investors were reluctant to get involved with the channel's current structure. Towards the end the ownership was almost three-quarters in the hands of a company that produced cement and concrete. Mind you, cement was big business in Switzerland given the number of nuclear shelters.

So the stakes had got higher. Most new television channels might have made a bigger push to boost revenues and perhaps started thinking about cost-cutting. But at EBC the opposite happened.

It was full steam ahead for ten hours of broadcasting within a fairly short timeframe. That meant employing many more staff, dozens from Britain. With the heightened and now glaring risk, that required even bigger salaries. Within weeks of EBC's final collapse, high-profile broadcasters were being invited over to Zurich with offers of six-figure salaries. One of those was Peter Day, who asked for my advice on whether he should leave the BBC and come to Switzerland. My answer was an emphatic no, but he came anyway and a couple of weeks later the channel went bankrupt. But at least he was able to resume his old job after receiving a useful pay-off.

The irony was that it was exactly the right time for a pan-European business channel. Huge political and historic tectonic plates were beginning to shift remorselessly in Europe. Economic weakness meant that the Soviet Union, under Mikhail Gorbachev, was not strong enough to prevent East Germans voting with their Trabants and joyously leaving their sick country in their thousands for the West. The Russians were not going to prop up the GDR's Erich Honecker any longer, there would be no tanks sent and soon afterwards the Berlin Wall came down.

It was history in the making and EBC covered developments for a few months, but it was beginning to face up to its own seismic event. EBC had always been pretty weird but it now became Alice in Wonderland. Fuelled by crazy expectations and completely unrealistic plans, the place was filled with hordes of highly paid and directionless staff.

In the real world, even rocket scientists were getting the science of rocketry wrong. EBC's hopes of greater distribution were hit hard by news that an Ariane rocket carrying a vital satellite had blown up on take-off. That set back forecast distribution plans by months.

A team from the giant US communications group Time Warner were also sniffing around and running up large bills at Zurich's stunningly expensive Dolder Grand Hotel. Speculation was rife. Were they planning a takeover, were they in Zurich to learn how not to run a television station or were they waiting for EBC to hit a brick wall and then pick up the pieces on the cheap?

In the end any plans for a takeover were blocked by the Swiss authorities. Time Warner broke off bid talks because they could not take a stake larger than 49 per cent under Switzerland's strict foreign ownership rules.

We continued to produce the daily morning programme but time was fast running out.

It was a brave, possibly foolhardy, decision to allow the tired and emotional staff to produce and broadcast a final edition when they all knew they had no jobs and nothing to lose. It was broadcast on a tidal wave of alcohol and floods of tears. It was actually well put together and entertaining, but is now lost in the ether of TV history.

With the last, emotional programme finally off air, the entire staff piled into the Wagi for *vielen grosses Bieren*. To emphasise the apocalyptic atmosphere, the skies burst, there was torrential rain and a dramatic electric storm. Amid the lightning and thunder, EBC's accountant came round the bar handing out wads of Swiss francs. Bankruptcy meant that the company's bank accounts had been frozen. It was a dramatic end to a brave project. It was said that EBC was 'ahead of its time'; it had certainly run out of time. The wads of francs were quickly spent.

So that was it. We had gone, as one local member of staff put it, '*Bruste nach oben*' or 'Tits up'. Following Will Hutton's well-timed departure, James Long had taken over as Editor-in-Chief. The London *Times* quoted him as saying, 'It is both alarming and horrifying that we have been put in a situation where no one now knows whether they can even get home to Britain with any dignity after two years of hard work putting together a highly respected programme.'

Many of the late appointments didn't have any contracts or work permits and even those with permits, like me, would now be illegal aliens because they had no work.

It meant getting the family out of Switzerland pretty sharp; selling the furniture and two cars, settling bills, taking the children out of school and returning to our house in Hove, which was then let out.

I stayed on in Zurich for a few more weeks, taking part

in a number of half-hearted meetings of former staff aimed at resurrecting some sort of 'Son of EBC'. If the channel's final days were set in Wonderland, those meetings were on planet Zog.

While the attempt to salvage something from the ashes was bold, it was also naive, particularly given what was looming on the horizon – the international recession that hit that year. The sharp downturn in the world economy would probably have sunk EBC however good it was.

6

HARD
LANDING

It was a jolt coming back to England – a move from 220,000 Swiss francs (£100,000) a year to zero; from a quiet, wealthy village overlooking the Zurichsee and the Alps to a frenetic and rather grubby Brighton and Hove (albeit by the sea); and from not worrying about money to being faced by some harsh financial realities, including rising debts.

The large group of business journalists who had left the UK two years previously with such high, if misplaced, hopes were all now back looking for work and faced with a certain amount of *Schadenfreude* from colleagues who had stayed. The recession was biting and no one was taking any risks or decisions. It was going to be tough. I didn't want to sign on the dole and, at the time, I didn't think I could anyway, having been abroad for two years.

In 1990–91, the housing market was sinking and there were gloomy forecasts of further falls to come. In an ill-advised attempt to wipe out all our debts and mortgage, we thought we'd put the house on the market. It was priced at £99,500 but attracted no offers. Just as well, as a mere 12 years later we were able to sell it for four times as much.

The tenants who had occupied the house while we were in Switzerland couldn't really be described as house-proud. Now the whole property and garden needed attention, which on zero income could only be financed by borrowing. At the same time American Express decided to immediately call in an outstanding loan of £2,500 – peanuts by subsequent standards, but it ushered in a long period of borrowing from Peter to pay Paul. I became very adept at ducking and diving but, however hard I tried, the burden of debt was always a struggle.

But my luck was in. After a few months of this financial bobbing and weaving, an offer came out of the blue to present Channel 4's *Business Daily* – replacing Dermot Murnaghan, who had moved on to the ITN-produced *Channel 4 Daily*. Despite vowing never to return to breakfast shifts and commuting to London, I was back to getting a taxi at 3am five days a week – a cab that I often shared with Carol Barnes, who also presented the programme.

The business element was produced by an independent company, Business Television. For a morning slot *Business Daily*'s output was a rather odd mixture, including cartoons and a recorded edition of *Countdown* presented by the late Richard Whiteley. This allowed plenty of opportunity for scurrilous handovers to Mr Whiteley without any chance of his answering back.

It was a slightly more professional operation than EBC, but not by much. The content was fairly dull and routine, glitches were frequent and the schedule was disjointed and fragmented. There was little time or room to get across a consistent feel to the programme and I felt twitchy and unsettled. It all just seemed to hang together rather oddly and sat uncomfortably with the dominant news at the time – the first Gulf War.

Once again the early starts and using alcohol as medication began to take their toll. To reduce the gloom of a 4am start, I began bringing a flask of coffee for the taxi journey up to town, but of course it wasn't just coffee. Occasionally I'd also do the midday business slot if my fellow presenter, Susanna Simons, was away. It gave me the opportunity, in the time between the bulletins, to nip up the road to a cafe that sold alcohol very early (for reasons that I never worked out). It made the later bulletin go a lot more smoothly – at least in my own mind.

As the studio and offices were in Soho, there was no shortage of watering holes within a few yards. Although the ebullient, champagne culture of the eighties was giving way to the rather more sedate and recessionary early nineties, there was still a small group that went for post-broadcast refreshment. On several occasions I'd share a few beers and a chat with a boyhood hero of mine, Bobby Moore, who must have had business in the area. He was always genial, relaxed company and, strangely, we rarely talked about football. I never did discover whether he thought England's third goal against Germany went in. Very sadly it was all over for Bobby a few years later.

My contract to present *Business Daily* was for six months at £5,000 per month, which kept the family finances going for a while but the deal was not renewed, mainly because the programme itself came to an end. It was yet another business television venture that had bitten the dust – and it would not be the last. I was on the job market again.

Family life was happy and comfortable and Judy and I had celebrated our tenth wedding anniversary. Both children were at the local state primary school, St Andrew's C of E. Judy and I always had separate bank accounts. All family bills and the mortgage were paid out of my account and on my credit cards, but for a while there was nothing coming in.

If I'd been a company, my credit rating would have been 'Triple A'. I was constantly getting offers in the post for new credit cards and for various transfer deals. Of course, I didn't have to accept. I was not blind to the clever sales techniques. I had a sufficiently good mathematical brain to work out APRs and the consequences of minimum payments. But I just took the view that if they were giving me access to funds I was not going to say no while I had the chance. I might not desperately need the money at that stage, but it was good to know that I could draw on it if things turned sour and my credit rating collapsed.

My first current account had been arranged with Barclays back in 1971 and I stayed with them for the next 35 years until bankruptcy. I was the ideal customer, borrowing frequently, but always paying back albeit with credit from elsewhere. It was the bank itself that urged me to take advantage of a Barclays Select loan which I could draw on whenever I needed to. The facility was for £25,000. I didn't need it at the time, but it gave me a marvellous sense of security to know it was there. I calculated that in total I could have instantly drawn on £100,000 of credit.

A vague fantasy wafted through my mind while walking the family dog along the prom... £100K in one day... a pile of clothes on the beach... disappear to some remote location. Lord Lucan... John Stonehouse... now Ed Mitchell. No! You'd miss the dog.

Judy and I were not profligate in our spending. We had a comfortable but ordinary semi, an ordinary car, children at state school, a moderate mortgage. Judy did not work then, but that was the way we both wanted it. We agreed that she, not a nanny, should bring up the children. Taking holidays remained sacrosanct, but the destinations were by no means exotic.

We ate well, but it was Tesco and Sainsbury rather than Harrods Food Hall. Judy cooked. We rarely had dinner parties. We drank wine, but it was bargains, bin ends or wine boxes. (Admittedly, I drank more than just wine away from home, but not excessively, I thought then.)

Throughout the house the windows were the original wood, not doubled-glazed plastic, and were not replaced in the 20 years we were there. The loft was only partially converted and there were no extensions. I painted, wallpapered, patched up the windows and tiled the bathroom and toilet. Judy did the gardening. The furniture was IKEA, MFI or DFS (or its equivalent then). I bought paperbacks, not hardbacks.

So what the hell went wrong? During our entire marriage I kept a very close watch on what was happening to our finances – always opening credit-card, utility and council tax bills when they arrived. My relationship with the Inland Revenue was up to date. My filing system was orderly, albeit hidden from view. I dealt with it, but didn't dwell on it.

What went wrong was that, after the collapse of EBC, my income became very patchy and yet we didn't really tighten our belts when there was nothing coming in, mainly because we didn't reckon that our belts had any notches left to tighten. (Of course, there were.) Anyway, something better would turn up. It always had done.

I'd had an above-average income for more than ten years, and certain habits of thought and expenditure had become ingrained. My attitude would be: 'Well, sensibly and realistically, we can't afford this or that, or go on that holiday, but what the hell! Tomorrow I might be diagnosed with a terminal illness, or the plane I'm in might crash or we're hit by an asteroid. Live for today! Something good is round the corner. Anyway I've got lots of credit I can draw on.'

I believed in my own luck. I had a charmed life. Someone was looking after me. In retrospect, of course, it's an extraordinarily dangerous way to think, particularly if you mix in a growing reliance on alcohol.

'My luck's in. I've been given some freelance work,' I called out to Judy. The phone call had just come in on a rather drab, depressing Monday morning in Hove. It was from a production company working for British Airways, offering me regular work.

The job was to present a monthly in-flight magazine programme about what British Airways was up to. It was typically one day's filming and half a day doing the voice-over, for which they would pay £600 per month – almost exactly enough to take care of the mortgage.

I just had to turn up, learn my lines and look excited about the latest news from BA. I didn't have to try hard, because it was exciting. The stories might be about how they trained their pilots on simulators, the new wine list (plus tastings) or food menus, the new interior design of Concorde (sadly, not leaving the runway), a new terminal, BA's presence at the Paris air show, what BA were up to around Europe, new uniforms for the cabin staff, training with the flight attendants, new designs for the outside of the aircraft and much more.

One particularly memorable monthly instalment involved going to New York with the camera crew. We had seats in business class and the section was virtually empty. The camera was switched on and I had the bizarre experience of doing a piece to camera that was synchronised with me doing a recorded piece to camera on the large cabin screen in the background. Well, unlimited free drinks from the galley made it seem amusing.

Towards the end of the flight I was invited up to the cockpit to experience the landing at New York's JFK Airport. The approach was down Long Island towards Manhattan and coincided with a glorious sunset. From the cockpit window I could see the Statue of Liberty in the distance, the Empire State Building and the World Trade Center's two towers catching the last rays of the sun.

The twin towers felt very familiar because, on a previous story, I had tried out one of BA's flight simulators. I thought it would be interesting to see if you could fly a Boeing 747 between them. The gap was 140 feet. The wingspan of a Jumbo is 195 feet 8 inches, but I didn't know that at the time and so lost quite a bit of my computer-generated wings. Tipping the plane at an angle might have just done it. Tragically, eight years later, the space between the towers wasn't of any concern to the 9/11 hijackers.

Previously I'd also tried to land a simulated Jumbo at Hong Kong's Kai Tak Airport. Having flown into there many years earlier, I remembered that it required a sharp right turn before bumping into Lion Rock. The manoeuvre needed skill to avoid the apartment buildings of Kowloon. Sadly I miscalculated my flight path and snagged some virtual washing hanging on the balcony, overshot the runway and ended up in the harbour – certainly the hydraulic system suggested I had made a serious error.

Having landed (in reality) at JFK, the pilot hadn't been told where to leave the plane. He just casually trundled around with his three-storey-high, 400-ton piece of kit, nonchalantly (to me, anyway) looking for a parking bay. Thankfully someone had just left, so we grabbed the space.

The BA job led to other plane-related opportunities, which I welcomed as I'd been a plane-spotter as a youngster. One was the role of presenter of the official video of the Farnborough Air Show. This was a full-time assignment for two weeks, covering the trade, press and public demonstrations of the world's latest aircraft and got me a brief flight in the new (and completely stripped bare) Airbus passenger jet. It also meant a memorable (and pointless) piece to camera directly below a hovering, roaring, hot Yak-38 Forger, the Russian equivalent of the Harrier Jump Jet. The straining plane was belting out flames and the stink of kerosene. The Yak was known (not officially) to crash frequently, but obligingly it stayed airborne while I delivered my inaudible lines.

The video was put together on a shoestring budget, which meant I presented, wrote the script and did the voice-over. I stayed in a local B&B. The job paid about three grand, which covered a few bills at home.

My work for BA was mainly with the passenger part of the group, but also with the huge and lucrative cargo division, which flies to 200 destinations in 80 countries. BA Cargo carries all manner of goods, including live animals, human remains and some dangerous items (which I hope they know about).

The cargo division was trying to achieve a particular Quality Standard qualification and, with this in mind, the plan was to tour the world and put together a video illustrating its strengths and weaknesses. The two-week trip included interviews at various locations in New York, Los Angeles and Hong Kong, flying business class all the way and staying in the best hotels. It was hell.

At that time quite a few big companies were going for Quality Standard certification. My next freelance job was for the electronics group Philips, making a nationwide tour of all its manufacturing and administration plants and offices. The company was well established and respected but its profits were faltering and it needed to retrench. Philips had always been impressive on the innovation and development side, but seemed to fail on making money out of its good ideas. Once again the purpose of the video was not only to secure a quality certificate but also to perk up company morale. For me it was another fortnight that briefly helped to perk up the domestic bank balance.

Given the precarious nature of my finances, I was willing to say yes to almost every offer of work and any proposal that might result in work. One such idea came as a result of a conversation in a pub in Hove, the Albion. I'd known Bill Smith for years from our days in the buffet car commuting to London. He'd been very successful in the property world, but times were a little harder now.

Bill had recently been to Russia with a small group of businessmen from Hove and they had made an influential contact with a senior government figure in Volgograd, formerly Stalingrad. The group had made some preliminary progress in sourcing some agricultural products. For example, mustard seeds were apparently plentiful and cheap, although there was some concern that they were growing downwind from an ageing nuclear power station. There was also the possibility of exporting from Russia works of art before any restrictions were imposed, watches and general Soviet-era memorabilia.

It was all rather nebulous; events were moving very rapidly in the new Russia in the early nineties, there were no established legal structures and the individuals involved didn't strike me as having a great deal of experience in international trade. The words 'league' and 'out of' kept coming into my mind. But the more pints of Directors Bitter I had, the more I wanted to get involved. It was suggested that I should investigate the media opportunities that existed there.

About ten days later Bill and I caught a BA flight to Moscow (and incidentally watched the latest edition of the in-flight magazine programme). We were met by representatives of Volgograd City Council and taken to a *dacha* somewhere in the snow-covered forests outside Moscow.

A feast was laid on with innumerable traditional Russian dishes, including bowls of beluga caviar. Inevitably we had to force down endless toasts of toothbrush-mug-sized tumblers of vodka. Until then I'd never really been a vodka drinker – certainly not neat and certainly not in those quantities. It was at the stage where we were all pledging undying international comradeship and getting very maudlin in a philosophical and poetic sort of way that I decided to wander off into the woods.

It was dark and icy and I had no torch. But the vodka had given me night vision and a miraculous fluency in Russian – a language I had been studying intensely on the three-hour flight to Moscow. The wooden, green-painted *dacha* with its windows lit up by roaring log fires disappeared in the darkness. I wandered around in circles until I could see flickering lights in a window in the distance. I thought I'd found my way back, so I knocked on the door of the wooden house and was warmly welcomed in by a charming old couple. The room was filled with heat and the wonderful aromas of wood smoke, spices and stew. The walls were covered in pictures of Lenin, Marx and Stalin. A vast vodka was thrust in my hand and we talked at each other animatedly into the night.

I must have fallen asleep, because I woke covered in a thick blanket. Vladimir and Maria – we'd got on first-name terms – had gone to bed. I quietly let myself out into the freezing night air and retraced my footprints in the snow with the weight of Russian history on my mind.

Very early the next day, Bill, three Russians and me climbed aboard the minibus for our journey south to Volgograd. The back of the bus was loaded with provisions for the 22-hour journey – loaves, sausages and tins of meat. Between the two of us on the back seat was placed a rusting metal milk crate holding 24 unlabelled bottles of vodka. We would feel no pain on the journey.

But we did. The pot-holes were the size of craters and relentlessly frequent. The single-lane road stretched to the horizon through snow-covered fields interspersed with hundreds of miles of birch woods – Russian grass. The scenery was mesmerising in its hostility. Huge, smoke-belching articulated lorries carrying chained-down loads of logs thundered aggressively towards us. Petrol tankers swayed drunkenly past within inches. Did they have their own vodka crates?

Rare villages stood out because of their huge, black puddles of oil from countless leaking lorry sumps. Toilet breaks in the snow drifts gave us the chance to view roaming wolves and sniff the cold diesel-laden air. Conversation flagged after the first 300 miles and my mind became numb and grey like the surrounding landscape.

I arrived feeling like an old sack of decaying root vegetables pickled in vodka. It was night time in Volgograd and it looked monochromatic and forbidding. Our hotel, once used by Party officials, was austere and unchanged since the 1930s. I assumed it was still fitted with its eavesdropping equipment. My snoring would give the Soviet technology a severe test.

What followed was an endless round of formal but unreal meetings and vodka-soaked social events. I was sure there was a technique for avoiding constantly having to empty full glasses of vodka, but I never found it.

It was impossible to be in Volgograd without being quickly aware that something horrific had happened there. The battle for Stalingrad was one of the most relentlessly brutal confrontations in military history – some 1.5 million combatants died there – and turned the tide of the Second World War. The heroically stubborn defence of the city had left deep scars mentally and physically. The tangible evidence had been preserved particularly around the steelworks where some of the most vicious hand-to-hand fighting took place. Walking among the silent ruins, it did not need much imagination to feel and absorb the fear and horror. I was sure I saw the glint of a sniper's telescopic sight and heard the double click of a rifle being cocked.

My interpreter, Irina, the attractive young daughter of the Mayor of Volgograd, accompanied me wherever I went. I was never really sure whether, apart from translating, she was always by my side to keep me out of trouble or get me into trouble. With the end of the Cold War, surely honey traps were unnecessary. Maybe she just wanted advanced English lessons.

We went to the colossal statue of Mother Russia on the Mamayev Hill overlooking the city, the world's largest representation of a full human figure, standing 270ft high.

Her sword alone, held aloft in a rallying and defiant gesture, is nearly 100ft of steel.

Dedicated to the Heroes of Stalingrad who fought there for 200 days and nights, the statue was clearly held in awe and reverence by visitors. The view from the hill of the vast, ponderous, steel-grey Volga, the snow-covered landscape and the austere, concrete buildings of the city, coupled with the cumulative effect of days of vodka and a chilling east wind, was profoundly depressing, and tears welled in my eyes.

Seventy years of rigid totalitarianism had rather dampened the vigour of the independent television production sector in Russia. So much so that Volgograd's television channel consisted of little more than a fairly quiet room with egg boxes glued to the wall and a handy-cam on a tripod. As the visiting big-shot media adviser from the rich and decadent West, they thought I might provide some investment. I offered my Visa card but it would not do nicely, thank you.

Stalingrad, I'd been told, was at one time the centre of the Soviet movie industry. I was shown around huge, echoing studios that must have churned out hundreds of uplifting films. In addition, I was allowed to view footage of the battle for the city which I was assured had never been seen in the West before.

On our final night the City Council really pushed the boat out. I'd grown to love cabbage, potatoes, beetroot and tinned meat. The vodka flowed like the Volga – it was impossible to swim against the current. Towards the end of the evening, after I'd pledged my undying loyalty to the New Russia and international brotherhood, we were whisked off in a convoy of ageing black cars ('limousines' would have been stretching it).

The journey took us down a long, narrow dirt track which

wound along the banks of the Volga. We finally arrived at a row of small, wooden fishermen's huts. Entering a smoke-filled room, we could just make out basic items of furniture and cooking equipment. There were busts of Stalin and Lenin and a framed picture of Zhukov. As the door closed we could see, pinned to the back of it, a poster of Samantha Fox – which neatly summed up the transition that was happening in Russia in the early nineties. I'm sure she will have been deposed by now in a Page Three putsch.

I couldn't remember leaving the fishing huts but had flashbacks of piles of steaming sturgeon, bowls of caviar, vats of vodka and an intense game of chess. I think I was beaten by the infamous Kopelzon gambit, though more probably 'Fool's Mate'.

Much to my relief, we returned by train to Moscow accompanied by tins of meat, a well-filled rusting metal crate, our young translator and no contracts.

Being freelance (unemployed), I had the flexibility to do anything and go anywhere, at any time. A pushier person would have been out there selling themselves, but that's not something I've ever been comfortable with. Anyway things had always seemed to come to me – a risky business model for a freelancer with a family and debts.

But the phone did ring now and again. I had a call from the BBC saying they were setting up the television version of the World Service, cleverly called BBC World Television. Would I be interested in presenting it? I'd always enjoyed broadcasting on World Service radio and I hoped that the same ethos would apply to the television version. Given that my position had always been to say yes to everything and work out the details later, I went for it.

There were a few months to get the thing up and running and there was a good, solid newsroom team with the now familiar enthusiasm for a start-up project. I was very much a 'presenter', which meant that, although I took part in editorial news discussions and was a fully qualified and experienced journalist, I was generally regarded as just the fluffy front man.

The launch programme went smoothly and the head of World Service television, John Tusa, congratulated us, saying we had made television history – well, a footnote at least. Tusa was someone I'd always admired as a journalist and broadcaster. His delivery was always polished and professional, so I was surprised to hear, when he was speaking to the assembled team, that he had a pronounced stutter, which obviously disappeared on air.

My shifts began seven hours before the evening broadcast, which easily gave me time to contact the Pronunciation Department and familiarise myself with half a dozen foreign names. ('Hmmm, that's ten minutes gone.') It was excruciatingly boring to sit in the newsroom staring into a computer screen pretending to prepare for one or two interviews and reading through scripts.

Not everyone would respond in this way, but the boredom and pretence got to me and so I'd take a stroll down to Shepherds Bush and have a couple of pints at the corner pub to pass the time. This became a regular habit and, not surprisingly, it began to show up in my presentational style. On one occasion I completely miscalculated my consumption (I'm pretty sure I was with Paul Gibbs) and made a complete mess of a story involving Azerbaijan, Kyrgyzstan, Kyzyl-Mazhalyk and a village in north Wales with a very long name. I seem to recall I'd left my flies open as well, which was, according to the small print, apparently in breach of my contract.

I was on the wrong planet for the World Service and the arrangement was brought to an end after three months, with the paperwork sent to me down in Hove (for economy reasons, I guessed!) by dispatch rider. A few days later a cheque arrived by post (no motorbike this time) for £15,000 from BBC Television to cover the three months' work. A week after that another cheque for £15,000 arrived to cover the same three months but this time from BBC World Service.

Nation might speak peace unto nation, but the two accounts departments were clearly not speaking at all. I had a brief moral dilemma but came down on the side of the angels and told one of the departments that I would tear up their cheque. Later, when my financial state worsened, I fleetingly regretted my honesty. It did give me a warm glowing feeling, though, knowing that 150 licence-fee payers hadn't had their money wasted. I expect they used my returned cheque to pay for a team-building managerial course in Hawaii.

My intoxicated exit from the BBC may have been forgiven, or gone completely unnoticed, but a couple of months later I got a call from Paul Gibbs asking if I wanted to fill in temporarily as presenter of its *Business Breakfast*. It was a regular morning update of business news and prices broadcast from the same studio as the main breakfast programme presented then by Nicholas Witchell and Jill Dando.

It was good to be working with Paul again and the business slot allowed a certain amount of personalised input. The output was an eclectic mix of items (including racing tips) with a great deal of handing over from presenter, to co-presenter, to interview down-the-line to outside broadcast.

One morning there was an item focusing on transsexuals, transvestites and related topics – an ideal subject for an audience getting the children ready for school and professionals wanting the day's top international news before rushing to the office. At the end of the report on the issues surrounding being a transgender, Nicholas Witchell looked up seriously from the monitor and said, 'And now for the business news. Here's Ed Mitchell.' I simply responded, 'Thanks, Nicola,' and continued. 'In New York, Wall Street was down 30 points overnight…'

My earpiece erupted. I could hear the director corpsing. But I kept a straight face. I thought it was just a little, albeit intentional, slip that might amuse the few who were concentrating. However, I misjudged the prevailing political correctness. I had committed heresy and was given a stern warning. It would be damp faggots at the stake next time.

A number of viewers who were probably benefiting from 'care in the community' wrote to the BBC – in green ink, naturally – outraged. There was then a programme that aired audience complaints presented by Sue Lawley. She phoned to get my response. I apologised if I had caused any offence, particularly because I did have a sympathetic understanding of transsexual issues – living near Brighton's Kemp Town, some of my best friends were trannies. Sue wasn't convinced.

One of the producers I worked with then on *Business Breakfast* was David Frank, who had started a company with another producer there, Richard Dove. They combined their initials to become RDF, which subsequently expanded to become Britain's biggest independent producer and a favourite of Her Majesty the Queen.

Back then RDF operated out of cramped offices above

some lock-up garages. David and his brother Matthew produced programmes and sold them worldwide to a variety of television companies. They phoned to see if I wanted to spend two weeks in Colombia putting together about five stories on the economy of the country. The cocaine industry was not one of the five topics. I jumped at the chance.

At the time – it was 1993 – my father, who was 69, had been ill for several months. He smoked about 60 cigarettes a day and had been diagnosed with inoperable lung cancer. He took it stoically, didn't complain and continued to smoke but not near his oxygen cylinders. We both knew his condition was deteriorating, but Dad didn't want me to miss the chance to go to Colombia. He said he would see me when I got back. As I left to go, he stood up and, completely out of character, we hugged and he kissed me on the cheek, saying, 'You've been a good son.' I could only manage to say, 'And you've been a good dad.' They were the last words we exchanged. Ten days later I got a call in my hotel room in Bogota telling me he had died that morning.

It chokes me now to write those words. He was a good man whose fate, like so many of his age, had been shaped by a military life and the Second World War. Towards the end we had the chance to chat over a few pints in the Crabtree pub up the road in Lancing. He talked animatedly of being evacuated, at the age of 15, under diving Stukas as the Germans invaded Jersey. He served in North Africa and Italy during the War, and afterwards in Palestine, Korea and Suez. There's no doubt his happiest years were in the Army.

When I mentioned to anyone that I was about to go to Colombia it automatically triggered two thoughts in people's minds – cocaine and danger. What most impressed me there was beauty (scenery and women) and friendliness. As for cocaine, I'd come across far more in George Street in Hove.

Colombia produces 80 per cent of the world's cocaine, worth about $5 billion, so it does have a distorting effect on the economy. But I was there to investigate coal, oil, coffee, tourism and the financial sector.

I'd have been foolish to ignore the danger in Bogota; the fact that we were accompanied on film shoots by machine-gun-toting guards was a constant reminder. I reckoned it was a good idea not to get pissed. On one occasion, though, I did have to go to the bank for the cash to pay our guide, local producer and kit hire. It was about £5,000 – not much, but when it was translated into Colombian pesos I thought I might need a wheelbarrow. Unaccompanied, my pockets bulging, I waddled along the city streets feeling pretty exposed. But perhaps I just looked obese.

My BP contacts from previous jobs gave us good access to the huge oil fields 90 miles north-east of Bogota at Cusiana and Cupiagua. The first stage of the journey was by light plane to Yopal, which had recently become a boom town thanks to oil. The natives were ambivalent about the benefits.

We were taken from Yopal to the fields by Bell Ranger helicopter, flying over the jungle where the rebel forces of ELN and FARC operated. We were accompanied by two former SAS men. The door was open for the journey and, being a bloke and a film buff, I did think *Apocalypse Now* and did loudly hum 'The Ride of the Valkyries'.

Unfortunately, as soon as we landed, the camera was switched on and the circuit board immediately burned out. The contrast in temperature from altitude to the steaming heat of the jungle had produced condensation and a short circuit. That lost a day's filming from an already tight schedule.

Another couple of days were spent in the far north-east of the country at the world's biggest open-cast coal mine. I hadn't realised it before I went, but Colombia is the fourth-largest coal exporter in the world and a significant amount is sold to the UK. Handling lumps of coal and looking macho in a hard hat made for a few gritty pieces to camera.

Colombia is an immensely rich country in terms of agricultural products and plants because it encompasses so many different geographical elevations. Almost anything can be grown somewhere in the country. So huge areas are ideal for the coca plant, but what's good for coca is also good for coffee and plantains. The coffee farmers we visited were perfectly open about their farming strategies. When the price of coffee fell they turned their fields to coca or plantain.

We were guests of the Colombian Coffee Growers' Association, who were very generous with their product. When I left Bogota I was given ten unmarked one-kilo packs of ground coffee – at least I think it was coffee. It was never checked, but I reckon the sniffer dogs would have picked up the aroma if it had been anything else!

The highlight of the trip for me was interviewing the President, Cesar Gaviria. A young, affable man who kept looking over his shoulder, he had won office in 1989 on an anti-drugs platform. Two of the other candidates had been shot dead by members of the drug cartels. The interview was conducted at the presidential palace in the centre of Bogota, which was surrounded by tanks and armed soldiers.

The interview was rather artificial in the sense that I was not allowed to touch on the subject of cocaine. But Gaviria did say that Colombia was doing as much as it could to combat drug trafficking but suggested it was up to the

American and European authorities to discourage the market for it. His argument was that nobody would grow it, export it or kill for it if people didn't use it.

Less than six months after the interview, the leader of the biggest Medellin cartel, Pablo Escobar, was shot dead by Colombian forces. Despite this, the cocaine industry is now bigger than it ever was and, Colombia being so fertile, there has been a significant increase in the production of marijuana and opium.

RDF were sufficiently pleased with the outcome of the two weeks in Colombia that soon after they sent me on a two-week reporting trip to Vietnam. The thrust of the story was that, after decades of war and isolation, the communist country was opening up to capitalism and tourism and was fast becoming one of the Asian 'Tigers'. The details of the stories and the trip were largely left up to me.

The assignment would involve a week in Saigon and its surroundings and a week in Hanoi. I was there with just one cameraman.

Having read so much about Vietnamese history, particularly the war years, and having seen so many films, I found it exhilarating to actually be in Saigon. Feeling like the Quiet American but English, I knew my first stop had to be the rooftop bar of the Caravelle Hotel, overlooking Lam Son Square and the Opera House. The square was packed with thousands of mopeds, each carrying three or more passengers, most of them young, attractive women riders dressed in silk pyjamas, large hats, white scarves and long white gloves.

Hanoi was beautiful in a rundown sort of way. The architecture was French in style but the houses and office buildings had become dilapidated and overgrown, the wide, tree-lined boulevards were pot-holed and filled with deep puddles.

I was able to speak to a former general from the North Vietnam Army. The interview took place in a large French-colonial house. It was completely quiet except for the sound of exotic birds in the palm trees outside the open veranda. Small, thin, grizzled and quietly spoken, the general explained that the Army had never allowed any doubts that it would achieve reunification of the country, however long it took. Vietnam had the time and single-mindedness. America, he said, had obvious growing doubts and a shorter political timetable. The outcome was inevitable. The Americans and the French should have made a closer study of history. He added it was never really about communism, but about a historic sense of nationhood. However, the future no longer lay with isolation.

Luckily, at the time there was an *Economist*-sponsored conference on in Hanoi. We were able to interview, almost conveyor-belt style, most of the country's leading business and financial leaders.

That left a fair amount of time to explore the sights and bars of the city. At night I'd hire a bicycle-drawn rickshaw. It teemed with warm rain every night, and my cycling chauffeur would take his drenched passenger and pile of take-out meals to some of the most obscure parts of Hanoi across the Red River. If there was danger, I was oblivious to it. I was preoccupied with reflections on what it must have been like to be under the nightly visits of B-52s.

Back in Hove, it was a return to job hunting and debt juggling. The phone rang less often.

At the BBC I'd met Rod Pounsett, senior producer of the

Today programme, a fellow traveller in the train's buffet car and, like me, an old boy of Worthing High School. After leaving the BBC he had taken up a lucrative consultancy with an international accountancy firm in Moscow.

Rod phoned to say he was in Berlin setting up a communications company that, to begin with, would operate out of a refurbished hotel next to the Cathedral in East Berlin's Alexanderplatz. The aim was to provide all the telecommunications needs for businessmen travelling through the booming city. He wondered whether I'd like to visit Berlin and see if I wanted to get involved. He also happened to be getting married.

Arriving at Tempelhof, one of the oldest commercially operating airports in the world and so closely associated with Nazi power and the later Berlin airlift, I was overwhelmed by a sense of history that was constantly with me for the week I was there.

I met Rod's potential investors at an alcohol–soaked lunch at an outdoor restaurant near the River Spree. I was expecting a member of the Hitler Youth to stand up and sing 'Tomorrow Belongs to Me'. Rod's backers were apparently making piles of Deutschmarks out of the rebuilding of East Berlin. Certainly the skyline, filled with a forest of cranes, suggested intense activity.

The hotel had once offered hospitality to guests of senior figures in the East German Government. The Stasi, the state police, had bugged all the rooms. I gave the mirrors in my room a suitable gesture in case they were still two-way. I kept my dressing gown on at all times.

During the evening we toured Berlin. Well refreshed, we climbed the ruined belfry of the Kaiser Wilhelm Memorial Church. This had been hit during an RAF bombing raid in

1943, but the tower remained and was known as '*der Hohle Zahn*', the 'hollow tooth'. Everywhere we went there were associations with the city's turbulent past. It was emotionally draining.

Rod's wedding and reception took place on a perfect sunny day down by the Grosser Wannsee, a large lake on the western outskirts of West Berlin. Beer and Rhine wines flowed freely at the crowded reception in a large house overlooking the water. I was overcome by a need for *Lebensraum*. I wandered off along the lake shore and stumbled across a large, chateau-like house. A notice said it was the Wannsee Villa.

I'd read enough history to know this was the place where, in January 1942, senior Nazi officials led by Heydrich and Eichmann had met to decide policy on the 'Jewish Question'. Their answer was the 'Final Solution'. I pressed my face up against the French windows and looked into the room where this momentous decision had been taken by a group of bureaucrats. It was a warm sunny day, but I was shivering.

Workwise, nothing ever came out of the Berlin venture for me. Eventually the East German property market collapsed, Rod's backers pulled out and a few years later business communications were completely shaken up by the Internet.

7

SOMETHING'S BOUND TO TURN UP

The phone had gone very quiet. The answer machine had no answers. Bills were my only mail. This was before the Internet and the mobile phone, but in my case they would have probably been inert if they had existed. I was sinking below the media radar. I knew I should market myself more, but reckoned that might look like desperation. I was desperate, but I didn't want to appear so.

I did have an agent, but there was a catch. I needed to be on television regularly to get noticed for freelance jobs, but I wouldn't have the spare time to do them if I had a full-time job. I had plenty of time for freelancing, but because I was no longer on TV people had forgotten who I was. But I had to keep myself available for well-paid short-term jobs – even if they seemed to have dried up.

The council, gas, water, electricity, building society, home and car insurance, life assurance, food, petrol, repairs, travel, children, dog – they hadn't forgotten me.

Just existing was costing about £3,000 per month. Looking at it another way, every month I did not earn, I was

£3K deeper in debt. I did apply for all manner of jobs, but only half-heartedly. The pay for local jobs would hardly make any impression on the mounting debt and I always held out the hope that something more lucrative would come along.

In the meantime I had to keep Family Mitchell Ltd afloat. Property prices had been recovering, which meant we had more equity in the house. The temporary answer to the immediate problems would be to remortgage. I was theoretically self-employed and on this basis put together some imaginative business figures. The building societies were keen on getting people to remortgage – the commission generated was a big incentive to the financial adviser. House prices would always rise, wouldn't they?

The agents encouraged customers to be liberal with self-assessments. ('Fifty grand? Yeah, that sounds about right. They never check!') They were keen to push earnings protection insurance at, in my case, a bargain annual premium of £4,000. It was sold as if it were a condition of the remortgage, but it was, of course, optional. Needless to say, under virtually no circumstances known to man would the insurance ever pay out. It was, I found out later while trying to make a claim, money down the drain.

So the remortgaging deal was done, and that bought more time. But time to do what? Well, I supposed, time to wait till something came along.

I'd been checking with British Telecom to find out if there was anything wrong with the line, when the phone rang. It was someone named Chris Graves, calling from Singapore. He explained that the wire service and newspaper group Dow Jones, along with some others, were setting up a pan-Asian business television channel to be called Asia Business

News (ABN). It was within weeks of launch, and would I like to come out for a few months and help with lift-off? Chris said he would have preferred someone Asian-looking, but my blond hair and blue eyes would have to do in the interim.

The deal was, I'd be put up in a hotel and paid 10,000 Singapore dollars a month, about £5,000. So there would be jam for tea. I accepted the offer immediately.

The hotel was the Amara, about ten minutes' walk from the studios in an office block in Singapore's business district and a couple of floors above a shopping arcade. The hotel itself had a second-floor swimming pool and several bars and was next door to a food hall selling every known dish in Asia (no dogs).

ABN's studio and newsroom were still being built and there were the usual problems with the computer system. The young team exuded the familiar cocktail of enthusiasm, start-up optimism and camaraderie. I was impressed by the studio – when I wasn't actually on camera I would be able to stare out of the windows across the ship-filled Strait of Malacca to the distant Indonesian islands. Not a lot of presenters could do that.

The launch went without crashing, but there seemed to be plenty of technical hitches built into the system, and all the while I was there they were never sorted out. It was a pretty good team – some of them had even worked in television before. They were mostly young Americans and Australians who seemed to be acting the part of television journalist.

I soon settled into a routine. I was given the early shifts, which was ideal. I'd get up about 4am and walk through the empty streets to the studio, past a Buddhist temple still pouring out the aroma of smouldering incense. It would be pitch dark and the air warm and filled with the sound of cicadas. There always seemed to be a tiny moon directly overhead.

I'd do a couple of hours of live broadcasting with the usual array of market and corporate interviews. One of them stands out in my memory. It was an interview with Richard Branson, who was unveiling a new Virgin service between London and the Far East. He'd been at some sort of launch party the night before, which fitted in nicely with my personal style of broadcasting. The interview was entertaining, informative and human, which was why I can recall it amid the conveyor belt of dry market pundits and corporate analysts saying much the same thing: 'The markets will go down and up, but not necessarily in that order.'

My shift generally finished at noon. I'd leave the studio, have a quick Tiger beer in a bar round the corner, hail a cab and head to the waterfront. There was a cable car between Singapore and the resort island of Sentosa, so I could be lying on the sandy beach under swaying palms with another beer in my hand in 45 minutes without breaking sweat. The sea was warm and safe. Close by was a variety of beach restaurants serving a huge array of cheap dishes from Indonesia, Malaysia and the Philippines. The day was my own to fill.

In the evenings I'd go to the restaurants or bars down along the Singapore River. One of them, Harry's, was frequented by foreign exchange, bond and commodity dealers. It was there that I often met a group of usually ebullient futures traders from Barings. It was only some while later that I realised that one particularly loud member of the group had been Nick Leeson, who subsequently brought the whole bank down. At that time in Harry's he was still probably confident that he could trade his way out of his exposed position – unaware of an impending earthquake in Japan.

For me there wasn't much socialising with other members

of ABN as I had to be in bed fairly early for the 4am start, but occasionally I joined the Aussies for a few tinnies. Some of them liked to round off the evening with an apparently traditional bar brawl. It was on one of those occasions that I sustained a fairly hefty blow underneath my right eye. It must have cracked my socket bone because I could see two of everything with that eye. I was convinced it was the punch, not the drink.

I had a good two hours' sleep but woke feeling like I'd gone ten rounds with Rocky Balboa. Maybe I had. Certainly I needed the skills of the corner-men before I went on air. I just managed to get through the presenting shift before the blood started flowing again and the ref stepped in.

Whenever I was in my hotel room I could hear the sound of drilling. I scoured all the corridors to find the source of the noise, but failed. The hotel staff were not aware of any improvement work or potential oil reserves. The result was that I spent most of the time by the pool or wandering around Singapore, which is a very walkable city. There were several exotic parks, the zoo was wonderful and it was thoroughly enjoyable to watch the cricket played on the spacious ground in the centre of town.

The whole idea was to spend as little money as possible while I was in Singapore and send the rest of my pay back to Hove to keep the wolves from the door. Once again a short-term job bought a bit more time and kept hopes alive that something more permanent might turn up.

On returning to Hove I resumed the financial plate-spinning. Life was still enjoyable but I knew alcohol was taking a tighter hold. I was becoming more reliant on it and both the night traumas and the morning shakes were getting worse.

Judy and I had been married 13 years and the children were not yet teenagers. We still did most things together: family meals, walks and picnics.

One picnic site had become a firmly fixed annual event. On the train journey to and from London I'd always looked out of the window as we passed over Balcombe viaduct, just north of Haywards Heath. From being enclosed by deep cuttings and trees, suddenly you're out in the open, about 80 feet above the valley of the River Ouse and with an uninterrupted view of the Sussex countryside for miles around. Below the viaduct were verdant fields and grazing cows. It looked idyllic and I'd always wondered exactly how I could get there on foot.

I found out the route and exact spot from the Ordnance Survey map and first took Judy there in August 1980. We returned every August for the next quarter of a century, taking first one child, then another and then Bella, the Dalmatian. For reasons that I cannot recall, Judy took a picture of me every year in exactly the same position and in exactly the same pose – looking at the camera, drinking from a bottle of cider and with the viaduct in the background. (There were a couple of years when it was apple juice.) It was an unbroken annual record of 26 photos showing the ravages of time. Two oak trees we planted there from acorns may still be growing.

Now, whenever I pass over the viaduct, I look down into that field and remember so many years of sandwiches and cider in the August sun.

As the months passed without work I was beginning to draw on some of the credit facilities I'd set up. The remortgaging had reduced the pressure slightly – sensibly, I'd used most of it to repay some of the debt with the highest interest rates. But just as I thought I was getting my head above water, the simple arithmetic – more was going out than coming in – reasserted itself and the sinking feeling returned.

But I hadn't been completely forgotten. Someone I knew from the train, Peter Spencer, had been involved for years in the more creative aspects of insurance and investment packages. He'd come up with the idea of a bond that would entitle the holder to unlimited bookings at a selection of hotels in the United States – Florida, to begin with – for a lump-sum payment that would be valid for a decade. Yes, a holiday bond.

The plan was in its very early stages and the word 'selection of hotels' was being optimistic. It also required an investor, which Peter seemed to have attracted. What was needed was promotion – and that's where I came in.

'Ed, do you fancy two weeks in Florida, all expenses paid and $2,000 in cash up front?'

'Ah, Peter,' I said cautiously. 'What do you want me to do, and is it legal?'

He explained the project and said he wanted me to produce and present a ten-minute promotional video outlining the advantages of investing in his bond and what wonderful hotels it would give access to.

It didn't need a financial genius to spot the weaknesses in the plan and my suspicion was that it would never take off, but a grey and drizzly Hove was no competition for a fortnight in Florida and cash in hand. Peter liked a few drinks as well. The answer was a sceptical yes.

'Pass the bottle, Peter. Leave me a drop!' We were motoring leisurely along State Route 50 with the roof down and ZZ

Top blaring on the radio. We'd landed at Orlando and were on the way to Melbourne Beach on the Atlantic coast of Florida.

Peter passed over the Wild Turkey and I finished off the last inch. There was another bottle in the glove compartment. Thoughts of *Fear and Loathing in Las Vegas* and Gonzo journalism went through my mind. I'd cobbled together some sort of script for the promo on the plane over. I hoped it made sense. It seemed to at the time, but that was after an extended in-flight lunch.

The hotel was spookily empty and looked seriously in need of attention. I think the script said 'spacious and recently refurbished'. We headed to the bar and met the camera crew – well, the cameraman, George. He explained that he had another job on at the same time, so he could only give us the odd hour here and there.

We did a few pieces to camera on the sandy beach and some general shots of the hotel, which had to be carefully framed to show the hotel at its best. I'd quickly sussed that this video was not going to impress anyone.

George went off to do his other job, which left Peter and me quite a bit of time on our hands. We sat at the beach bar and immediately attracted a small gathering of fellow drinkers who had seen us filming earlier. There's something about someone talking into a camera on a tripod that still impresses people. So did an English accent.

It was obvious, though, that our new friends at the bar were complete wackos. Assuming that we were making a big-budget movie – a misconception we made no attempt to rectify – they poured out all their ideas for plot lines. One of them even had a grubby and well-thumbed screenplay on him. A glance at the first few pages – something about flying mechanical insects flown by scantily clad female pilots

Above left: One car that I managed not to crash ... me at eight months old.

Above right: With older brother Les outside our army quarters in Donnington, Shropshire.

Below: Having Les as my older brother was like having a pathfinder.

Above: Senior Man at Castle, Durham, 1974. I'm next to the Master of the College with the shield.

Inset: A taste of things to come? Taking the chill off at a University rugby match.

Above: Dragon Boat Day at Stanley Beach, Hong Kong.

Below: The streak that landed me in court and on the front pages.

Above: New Year partying at the Hong Kong Club.

Below: Meeting Judy for the first time in Hong Kong. A car crash just before arriving produced the head wound.

Above: In the Financial Unit offices at Broadcasting House.

Below left: Broadcasting for the European Business Channel in Switzerland. The glass on the desk in this photograph says it all.

Below right: With my family in 1998: my daughter, Alex, Judy, and my son Freddie.

Above left: All that was left after rolling the MGB Roadster in 1978.

Above right: The end of my Morris Minor a few months later.

Below: Working on *The Business of Sport* at Brands Hatch in 1997. A car I didn't get to drive.

Not long before my exit from CNBC … escorted by security.

Some stills from the documentary *Saving Ed Mitchell*.

Above: With the late Carol Barnes in Hove during the making of the documentary.

Below: Contemplating a rough future. Brighton beach, December 2007.

carrying ray guns — and I began to get nervous. His wild, swivelling eyes, manic grin and leaking saliva didn't help.

Everywhere we went on Melbourne Beach we came across locals with time on their hands, an insatiable desire for alcohol and deep pockets. It was La-La Land and we were powerful, British movie moguls looking for new stars.

George never reappeared and Peter had gone off to see friends he'd met from a previous visit. That left me with days to wander up and down the endless white sands watching the sea pelicans or swimming in the over-chlorinated hotel pool, which gradually turned my hair bright green. I looked and felt like a sci-fi alien — blending in nicely with the natives. The proximity of the Cape Canaveral Space Center further up the beach added to the extraterrestrial atmosphere.

The promo video never saw the light of day, the hotel bond never launched and the wealthy investor saw sense and pulled out. But Peter did pay my fee. He went on to have many more bright investment ideas, underwriting insurance packages for sub-prime housing loans in Louisiana, I believe.

Back on earth in Hove, I felt disorientated. It might have been the amount I'd had to drink in Florida, but I knew that another drink would sort it out. After a few days back opening a pile of credit-card bills — a task that was impossible to tackle without a bottle of something — the phone rang.

'Hi, Ed! It's Jeremy. You remember me, don't you? How would you like to make an advert about detergent? It's a big name, it's a big shoot and it's only a day's work. They want someone with a bit of gravitas.'

Jeremy was someone I had done a few corporate things with in the past but hadn't heard from in years. There must have been quite a few refusals for him to have come to me.

Somehow the words 'soap advert' and 'gravitas' didn't sit together comfortably – maybe the detergent was called Oxymoron. One glance at the pile of credit-card bills prompted the only possible answer: 'Yes, I'd love to Jeremy! It's what my career has been building up to. Thanks for ringing.'

It was one of those film shoots that has hordes of extras, dozens of girls called Caroline running round with clipboards, a gang of professional oily rags making the most of the bacon rolls from the food van and a harassed director in a constant flap.

I really didn't understand the plot, but I think I was supposed to be a chat-show host discussing laundry with expert guests in front of a large, noisy studio audience. The whole thing breaks down in chaos and clouds of soap bubbles. Well, that's certainly how it did end. I just hoped that was the intention. I never saw the finished product and I had serious doubts that it sold any detergent. The cheque was 'in the post' for several months. It's uncanny how Royal Mail knows which sealed envelopes contain cheques and then slows them up.

Towards the end of 1994 ABN phoned to ask whether I'd be able to go back out to Singapore for a few months to do some more presenting shifts. At the same time I'd heard rumours that Dow Jones was planning to set up a European version of ABN, possibly starting in January 1995.

I had mixed feelings about going back to Singapore. The city was safe, relaxing and clean (I could accept not being able to chew gum) and it meant a reasonable pay packet that would keep the ship afloat a bit longer at home. But, if the newsroom, computers and production standards were the same as last time, it was going to be pretty frustrating again.

Changi Airport was its usual cool, efficient self and I was quickly speeding along the East Coast Parkway with Singapore's skyscrapers shimmering in the distance. I say 'speeding' but only in Singaporean terms. There was the near-constant sound of a bell in the cab warning the driver he was about to exceed the speed limit. But that says a lot about the city – unlike, say, Bangkok or Jakarta – as at least there was the possibility of speeding on the refreshingly clear roads. Good enough for a Grand Prix.

I arrived at ABN's offices and sat unnoticed at the back of the newsroom listening to a meeting of staff and management. The heated exchange of views, complaints and criticisms was an exact repeat of everything that had been said the previous year before the launch. Nothing had changed. It had the feel of several other business television channels I had worked with – poor content, patchy distribution and well-below forecast revenue. Despite good intentions, I had the suspicion that Dow Jones was not in it for the long haul – which, in the end, it wasn't.

I left the newsroom and returned to the Amara Hotel to get some rest after the long flight. As my head touched the pillow I heard the sound of drilling somewhere in the building. I knew from my last stay that no one was actually using a drill because there was no one there to use it. By now I'd come to the conclusion that there was something buried in the fabric of the building that produced the noise – ghostly coolies condemned to drill for eternity.

Sleep was impossible, so I took a stroll towards the city centre, along the litter-free and tree-lined streets. As Singapore is almost exactly on the equator, the sun was directly above, but the air was comfortably dry. I had no route in mind but unconsciously headed for the high point of the city – Fort Canning Hill, named after its Governor General in the mid-19th century, Viscount Charles Canning. It was noticeably cooler there. Beautiful aromas wafted on the breeze from the botanical gardens and huge, languid butterflies floated from bloom to bloom. The founder of Singapore Island, Sir Stamford Raffles, built his bungalow up there in 1822, which was handy, because the hotel named after him was just down the hill and I needed a drink.

Singapore 'Slings' were a bit weak and aimed at tourists so I just had several large Tiger beers served in a glass vessel held up by a wooden frame like something in a chemistry lab. The bar was overly air-conditioned and felt very artificial, like something out of a theme park. Not even the floor strewn with monkey-nut shells gave it any authenticity. I headed back via the river, which, even in less than a year, had acquired dozens of new bars and restaurants. I went back to Harry's but I couldn't spot Nick Leeson – maybe he had other things on his mind.

Being alone in Singapore and having pockets bulging with wads of dollars, I could have drunk myself stupid, but the discipline of getting up at 4am was useful and the need to send as much money back home kept me in line. Another strong incentive was to avoid fouling up and ruining any chances I might have of working for the planned European Business News channel in London.

My contract in Singapore came to an end without any drink-related incident – the Aussies had obviously grown bored of punching their co-workers – and I was back in Hove with the family for Christmas.

The studios and offices of European Business News were in a new development called Fleet Place, just off Ludgate Circus at the end of Fleet Street. It was actually above the old Fleet

Prison, where, a couple of centuries earlier, debtors and fraudsters served out their time. It was an area I knew extremely well, having worked just up the road at Reuters some 20 years earlier.

I was interviewed by the Editor-in-Chief, Michael Connor – I'd known him as a *Wall Street Journal* contributor to EBC in Zurich – and by the editor, Rob Beynon, with whom I'd worked at ITN. Both were affable and I knew them to be highly professional. I got the impression they thought that employing me would be taking a bit of a risk. There were a number of stories circulating – some accurate, some embellished – about my drinking, including a barely recognisable tale of my being in a fight in Singapore. Absurd.

Anyway they chose to take the risk and I started as one of the presenters soon afterwards.

A large, keen team was put together. The female members were almost all young and attractive, which may have said something about Rob's selection criteria! The new staff were full of enthusiasm, bursting with ideas and able to speak in many tongues. Not many of them were journalists and even fewer had worked in TV. My impression was that they were there to learn the business, improve their CVs and move on, which almost all of them did.

Naturally it's important to have high hopes and ambitious plans, but my experience was that realism and pragmatism were far more important. Start small, tight, professional and low-budget and then expand step by step. Design a tough, workmanlike newsroom and computer system and use experienced journalists who know what they're doing, even if they cost more. It should not be a training college. EBN, just like EBC, did the exact opposite.

So we launched with a vast team, producing lots of glossy

magazine programmes as well as the morning news and some of the most stunning (and expensive) graphics, studio designs, logos and promos that the industry had ever seen. The invoice from the design group, Lambie-Nairn (famous for its frequent makeovers at the BBC) was reckoned to be the size of the GNP of a Third World nation.

Quite a lot of the programming made good television and many of the innovations were copied elsewhere. But the channel needed more viewers – or at least solid, empirical proof of audience sizes – as advertisers were scarce.

It's never very long before financial reality sets in and gradually the cost-cutting began and a number of the magazine programmes were shelved.

I worked on the various morning business news shows which had different and changing titles but were all really pretty much the same thing. They covered the markets that were open and interviewed a steady supply of market pundits and analysts. I'd get through about 40 live interviews a week, plus innumerable down-the-line chats with our market reporters in Frankfurt, Paris, Milan and New York. There was plenty of room for technical and factual error – and the mistakes and glitches were frequent – particularly because the new computer system baffled most of its users.

There was, in the early years, a great atmosphere at EBN. Rob was a capable editor who pretended to be tough and demanding but who wasn't really. Nobody needed any encouragement to party. The studios were about 53 yards (I counted them) from Corney & Barrow's wine bar across the square in Fleet Place. It became known as 'Studio Three'. My regular drink there was a large white wine and soda (easy on the soda) with just one piece of ice to avoid taking up space. This became known as a 'Spritchell'.

My shift meant catching the 5.57am train from Hove, then broadcasting for two, three and just occasionally four hours without a break (I had a strong bladder in those days). As presenters we operated our own autocues by foot and were able to change scripts live with laptop computers. We didn't pretend to use them just for the camera. You had to know your stuff, be on the ball and preferably sober. It was mostly good fun and wasn't like real work in a pit-face sort of way. As was the case with almost every job I've ever had, I found it hard to take it seriously.

Coming off air, I'd always need a drink to dilute the adrenalin and then prepare for the recording of my afternoon programme *Media Report.* This went out five days a week and, as the name suggests, was a round-up of news, views and developments in the media world. I just did a couple of interviews and read the links and tried to look cheerful and relaxed, and that was about it. The programme had a competent editor, Adrian Smith, who did most of the work and had a benign attitude towards my liquid lunches, some of which he was present at. He went on to greater things at CNN.

As part of a *Media Report* special and as a way of promoting EBN, a large team of us went to MIPTV, a major television festival in Cannes. I had worked in that city before and knew most of the bars, including the infamous Barracuda. The promotional activities tended to involve champagne, and at that time I thought it was bad manners to leave any.

However, I was there in a professional capacity to conduct serious interviews – particularly with the head of the whole event. Sadly the night before the interview I overestimated my staying power and fell asleep on the wooden floor of the Barracuda. I woke to the sound of vacuum cleaners and the smell of disinfectant. I glanced at my watch and saw I would be late for the big interview. My heart was pounding, my head throbbing, my sweat was pure alcohol and I looked uncannily like someone who had slept on the wooden floor of a bar. I dashed round the corner to the Hotel Martinez, bought some shaving kit and deodorant and sped past the fashionably kitted morning joggers along the Croisette. Too late – I arrived to see one of my colleagues conducting the interview. Informed that I was now surplus to requirements, I caught the evening flight from Nice back to London, but not before making the most of the rest of the day in Cannes.

I held on to my job but only just. I kept a low profile for the next few months and made sure my drinking wasn't noticed. It didn't stop me drinking, though.

Having a steady income helped the family finances, but it didn't solve the debt problems. When I began at EBN I was paid £60,000 per annum. That meant £5,000 per month, or not much over £3,000 net. Outgoings, including servicing debts, were almost exactly that amount. So, in effect, we were treading water.

But I reckoned we all deserved a holiday. Life's too short, live for today, tomorrow we die, life's not a rehearsal... We chose to rent a bungalow in a small coastal town called Osterley on Cape Cod on the eastern seaboard of the USA. Set back from a quiet road in large gardens and surrounded by trees, it was just ten minutes' walk from the sea.

There's something special, almost magical, about Cape Cod; it's a combination of the light, sand dunes with marram grass, white clapboard houses, preppy fashions, wealth, the presence of the Kennedys and a laidback atmosphere. Irrespective of their politics, I'd always been impressed by the photos of the Kennedy family out sailing or on the beach looking tanned, healthy and sporty as if they were in an advert for Ralph Lauren. It was a great – professionally created – image, if slightly adrift from reality. Some of our family snaps nearly caught that sixties 'Camelot' look.

Our children were 13 and 10, so at the ideal age – not yet sullen teenagers (fortunately they never became so) and not so young that they needed constant attention.

We hired a car and, helped by Judy's reliable navigating skills, went to all the places a tourist should on Cape Cod and the surrounding area: Hyannis Port, Provincetown, Martha's Vineyard, Edgartown, Chappaquiddick and so on. Like all holidays, I hung on to every day and dreaded the return to work. Like most people, I'd always thought, Why can't life always be like this? I've only got one try at life on this planet – why do I have to go back to drudgery? The answer was, of course, to pay the bills, but the nagging feeling that there must be a better way was becoming more insistent.

EBN soldiered on for the next couple of expensive years without producing much revenue and Dow Jones began to lose its nerve. The channel was up against the same basic problems that all business television channels had faced previously and would face subsequently. It was costly to produce but never reached an audience large enough to attract advertisers. The international advertising spend was increasingly being shared out among an ever-growing variety of media. The Internet was beginning to make its enormous potential presence felt.

Dow Jones looked as if it wanted to ease out gracefully from its exposure to broadcast television and began talks with the American TV network NBC, owned by the vast international conglomerate General Electric (GE).

Before long, EBN began to feel the influence of NBC. The Yanks were over here and overbearing. It was strongly denied at the time, but the ultimate aim was to turn EBN into a replica of CNBC, with all its shrieking, plastic presentation and screens packed with mesmerising data. Out were reporter packages, most magazines programmes and subtle humour.

The channel's future was getting cloudier and the absence of any announcements fuelled rumours that were further elaborated during endless alcoholic gatherings in Corney & Barrow. There was a growing and cynical 'escape committee' mentality. But, while there might have been some belt tightening, EBN's budget always stretched to regular parties.

I was probably seeing the whole thing through 'wine goggles', but I was feeling rather detached from the project and possibly reality. My drinking increased and it was compounded by the daily four-hour commute, early starts, endlessly juggling with credit-card bills and the inevitable arguments with Judy.

It was at one of the many EBN gatherings that my drunken behaviour must have caused a scene – I say 'must have' because I had no idea what had happened, yet had that vague, sinking feeling that something very embarrassing had occurred. As far as I could tell, it didn't involve puke, nakedness or violence, but beyond that I never did find out. It was probably an inarticulate critique of the company's failings. It played on my mind when I woke up in the sidings at Hastings.

The next day I was called into Rob's office and he quite reasonably said I needed to sort out my drinking. It was made clear that unless I tackled the problem I'd be given notice to quit. He recommended someone called Dr Brian Wells at an address in London's Cadogan Place. Given that I had been relieved of duties that day, I went straight there.

Dr Wells was an amiable man a few years older than me. We sat in his quiet, book-lined consulting room and he listened with an expression of complete, unwavering but sympathetic concentration. Without saying very much, he indicated that he had relevant professional experience of the problem, had treated many high-profile media types (Eric Clapton's name was mentioned) and suggested that my drinking had become uncontrollable and that I needed to be hospitalised.

My stomach churned and my brain screamed, But that's not possible! I've got work to do. I'm really not that bad! What will people think? Dr Wells didn't give me much of a chance to respond. He was on the phone to the Priory at Roehampton, south-west London, and simply said, 'There's a bed for you at the Priory tomorrow. It can be paid for on your company insurance. Go home and get a change of clothes and your overnight kit. The rest can be brought later. I'll contact EBN. By the way, you might as well have a drink. Most people do. It'll be your last, with any luck.'

A jumble of emotions went through my head. How do I explain this to people? What on earth happened at the party last night? What the hell am I in for? At the same time I had a much more positive feeling of relief and optimism. Maybe this would get me out of the hole I'd been digging myself into.

The next day my taxi turned into the tree-lined drive of the Priory and I saw for the first time the impressive white architecture of the main entrance. I thought I would be there for a few days, but it turned out to be almost five weeks. What I could not know then was that I would be back ten years later in very different and more desperate circumstances. What actually happens in the Priory, I'll talk about later in the book.

I came out of the Priory feeling on top of the world. Sleeping and eating well, no early shifts, no commuting, no frustrating and nerve-racking live broadcasting and no booze – all these together had done the trick. I didn't really understand what group therapy had been all about, I hadn't grasped what a Higher Power was and AA (Alcoholics Anonymous) meetings seemed a bit of a chore, but I felt bloody good.

But it was straight back into the same life – bills, commuting, family and the drinking environment at work. All the factors that had contributed to a dependency on alcohol were still there and I wasn't convinced that my attitude towards drink had changed that much.

EBN was in transition to CNBC with all the associated changes of work practice. There was a team from the US to instil the 'new ways' of broadcasting. They pretended to allow a bit of adjustment for the European audience (not that there has ever been anything resembling a homogenous 'European' audience), but it was perfectly clear that it was going to be the American, 'NBC' way or else – acres of beaming white teeth, cheesy, obvious humour, plastic banter, a lot of standing up, loads of 'This just in', 'Over to you', 'Back to you' and a kaleidoscope of graphics (not for those prone to epilepsy) that occasionally reflected what was happening on the markets. Irony – if noticed or understood – was heresy.

One of the first casualties was the regular morning contribution from Mickey Clark, stock market reporter from the *Evening Standard*. I had worked with Mickey on just about every broadcasting job I'd had. He knew his subject thoroughly, was quick-witted and highly amusing in a streetwise, Jack-the-Lad sort of way. We'd chat about the London markets in a relaxed and casual manner and would frequently reduce each other to tears of laughter. Judging by the emails, letters and phone calls, the audience got a lot out of it. But the NBC people didn't 'get it' and so it was axed.

Now that I was officially a recovering alcoholic, I was given more responsibility. Apart from the morning news and *Media Report*, I was asked to present a programme called *The Business of Sport*, which was put together by (and occasionally presented by) Ross Westgate. As its title suggests, it was all about the financing and economics of sport. It meant various stories on football, boxing, motor-racing, rallying, horse racing, skiing and so on. For a while I presented the programme with Sebastian Coe, whose fee was more than those of the rest of the staff put together. I was sure his charisma pulled in the viewers, though. My sobriety also gave me the green light to go abroad again – a highly enjoyable, alcohol-free trip to the French Alps being among the most memorable excursion.

Judy and the family preferred me not drinking and we had a good two-week holiday in Turkey – the first holiday during which I didn't have any wine or beer. But I could hear the old voices calling. Alcohol, despite all the evidence to the contrary, was still associated in my mind with good times. The voices became particularly insistent on an organised picnic on a Turkish farm up in the cool of the hills inland from the coast. Judy was feeling ill and stayed at the hotel. I went with the children and a group of other holidaymakers. We sat under the flowering fruit trees, in the lush grass dappled by sunlight and with a warm breeze blowing from the distant sea. The food was delicious, the limitless wine was free and Judy wasn't there. Why not have a glass?

Well, I didn't, but it was a close-run thing.

The takeover by NBC proceeded and all remaining vestiges of EBN were scrubbed out. The top level of management, including Michael Connor and Rob Beynon, was purged and replaced by Americans. I wondered at the time how long before I was chopped and my photo in the foyer was airbrushed out.

About ten months after leaving the Priory, I had a glass of wine. It wasn't for any particular reason, I just felt I could handle it. Well, I could easily handle that glass of wine, but I was quickly back to my old consumption levels. The wrestling match to control it resumed. I kept a diary noting whether I'd had a drink or not, but started putting in ticks for no drinks, when there should have been crosses. Who was I kidding?

The exhausting battle continued for the next two years at CNBC. The night sweats were getting worse and the morning jitters could only be controlled by more drink. It made me frightened to go to bed and even more frightened to wake up. I desperately needed that morning drink and was regularly throwing up the first mouthful, but the insanity of alcohol dictated that I would have another slug until I held it down. If Judy found my secret supplies, she would pour them down the sink. In desperation, I resorted to Listerine mouthwash, which contains 27% alcohol. It doesn't mix well.

Although I was holding the job down, I was having to draw on diminishing mental resources. I joined the gym near the office, became obsessive about the rowing machine and joined a competitive rowing league. After a gym session I'd return to work via the nearest bar and down several pints to 'replace the fluid'.

I had a few close shaves at work but, in what was to be my final few months there, I was given a merit award which brought my salary up to £80,000 a year and was given an extra, hour-long lunchtime programme to present directly after two or three hours of rolling news in the morning and before *Media Report* in the afternoon.

Somewhere in the recesses of my mind I expected the fragile edifice to collapse. Perhaps in the deepest part of my subconscious, I wanted it to collapse. My salary kept the finances going and I was able to acquire more credit cards – not so that I could buy things, but to secure more borrowing capacity for this subconsciously expected financial Armageddon.

Meltdown might be round the corner, but that wasn't going to stand in the way of another family holiday. The way I was thinking, it might be our last. We chose the small island off Tenerife called La Gomera. It's an absolutely beautiful island and, unlike its bigger neighbour, was wonderfully quiet. The children were old enough to look after themselves and I was able to find solitude, read and, naturally, drink.

Lying awake at night with my brain madly chattering, I knew I was at breaking point, but I was also aware of the stark reality that I had to tough it out at work, because without that salary we would have to sell the house. Judy had started work but her income would cover only a fraction of the outgoings, a big chunk of which was simply interest payments.

I tried to relax back at work, but there were too many things driving me mad, not least the irritating way the company was being run. The fragile technical systems, overstretched production staff and HAL-like computer system meant a daily tightrope walk for the presenter.

It was just a routine day and I'd finished my morning shift, come off air and got out of the building as quickly as possible into Corney & Barrow for a Spritchell or two. I should have been heading home ready for the next day's shift, but one glass led to dozens and I wasn't thinking much sense. My autopilot kicked in and after about six hours of drinking I thought I'd head back to the office and pick up my briefcase for the journey home.

The newsroom was empty except for the Editor-in-Chief, whose name has now been expunged from my memory. I very rarely saw her and she had no hands-on role with the output. I should have picked up my bag, turned around and gone home. Instead, I went into her 'glass-box' office, slumped down and explained to her where CNBC was going wrong. I was sure I was making sense but I must have slipped into Urdu, because she just stared at me wide-eyed and kept mumbling 'inappropriate' (the mother of all weasel words). I thought I was calm and articulate, but I guess I must have come across as a repetitive, gibbering psychotic. I got the impression she hadn't a clue who I was.

Twenty years ago an editor might have said, 'Oh, for Christ's sake, Ed. Get yourself sorted out and I'll see you in the morning.' But, in these more enlightened times, she called Security – perhaps she thought I was an intruder, or Beelzebub – and I was expertly poured out of the building. I'd forgotten my briefcase.

In my inebriated state I caught the train to Hove, fell asleep on the station, woke up, thought it was just another day and boarded the 5.57am train back to London for what I thought was a normal day's work. I could sense by my reception that it wasn't a 'normal' day.

On page 12, paragraph 3, sub-section 2A of my unread contract, being drunk on the premises was classed as 'Gross Misconduct' and so my relationship with CNBC was terminated. The game was up. The house of cards tumbled.

I made a half-hearted attempt at an appeal on the grounds that, after five years' service, I should have been allowed to resign for medical reasons. Alcoholism, I argued, was a disease. It didn't wash and so I was given just one month's pay. Ironically, my back-dated merit award arrived a week later.

It was back to being freelance (unemployed). I had a mixture of reactions. I was embarrassed, aggrieved, I felt a bit of a fool – but there was an underlying sense of unburdening. I wouldn't have exactly chosen to leave CNBC in that way, but self-sabotage had produced the same result. Thank goodness commuting and relentless live broadcasting into a vacuum were over. Maybe now I could get a grip on my drinking.

The financial arithmetic looked bleak. Somehow I had to get us out of this mess – a mess which, I was constantly reminded, was of my own making. No amount of self-help books or studying the works of Buddha would stop me waking in the middle of the night writhing with worry and bathed in sweat. It's been written, 'Don't sweat the small stuff', but to me at the time it wasn't small, it was all-consuming. This man wasn't sweating, he was drowning.

I was doing everything I thought I could given the circumstances – opening the mail and keeping it filed, paying the mortgage (with borrowings), paying the minimum on credit cards (using other credit cards) and always paying higher-interest borrowings with lower-interest borrowings. It didn't take a financial genius to spot there was an important factor missing – income.

But temporary salvation came again. I answered an advert in *The Times* for Head of Public Relations at a City financial company. It could have been anything – I was using a scatter-gun technique in applying for jobs.

It turned out to be the 'retail financial derivatives' company City Index. It's a company that gives customers the chance to gamble on the financial markets by betting that an index or a price (stocks, commodities, bonds, precious metals and sporting fixtures) would be above or below the spread quoted by the company at a certain given time in the future. The more right you are, the more you win. If the price, index, or whatever, was within the company's quoted spread, it won.

City Index and its sister company, Blue Square, were owned by ICAP, the world's largest money brokers. The biggest shareholder in ICAP was one of the UK's richest men, Michael Spencer. The CEO of City Index itself had already offered me the job, but it had to be cleared by Spencer, who appeared to be regarded as a God-like figure within the group.

He looked the stereotypical City dealer from the preceding decade. The wide, red braces could only have been an ironic nod to Gordon Gekko. If 'greed is good', then bad language must be too. During the brief interview he used 'fuck' gratuitously several dozen times.

Well, I got the effing job and was given a salary of £70,000, which would tide things over. With an established salary I moved quickly to remortgage yet again, buying more time. In effect, I was extending the mortgage to pay off the credit cards I had been using to pay the mortgage.

It meant going back to commuting 20 hours a week and putting in pretty long office hours, which, for me, would produce the inevitable increase in alcohol consumption. In a desperate attempt to combat that, I started going to AA meetings in London at 7.30am, and that meant a very early start from Hove. There were some desperate characters at those meetings. I was one of them, but I didn't manage to keep up attendance for long.

It was unclear to me (and to them) exactly what my new job was. I was supposed to be spokesman for City Index, but was rarely allowed to speak. I ended up handling their advertising budget, which was quite large and loose. Michael Spencer was a generous man and I was told his preferred charities were devoted to children. I got involved in organising a big evening bash for the Euro 2000 football championships. City Index had to sell some 40 tables of 10 around the Square Mile and was then to give £50,000 to the children's charity Barnardo's.

Ticket sales were extremely slow and when England were knocked out of the competition sales dried up completely. The evening event was cancelled but the company, to its credit, honoured the pledge to Barnardo's. I took the flak for the event's failure. I blamed England's 4-4-2 system.

Another requirement of the job was to be available to any television or radio channel to give City Index's view on what was happening in the markets. Having done many hundreds of interviews with financial pundits, I found it odd being on the other side. A new business channel, the Money Channel, had been launched with a great deal of press coverage, helped by the fact that Adam Faith was a major shareholder. From being a highly successful pop star and actor, he had turned into a financial commentator, adviser and investor.

In my role as a City pundit, I was invited to the Money Channel's expensive studios in Docklands' Tobacco Wharf. The company had a large staff of keen, young, ambitious journalists who were brimming with bright ideas and enthusiasm. I recognised a few faces from EBC, *Business Daily* and EBN. It was deja vu all over again. I mentioned to Adam that I'd worked on several business channels and they had all made the same mistakes – too expensive, didn't reach the target audience and generated little revenue. He said this time it would be different.

Working for a financial betting firm, I jokingly offered a spread on its survival of 16–20 months. It went bust after exactly 18 months. Sadly, Adam Faith went bankrupt, reportedly owing £32 million, and died two years later.

City Index had a unique hospitality room – 'unique' because no one else in their right mind would have designed anything like it. It made a 19th-century Parisian bordello look Swedish minimalist. It had a well-stocked bar and I had a set of keys. It was a good place to get some peace from the manic trading room.

The company's USP was giving small punters access to the big professional markets with small margins and potentially huge winnings. I regularly saw a customer's position go from £100K up to £100K down in the space of a trading day. It was a high-octane atmosphere and, even to a non-gambler, it was fascinating, tempting and ultimately infectious.

I didn't have the wallet or the nerve to spread-bet. I did start doing straight single bets on the FTSE, Wall Street, bullion and so on, and unfortunately I tended to win – which for a beginner can be disastrous. It's a bit like enjoying your first taste of alcohol. In gambling, there's nothing worse than believing your own luck or experiencing that first dopamine rush of winning.

I never felt comfortable at City Index and my drinking worsened. By mutual agreement we parted company after a year. Before the end came, though, I managed to fit in a wonderful holiday with my family (our last) in a large private house owned by a well-known Indian artist on the beach in Goa.

Meanwhile, I was still battling to control my drinking. I wasn't so hopelessly stupid that I couldn't see what it was doing to me and the family. On a number of occasions Judy insisted I go to my GP for help. Being a bloke, I was always reluctant to go to the doctor and anyway I was sure I knew what he would say. He was a perfectly pleasant and professional man, but the upshot was always the same: 'Well, you know, in the end it's really down to you.'

He did arrange six months of counselling through an organisation called Addaction. It was weekly, one-to-one counselling, in a seamy part of Brighton, with a pleasant, middle-aged woman who was herself a recovering alcoholic. There was nothing wrong with what she said. It was all sensible stuff and I was able to talk through my feelings to someone who listened and understood. But my overwhelming reaction on coming out of each session was: God, I need a drink – make it a large one! I stopped going after about four months.

Out of the blue I was phoned by a friend of Peter Spencer (the chap behind the hotel bond in Florida) who said he had a sure-fire winner of an investment idea and would I like to be involved in promoting it? This chap, Tony Forster, explained that he had set up the scheme in league with Delta Airlines to market a form of business travel bond. The plan was that companies would pay $50,000 for unlimited travel on Delta and several other airlines for five years. ('See the small print for exclusions.') Delta, like all other North American airlines, was deeply in debt and flying at a loss – effectively in administration. It was desperate for passengers.

The proposed company, Global Business Pass, was based in Bermuda, but operated through a UK company which had offices in the City overlooking the Tower of London. At that time international crude oil prices were about $40 a barrel. As I write, they briefly approached the $150 level and that has been reflected in increased airfares, so a bond that fixed ticket prices for five years was theoretically a good investment.

I flew out to Bermuda and stayed for a week in a small cottage overlooking the harbour of Hamilton, bristling with luxury yachts. Tony had lived there for years and was something of a local celebrity. My impression was that GBP was regarded as just another of his schemes and would probably never come to anything. The fact that the company's main investor, AIG (the world's biggest insurance company), didn't buy a single Business Pass might have been a warning sign. AIG, of course, was subsequently bailed out by the US Government.

I was with Global Business Pass for about four months and helped to launch the plan. To my knowledge, no bonds were ever sold.

I was in my early fifties and unemployed again. (In the UK one in three men over 50 is unemployed.) I could pretend to be a freelance journalist but the work had dried up. I did get a three-month contract with a local business communications company, Inside Page, writing material for the Visa credit-card website. I certainly had experience of credit cards. The company was run by a husband-and-wife team from a cramped office on the Brighton–Hove border. It was a strange set-up with the making of money being of low priority. The small team was made up of intelligent, genial, librarian types. They all ate lunch noisily at the closely positioned desks and coughed a lot. I didn't need any excuses, but I was always gagging for a drink. It was a relief to leave, despite needing the money.

Faced with approaching financial doom, I was fighting a rearguard action the outcome of which was obvious. I enjoy a game of chess, so I was aware of the concept of Zugzwang, a position in which a player is reduced to a state of utter helplessness. He is obliged to move, but every move only makes his position worse.

My next move was to get a job delivering new cars all over the country for a local VW showroom. The work was patchy and paid just £4.95 per hour. On the other hand, the advantages were that I couldn't drink while I delivered a car – frequently as far as Manchester or Liverpool – and I continued to earn the huge hourly rate on the train home, although I could spend at that same rate in the buffet car.

On a good day I could clear almost £40, which nearly covered the minimum payment on one of my two dozen credit cards. Another plus was that, if I set off very early, I could plan the route to take in historic sites and places of interest. One morning I managed to be at the top of Glastonbury Tor by 10.15am, looking out across a mist-covered Somerset before going on to deliver the car to a customer in Exeter. Another day I spent hours browsing through the bookshops of Hay-on-Wye. Fortunately the customer wasn't in a hurry for his new Beetle.

I never understood why VW couldn't deliver new cars more locally, which eventually they did and the job ceased to exist.

Through an agency I got three months' work as a postman delivering mail around Hove. Having done breakfast television for years, I was used to the early starts. I enjoyed the mostly good-natured banter in the sorting room and getting the mail (mostly junk) in the right order on the rack was more easily done without a hangover. With everything bundled up, ordered and loaded into the trolley, it was exhilarating to walk out into the open air – rain or shine – and to know that, for the next few hours, I was my own master.

I got the big, hilly rounds in the Dyke Road area, where the rich folk with long gravel driveways live. One 'morning' round ended at 6pm, partly because I managed to get myself locked in behind the giant security gates of a particularly grand house. It almost certainly belonged to a drug dealer, so I thought being caught on the security camera clambering over the walls with a big sack was not a good idea.

For several months in the heat of the summer, I worked as a landscape gardener in Worthing, again at the minimum wage. I didn't do much 'landscaping' but an awful lot of digging alongside a growing number of Poles, Ukrainians and Lithuanians. It was tough but I reminded myself I was from peasant stock and occasionally it felt good to be turning sods of earth, especially after a few pints of cider at lunchtime. To save paying the train fare, I did the 24-mile round trip from Hove by bicycle, which was healthy but tended to work up a thirst. It was difficult to pass the more than 20 pubs and 15 off-licences along the way.

At one stage I applied to be a road sweeper and beach-litter picker with Brighton and Hove Council. It struck me as being the ideal job – out in the open air and doing something positive for the environment. All I would have to do was wear sunglasses and a big hat to avoid being recognised. I went along for the interview at the Town Hall and was confronted by a panel of four inquisitors who asked endless questions about Health and Safety and how I would relate to my fellow environmental operatives. I thought I'd handled the probing questions well and had come across as passionate about clean streets, but I was turned down. I suspect they thought I was an undercover journalist looking for dirt, but not to sweep.

None of these low-paid, short-term jobs was ever going to make the slightest difference to our finances in the long term – it was just about keeping up my pride and confidence. I had to come up with something more long term. One of the biggest industries in the Brighton and Hove area (indeed the third biggest export earner in the UK) is teaching English as a foreign language. To teach, I would have to get the qualifications. Using money from credit cards, I financed a six-week course which resulted in two certificates (with distinction), to teach English as a second language to adults and to teach business English.

For a beginner in the profession, the pay was generally £10 per hour, but each hour of teaching needed an hour of preparation and few teachers put in more than three class hours. So a full day's work would produce only about £40 at most. Most of the jobs on offer were in China or Japan. They were useful qualifications to achieve and the six-week course was enjoyable and good for my confidence, but it was never going to turn the tide.

It was glaringly obvious that after two remortgages, cashing in a poorly performing endowment policy, shuffling credit cards till they were incandescent and lacking a permanent well-paid job, the only option left was to trade down the housing market. House prices had been rising strongly and there were some forecasts they were set for a correction.

The house sold within a few weeks. We had been at the same address for 20 years. For the whole family, it was an emotional wrench made more so by the fact that it was the only house the children had known and, not long before we moved, our Dalmatian, Bella, died aged 13.

The first step was into a rented property. We were

incredibly adventurous and moved ten doors up the road into an exact replica of our old house. It was close enough to move everything by hand in several hundred journeys. We had 20 years of accumulated clutter, a big chunk of which we got rid of one way or another. But at £1,200 per month renting was not a sustainable option and was eating into the equity from the house we'd sold.

After nine months of renting we bought a cheaper house in Portslade. It was in an area of parks and trees, five minutes from the South Downs and just round the corner from the Emmaus community and St Nicolas's Church, both of which I would later get to know more intimately than I thought. The village had everything; two pubs, an off-licence, a Ladbrokes betting shop, a post office and a chip shop and was just a short stroll down the hill from the house. Although only three years old, it needed completely redecorating and carpeting, which kept us occupied for several weeks.

The difference in price between the two houses released some money – a lump of which was swallowed up in the move itself – but it did buy more time until something turned up. I was painfully aware that it only delayed the inevitable. There was simply no escape from the immutable balance sheet – money out exceeded money in, however tight belts became. Even ceasing to exist would leave us worse off.

The money I could earn from local jobs was just a drop in the vast ocean of red. Having worked at City Index, I'd developed a bit of a taste for horses and virtual roulette. My first forays were successful and on the virtual roulette machine I could win more in a couple of minutes than I could spending days digging floral gardens or posting thousands of Readers Digest offers for the Royal Mail. I would frequently walk out of Ladbrokes with more than £1,000 in my pocket. It became addictive even though logically I knew that the virtual bank would always win given enough time.

Playing virtual roulette is a metaphor for life. Is the wheel truly random? Or does the software contain hidden patterns and meaning designed by a Divine Numerical Author (DNA). Play often and long enough and patterns do apparently emerge; there seem to be relationships between numbers – or is it an illusion? The pleasure of predicting and winning produces a form of superstitious belief that lasts well beyond the many times the predictive system fails to win. Failure to win produces the belief that the machine is being 'nasty', is in a 'bad mood'. It 'senses' that you, the player, are a loser. It needs appeasing.

But how many lottery tickets must we buy with meaningful selections of six 'lucky' numbers before we accept that the numbers have no meaning, do not 'know' what they are or if they have won before and that the National Lottery's odds of 14 million to 1 against are well on the way to being impossible to beat. But, we're told, 'It could be you!' And, if the numbers do not 'know' what they are, why hasn't the sequence 1, 2, 3, 4, 5, 6 ever been drawn? It's just as likely as any other combination. Instead there is always an uncannily even spread of numbers. Weird.

I got into the pattern of going to one of the village pubs, the Stag, just two minutes from the bookies. It was a traditional pub, unaltered by time, used by locals and with a larger-than-life landlady, Eileen. There was an active chess group – a game that is completely absorbing in its own right but even more so after two pints of Old Rosie.

The combination of virtual roulette number patterns, chess moves, credit-card figures, lottery numbers and alcohol filled the night-time hours with crazy, feverish numerical dreams. I was an out-of-control computer faced with an insoluble conundrum but whose software instructed it to solve the problem or self-destruct.

Judy had banished me to the spare bedroom by this time. The room was spare because Alexandra had left home. At 23 she could be expected to take off, but the increasing arguments about drink and money had probably hastened her going.

My snoring didn't help things. I'd been snoring at night all my life. I have vivid memories of my brother hurling objects at me in our shared bedroom to get me to stop. I wasn't overweight, but I did have sleep apnoea, which would wake me (and Judy) many times a night. I'd been in hospital for an overnight sleep investigation and the result was: 'Yes, you have a sleep problem.' And that was that. I'd been to Harley Street to see if laser treatment would work. They examined me and took a £200 deposit, saying that I should have the treatment but warned that it was painful, didn't work for long and cost more than £1,500. In the end, I went for a gumshield, which did work but gave me endless dreams about having a mouthful of chewing gum and choking.

For many years I'd been responsible for the family finances and so was aware of what was happening on a daily basis. Judy had left things to me, but she was taking more of an interest now that we were approaching a crisis. My last throw of the dice was to raid my personal pension plan, now that I was over 50. The money raised – about £30,000 – helped to service bank debts and pay the mortgage. It gave us a brief breathing space, but, of course, solved nothing.

Arguing with Judy was pointless, but that didn't stop us arguing. The discussions followed a well-trodden circular path and got nowhere except a lingering, frosty silence. Walking away from arguments didn't seem to work. Nagging about drinking and money problems had always struck me as counterproductive.

Our heated 'discussions' always ended with the words: 'It's all your fault, you drink too much', leaving very little room for cool debate. I felt powerless to turn our financial situation around. I felt powerless over drink and I felt unable to articulate my point of view. Everything, including global warming, world poverty and Original Sin, stemmed from my drinking. All the good times we'd shared had been forgotten – or at least reinterpreted in the light of our current problems. Inside I was screaming with impotence and frustration.

I was bashing my head against a brick wall and using alcohol as an anaesthetic. I'd escape to the solitude of the walled garden, a game of chess at the Stag or, to really add to the gloom, I'd go to a pub at the bottom of George Street in Hove. J.D. Wetherspoons, known as 'Spoons', is a dark place where people go to die but forget to. It's God's waiting room, but the Almighty is reluctant to call the next patient.

But the beer was good and cheap. It was there that I bumped into Mandy (occasionally literally). We shared an interest in Spoof, drink and laughter. She always seemed sunny, happy and was rarely critical. It felt like a breath of fresh air despite the funereal surroundings. But, of course, I was aware that drinkers tend to seek out fellow drinkers and we fed each other's needs.

I'd known for quite some time that the fight was lost. Judy quite understandably was tired of the whole thing, and at one stage said, 'I just want to get out of this. All I want is a little place of my own.'

And so did I, but at the time I didn't imagine how little.

We went to a few sessions at Relate, but the female counsellor would always arrive at the same conclusion – there was no hope unless I gave up drinking. Maybe by that stage I didn't want hope.

But she was right, of course. At one easy stroke, abstinence would wipe out more than £200,000 of debt, find me a highly paid job, stop the endless circular arguments and bring love back into the marriage.

The next stage was to get free legal advice about a divorce. I was certainly not going to contest it and we rapidly, and without much friction, agreed on a split of the equity in the house – Judy would get 60 per cent and I would get 40 per cent. She would get the car and furniture and I would get all the credit cards and bank debts that were in my name.

A quarter of a century of marriage came swiftly to an official end on the grounds of my 'unreasonable behaviour' and the house was sold within a week.

Judy found a comfortable flat of her own just across the park in Portslade. I knew, as I had done for some time, that my only option was to eventually petition for bankruptcy. But I would keep the financial house of cards going a bit longer with my share of the equity in case something came along. I hadn't arranged anywhere to live, but as usual I reckoned something would turn up.

It had all happened so quickly – almost as if it were a dream.

8

AWAKENINGS

How long had I been asleep? My limbs and back had become stiff and cold on the stone church floor. Maybe rigor mortis was setting in. Through vodka-misted eyes I could make out three ethereal figures near the altar. It was 12 December 2007 – two weeks to Christmas; had the Magi arrived early?

As my vision cleared I could see they were from the East (Hove, actually) and they were bearing gifts – water and Marmite sandwiches. It was Mandy and her mother and father, Ann and Bernie. Apparently I'd phoned and been speaking in tongues which, roughly translated, said I was on the point of collapse in St Nicolas's Church, Portslade. They had come to check if I was still of this world.

I felt gratitude, but it was outweighed by embarrassment, so I thought I'd make my excuses and leave. I had another day to fill and anyway my vodka bottle was frighteningly empty and the off-licence had been open a whole hour.

Shouldering my rucksack and new sleeping bag, I headed down the hill into the village. I noticed the weathervane on the church tower had changed direction and was now pointing north-west, which usually meant clear air, good visibility and a bracing wind, at least for the next 24 hours. I just hoped that the change in the wind might produce a change in circumstances.

That day I had the luxury of an all-day bus pass. It was the scratch-card type of pass, which was not only 20 pence cheaper than buying a ticket on the bus but, with a well-placed scratch, could be made to last two days.

My first stop was First Base's day centre in Montpelier Place. I was reasonably early and managed to get in the shower. I had by now mastered the technique of keeping the short-timed, press-button water constantly on and so was able to shave at the same time. Feeling and smelling like a new man, I had a bowl of porridge with some honey that I'd been given.

The last time I'd spoken to Debbie, the housing expert there, she'd said my chances of getting anywhere with the Council were slim – nothing was going to make me a higher priority. And that's the way it remained. There was not going to be any progress on that front until the New Year and maybe not even then.

But there were two bits of good news. One of the team helping rough sleepers had applied for and received a copy of my birth certificate. The original had been lost in the various moves I had made. That meant I could apply for a passport to replace the one that had gone missing. Finding more than £70 was going to be difficult, though.

The second bit of good news was that I'd been given my ticket for the Christmas Dinner at First Base. It was a ticket-only event because the previous year it had been open to all, which led to overcrowding, disputes and a riot which needed the police to break it up. Yuletide drinks may have been a contributory factor. This Christmas it was going to be strictly peace and goodwill unto all men.

As I had all-day travel on the bus I went further into Brighton, to the new library. It's a fine piece of architecture, but the first impression you get is that there are no books. I felt sure they were there somewhere. It certainly had a very pleasant and relaxed area for reading the newspapers. It's also got good, clean toilets. On my last visit some of the cubicles seemed to have had more than one person in at the same time, but that may just have been my imagination.

That day I was due to have lunch with an old friend, Neil Winton. I'd worked with him years ago at Reuters and he is godfather to my son. Neil had spent his whole working life with the company and took early retirement some years ago. On one occasion about six months previously he had put me up for a night at a B&B in Findon, where he lived. It may have been just for one night, but I was relieved and grateful, given the particularly difficult circumstances I was in at the time. I looked forward to having a normal conversation about something other than the problems of homelessness and street survival. I also looked forward to having a proper meal – and, naturally, several glasses of wine. Neil knew I couldn't pay.

On the way over to the restaurant in Hove, I got a phone call from someone called Jessica, who was a reporter with the *Argus*. My mobile number had been passed on by her colleague, Andy, whom I'd met the night before. Could we meet somewhere in the afternoon for a chat? I suggested the bar of the Babylon Lounge. More free drinks, I hoped.

After an excellent lunch with Neil, I felt human again. And as I'd had a shave and a shower that morning, the only visible sign that I was a tramp was my rucksack and sleeping bag. Maybe the other diners hadn't noticed my overnight kit.

I reached the empty bar along the promenade ahead of Jessica. She quickly recognised me when she walked in. I must have been Googled. Maybe I hadn't aged that much. I gladly accepted her offer of a drink and chose a pint of cider.

She asked all the right questions and took impressively fast shorthand notes. How had I got into this position? Who had I worked for? What was the most I had earned? Who had I interviewed? How was I coping with being homeless? Why couldn't I find accommodation?

The focus of the questioning was on how I had racked up such debts because, at that time in the media, there were endless stories running on the expected debt crisis when the Christmas credit-card bills arrived through the door in January. The *Argus* had also always been a champion of the homeless – so the combination of a fallen, highly paid broadcaster, a local family man, now living rough just round the corner from his former house and having gone bankrupt with massive debts, was an absolute gift from a journalistic point of view.

Despite the fact that I was sitting at the table with my second pint of cider, the subject of alcohol, and its possible contribution to my downfall, never arose. And at that stage I wasn't too keen to volunteer the information. I remained economical with the truth, because I was never asked.

Jessica had also brought along a photographer, Tony Wood, who took a series of shots of me walking along the beach and looking a bit glum sitting on my bench. We said our goodbyes. Jessica reckoned the story might make a few column inches.

Having had three hours of intelligent conversation and a fair amount to drink, I was feeling pretty good. As an alcoholic, that made me think that I wanted more. During the morning I'd stopped to chat to a street newspaper seller, George – someone I'd served an extra-large portion of egg and chips to at the Emmaus cafe. He knew that my circumstances had deteriorated and kindly 'lent' me £5. I headed straight for the Londis off-licence to stock up for another night on the bench.

Rucksack loaded with several litres of apple-flavoured aviation fuel (cheaper than petrol), I headed to Off the Fence on Portland Road. Behind the net curtains the usual suspects had gathered for a chat and free coffee and rolls. I thanked Merv for last night's visit and mentioned that my new sleeping bag had done a good job. He had also kindly organised a short-term loan of £3 for an all-day bus pass the next day – I couldn't risk using the same ticket for another day.

One of those in the 'office' was Mike, whom I knew from Emmaus. He had been expelled for some alcohol-related misdemeanour and was on the streets again, having been given his 'redundancy' money. He suggested we could maybe share a bottle in Portslade cemetery. It was a sunny, if bitterly cold, afternoon and the cemetery was a pleasant, relaxed place to contemplate mortality – perhaps even our own. Mike would go to the cemetery via the supermarket. He turned up half an hour later with two bottles of Tudor Rose British wine, a robust tipple that was more like cooking sherry, but, at 17 per cent alcohol, the taste was of secondary importance.

We sat on a bench beside the cemetery's chapel, watching the westering sun cast pink light on the statue of a standing angel.

'You know, Ed, I don't really know what to do next,' Mike confided. 'I don't give a toss about being thrown out of Emmaus. I was going to leave anyway. I've been at almost every Emmaus in the country and broken every rule in the book. When you're a companion, you just get, you know, stuck and lazy. The pittance they pay goes in days on booze and fags. At 58, no one's going to give me a job... I couldn't stand being told what to do anyway. I'll just have to hang on until my pension comes through. God, when I think of the money I've pissed up against the wall...'

He went on, 'Did I ever tell you about the time I lived in Israel...?'

The Tudor Rose was doing its job.

'Yeah, you did.'

'Do you know I can speak fluent Hebrew?'

'Yeah, I know. You've mentioned it a few times. And I can speak Aramaic after a bottle of this stuff.'

A long, contemplative silence.

'Shall we head for the soup run?' I suggested.

'Shalom,' he said in fluent Hebrew.

Our exodus was by bus. The soup run, which in fact offered a lot more sustenance than just soup, took place most evenings at 7.30 in the seafront shelter nearest the Peace Statue on the old border between Hove and Brighton. We were a bit early, so we had a slow pint in the Iron Duke in Waterloo Street. Nearer the time, we wandered down to the promenade, where a small group of rough sleepers were beginning to gather.

That night the coffee, tea, soup, sandwiches and chocolate biscuits were being handed out by a devoted and altruistic individual who had been helping the homeless for years. He financed it personally. Some said he had once been homeless himself, but I never knew whether that was true or not. His kindness really moved me.

It was also the night that the St John ambulance turned up – well, a converted ambulance that had a mini-kitchen serving more tea and coffee. They also had a big supply of hats, socks, gloves and scarves. I was beginning to build up quite a winter wardrobe. The group of homeless dispersed as soon as the goodies had been dispensed. I wondered where they all went and what sort of night they would have. It was freezing cold, but at least the sky was clear.

Mike and I sauntered back west along the prom. The Babylon Lounge was about two miles away. He decided to bed down along the way at the Hove and Kingsway Bowls Club. I carried on further to the garden at the back of the nightclub.

As it was getting closer to Christmas there were now nightly events at the Babylon for various companies and organisations. That Tuesday it was a girls' night, noisy but at least there was no danger of being beaten up or set on fire. Then again, ladettes these days…

By 9pm I was in my sleeping bag on my usual bench, fully clothed and as unobtrusive as possible. It might have been zero Celsius, but the prevailing clubbing style was short skirts, bare midriffs and pink cowboy hats. Ugg boots were the only concession to the frosty night air. Mind you, they apparently do the opposite in the summer.

At nearly 2am I heard the strains of Boney M's 'Rivers of Babylon', which meant it was chucking-out time, and that was when the shrieking began. Just how many times does a person have to scream, 'Goodbye', 'Merry Christmas' and 'Love you, Emmaaah'?

After the last of the over-revved engines and squealing tyres, peace and darkness returned. The flickering, blue and partially functioning neon sign was switched off and I could see the clear, starry sky. I could hear and feel the nearness of the dark, empty sea.

The dominating winter constellation of Orion was high in the southern sky. Under the influence of Frosty Jack, my mind was beginning to wander.

I could make out Orion's belt – a line of three stars like the Pyramids. My thoughts were jumbled. Hercules… Strength… Power over Babylon, the ancient city of the Jewish exile. Victory over exile. Orion rising over Babylon. The Great Hunter tracking down his quarry.

I had exiled myself and I was powerless over alcohol.

I felt tired and old. I was an Old Astronomer and my star was setting…

… But I have loved the stars too fondly to be fearful of the night.
I have sworn, like Tycho Brahe, that a greater man may reap;
But if none should do my reaping, 'twill disturb me in my sleep.
So be careful and faithful, though, like me you leave no name;
See, my boy, that nothing turn you to the mere pursuit of
*   fame.*

I must say Goodbye, my pupil, for I cannot longer speak;
Draw the curtain back for Venus, ere my vision grows too weak:
It is strange the pearly planet should look red as fiery Mars,
God will mercifully guide me on my way amongst the stars.

My soul began to set in the darkness of sleep. I could only hope it would rise in perfect light. And, if I should die, take me and cut me out in little stars. I will make the face of heaven so fine, that all the world will be in love with night and pay no worship to the garish sun.

Several times during the night I rose in pitch blackness to water the palm trees. Getting comfortable in a sleeping bag with at least three layers of clothing was always a struggle and having a demanding bladder was a bind. It's an age thing.

I lay awake on the bench with only my eyes uncovered. I was wearing three hats and my new Thinsulate gloves. I nibbled on the remains of the donated sandwiches from the soup kitchen and a small Kit-Kat. A hot, steaming coffee would be heaven – but that was two miles away at First Base. I then realised that it was Thursday, so they would be closed. Chilled cider would have to do.

I also remembered it was my brother's 57th birthday. Well, we haven't given each other presents for half a century, but I'll see if I can get him some sort of card, I thought.

In the east the sky was an electric blue and Venus had replaced Sirius in the south-east – it shone even brighter. I heaved myself upright and unzipped my sleeping bag, letting the cold morning air disperse the familiar cidery smell – at least I think that's what it was.

I'd become pretty good at folding up my sleeping bag and squeezing it back into its small carrier. After strapping it to my rucksack I put back on my extremely comfortable shoes – £12 from Asda.

Kit packed, rucksack comfortable and bench checked, I was ready for the off and whatever the day might bring. It was always a moment that felt good. I'd made it through another night and had woken up breathing. I felt self-contained and with nothing left to lose. I had little to worry about except the source of the next drink and sandwich.

Anything more than that... well, the future would have to look after itself.

Back on the prom I bumped into the rough sleepers' team, who had been checking horizontal bodies further along the seafront. I was chatting to the two of them when I heard a loud scream coming from Ma Mop's toilet. It was the lady herself.

She rushed out of the Gents' waving a newspaper – the early edition of the *Argus*.

I could see that the entire front page was taken up by the story of my homelessness. 'Blimey!' she said. 'I didn't know I had a television star in my lavatory!'

Bloody hell! I thought. They've gone for a splash. It must be a slow news day. I hope Jessica hasn't made me out to be a complete loser.

I could just see the headline 'Lost It All' and a picture of me walking along the beach in my leather jacket and red scarf.

Well, that's an end to anonymity, I realised. Everyone will know now. What on earth will people think? Then again, what the hell? I've got nothing to lose and I'm sure it'll all blow over quickly. Maybe some good may even come out of it.

I was heading for the newsagents anyway, so I thought I'd pick up a copy and check that Jessica hadn't stitched me up. I knew professionally how easy it was to distort reality.

Bylined 'Jessica Bauldry', the article said, 'Seven years ago this man was a high-flying television presenter earning £100,000 a year. Now he sleeps on a bench. Here he tells his moving story so that others might avoid the misery of spiralling debts.'

Running to about 1,200 words, the piece took up the whole front page and most of page 15. To my relief, all the quotes had been accurately taken and had concentrated on the debt issue. There was no mention of alcohol.

'While credit cards and banks are pushing the idea of borrowing money, the 21st century tramp is now white collar and there's going to be a whole load more that will struggle with their debts.

'"I'm speaking for the tens of thousands of people that are going to go through what I've been through. You may think, how does a high-flying presenter find himself on a park bench? But it's not far away from anyone."'

Well, that seemed perfectly OK. I had said all those things. As I chatted to Jessica the day before, I'd guessed what phrases and expressions might get picked up. If I were in her position that's what I'd want to hear, because it would fit my story. At that time, in the days before Christmas, the current issue was the 'time-bomb' of personal debt, and now the story could be really personalised. 'Look what uncontrolled debts did to an intelligent, professional family man (a business expert no less) … it made him destitute. It could easily happen to you.'

It was the truth, but not the whole truth. Being an alcoholic hadn't helped my case – it was possibly even the main cause of my decline. But there was no doubt in my mind that juggling with unmanageable debt for 20 years had worn me down and increased my alcohol intake. Then again, I didn't really need any excuses to drink.

That morning, drink was at the forefront of my mind. As well as the *Argus* I bought a quarter of Chekov for £2.99, which left me with virtually no cash.

I went further into Hove to meet Mandy at her parents' flat and she came out with a very welcome coffee. When I showed her the local paper, she said, 'Well, I wonder what the reaction to that's going to be? This could change everything.'

At that moment my mobile rang. It was someone called Phil Mills, who ran a local picture and news agency called Snap. Having worked for years at the *Argus*, he'd got my phone number from Jessica. Phil reckoned this story had some mileage in it, so would I like to meet? We agreed on the Café Nero on the corner of the Drive and Church Road. Phil came across as a decent bloke and an experienced journalist and it turned out we had mutual acquaintances in the business. He predicted that the story could take off. Would I like to sign up with Snap and he would handle things? He had a partner, Sid, who did the photographic work.

I met Sid down at the bench at the Babylon Lounge and he took several pictures, including one of me lying in my sleeping bag with my blue wool hat on (see back cover). It was still early and I looked tired and dishevelled, which is pretty well how I felt. It was a useful image for the media because it fitted the story. The photograph would be used hundreds of times, all over the world.

Sid wanted any pictures I had of my past life as a news reporter and presenter and any snaps from family albums. I knew I had a few, but they were stored somewhere in my mother's garage in Lancing. We raced over there, stopping on the way to pick up a birthday card for my brother – he was at my mother's that day.

It was a whirlwind visit and rather difficult to explain. My mother had never really grasped the fact that I was street homeless. Maybe she was putting the whole thing out of her mind, but she didn't really understand that the statement 'I have nowhere to go' did actually mean that I was sleeping rough outside.

I took the view that she didn't really need to know and I wasn't going to create more hurt by attempting to explain.

She just wanted the best for me but felt powerless to do anything to help. The less said the better, I thought.

With his top-of-the-range digital camera Sid was able to take photos of old pictures without much loss of quality. Two key ones had a big impact in terms of illustrating the story. One was a studio portrait taken by a professional when we lived in Zurich. It showed Judy and me with Alex at seven years old and Freddie at four. All of us were healthy and smiling. It captured perfectly the image of a happy family, which, 17 years previously, I guess we were.

The second was even more influential. It was the photo that had been published in 1988 in *TV Times*, showing Alastair Stewart, Carol Barnes and me, that year's ITN Budget team, standing outside 11 Downing Street. It was a picture reproduced over and over again – ultimately in circumstances that I couldn't then have possibly imagined.

On the way back to Hove my phone never stopped ringing. The first call was from the Press Association, which supplies stories and information to all media outlets. This meant that the next day my story would be in the national papers. Depending on how these treated it, it was very likely to be picked up by radio and television.

Everyone wanted exclusives and I knew they would all want their own angle on the story. Journalists being journalists, they'd start digging. I accepted that it wouldn't be long before the alcohol issue would come out and not long either before someone would want Judy's side of the story. Given that I had absolutely nothing left to lose, I took the view that I'd answer all questions honestly but wouldn't offer anything more than was asked. And I wasn't going to say anything bad about anyone else, because I had no cause to. I knew where the fault lay.

Also, I knew perfectly well that if I were just an anonymous vagrant there wouldn't be the slightest bit of interest. My plight in the days before Christmas would have gone unnoticed, like that of the rest of my fellow travellers on the benches around Hove and Brighton. The homeless have always been there and almost certainly they always will. Although some may choose that life for the freedom, the vast majority just simply cannot get out of the mire they're in.

I might have been an alcoholic, but I certainly wasn't going to come across as hopeless or pathetic. I was the only one who really knew how I had got myself into the place I was. If this media attention got me out of that mess, I wasn't going to say no. There had been no way out for months – indeed, the relentless downward spiral had begun years ago – and there had been little prospect of escape under my own steam. The words 'gift', 'horse' and 'mouth' came to mind.

Phil Mills had spoken to the *Daily Mail* and *Daily Express* and he had heard that the *Mirror* and the *Sunday Mirror* were trying to get in touch with Judy. I was told that a reporter had already turned up on her doorstep, but she had sent him packing.

At this stage I'd acquired a bit of cash. Given what was happening, I desperately needed some credit on my Tesco mobile phone. I also desperately needed another drink, so I popped into my favourite off-licence, Mulhollands, opposite St Andrew's Church.

'Ah, Ed, I see you're famous again. I didn't know you were a tramp. Is it still the usual, then? Or can you afford the Moet?' It was the owner of the shop, Mr Mulholland, who, in a previous life (with his taxi-driver hat on) had driven the family up to Gatwick at the start of our holidays.

'I'll stick with the usual, thanks. I've grown to love that oily flavour of industrial vodka.'

I popped into Hove Library next door and took a big slug of the burning liquid in the disabled toilet. Fully able, I headed next to Off the Fence.

Merv and Phil were impressed by the coverage in the *Argus* and mentioned that a radio reporter from Southern Counties Radio would be paying a visit to the Babylon during the night.

While I was there I got a phone call from a researcher on the BBC's *South Today* programme, asking if I'd be willing to be interviewed the following day somewhere near the bench for the lunchtime and evening news. By now I was pleased to say yes to everything and then work out what I was going to say.

Another call came in from the *Argus*, asking if I'd come up to their offices on the Hollingbury industrial estate outside Brighton to do a video interview for their website. I met the paper's editor, Mike Beard, who offered me a week's work presenting the daily video news reports for the site. I was due to start the following Monday, but events rather overtook the arrangement and it actually never happened.

After a whirlwind day, it was the usual bench that night, but it certainly wasn't a normal night. Word had spread rapidly around the homeless fraternity and, instead of the usual two or three at the Babylon, there were eight or nine. It may have been a genuine desire to get a variety of opinions about the plight of the homeless across to the media, but there was also probably the thought that there might be a bit of dosh around for a few drinks.

The Off the Fence team turned up, along with the radio reporter, and there was a good-natured scrum in which a number of views were expressed enthusiastically. Mike was keen to let the reporter know that he had been in Israel and

FROM HEADLINES TO HARD TIMES

spoke fluent Hebrew, which that night he seemed to have slipped into effortlessly. We had a couple of visits from members of the public who came bearing early Christmas gifts of toiletries and warm clothing. One very kind elderly woman came along with a few small bottles of Napoleon cognac.

Over the next few days quite a number of presents and cards were left on 'my' bench – acts of generosity that I will never forget. (I'm still using the razorblades.)

It was another freezing night on the bench, but fortunately the combined noise of half a dozen snorers drowned out the usual sound of the traffic, the chucking-out record 'Rivers of Babylon' and the screams of goodbye to Emmaaah.

I woke early to another clear, crisp sky and condensing breath. Washed, shaved and moisturised (Nivea), I made my way along the prom to the newsagents. The *Argus* story had gone well and truly national now.

The *Daily Mail* was running the headline 'The ITN Man Reduced to Sleeping on the Seafront'. It was just a rewrite from the *Argus* and PA, and so made no mention of alcohol problems. It was much the same story in all the other nationals.

The *Argus* had a follow-up story and an editorial which read: 'The difference in lifestyle between earning £100,000 a year while staying in five-star hotels, and sleeping on a bench in the freezing cold, is significant.

'But perhaps that is not what has caused the collective shock and sharp intake of breath. Mr Mitchell's sad story serves as a powerful reminder that being homeless can happen to anyone at any time.

'Many homeless charities say we are all just three pay cheques away from sleeping on the streets.'

Once again that seemed fair and balanced, but, of course,

188

still didn't include alcohol as a factor – because no one had asked. It wouldn't take long, though.

Later that morning I was due to meet the *South Today* TV crew on the seafront. The plan was to do a 'live' interview for the BBC's local lunchtime news and then a longer piece for the early-evening news. The 'live' part meant a links van, which, in my time in television, meant quite a commitment of resources to the newsdesk, but maybe TV technology had moved on and it was now relatively cheap.

The filming went smoothly and involved predictable shots of the bench, packing rucksack, looking thoughtfully out to sea and walking. The close-ups of my feet, I was sure, would make my George at Asda shoes fly off the shelves.

In the interviews I tried to get across the idea that almost anyone could find themselves homeless if all their options ran out. I borrowed the line 'We are all just three pay cheques away from sleeping on the streets.' Not everyone wanted to stay on friends' sofas for any length of time – least of all the friends. The central point was that the Council had no 'duty of care' to house people who were not considered vulnerable – a rather subjective term. That generally meant any males between the ages of 18 and 65 who were not disabled or mentally impaired were always going to be classed 'non-priority'. No amount of applications, referrals, meetings or letters were ever going to change that bald fact – as I had discovered.

For the filming I'd switched my phone off. Back on, it showed half a dozen missed messages – presumably my number had been passed on by the *Argus*. Several more daily newspapers, and now the Sunday papers, had been on to me wanting further information and, more importantly, new angles and possible exclusives. I wasn't sure how all this squared with the arrangement I had made with the local news agency, but since no money had changed hands I thought I'd still carry on agreeing to everything and working out how to do it afterwards.

For me this was not the easiest of things to organise at that time. Living out of a rucksack had always meant keeping up to date with personal administration was rather tricky and being destitute precluded having a BlackBerry. The result was that I just said the same thing to everyone: meet at a certain pub, at a certain time, hoping that my drink-impaired brain would remember. And there was a lot to remember as I was getting dozens of calls.

All the journalists I'd spoken to turned up at an agreed pub near Brighton Station. After I'd had a few pints of lager on others' expense accounts, the gathering became a strange sort of press conference with questions being fired from all directions.

We then packed into cars and roared off to the Babylon for more photographs on the bench. On the way the *Guardian* reporter Robert Booth turned round to me in the back and said, 'This whole thing isn't a big scam, is it?'

'Absolutely not! Being homeless is simply having nowhere to sleep. I'm not on a bench every night by choice. It makes no difference whether you look clean and can string words together or not. Should I be unkempt and inarticulate?' I replied.

Mind you, I didn't blame him for having that thought. I was painfully aware of the reality of being homeless, but, having read numerous stories about myself, I was beginning to think, Do they really mean me? Am I that vagrant in the headlines?

It was a feeling of surreal detachment that was to increase

over the next ten days; that odd experience of being a spectator again.

That afternoon I had several more calls. One was from Southern Counties Radio, who wanted me to do an interview on Gordon Astley's show. Another was from a researcher on Radio 4's *Today*. Apparently John Humphrys wanted to do the interview himself. He may or may not have remembered me, but I certainly recall some advice he gave me when I was at the BBC and being considered for a job presenting *The Nine O'Clock News*: 'Whatever you do, Ed, don't become a newsreader. It's not a job for a grown-up.'

A third call came from someone called Amanda Stocks, who ran her own press and PR company, Exclusive. She had previously worked for the *Mail on Sunday* and asked if I wanted to take the story forward and agree to an exclusive with the newspaper. I had a fairly good idea what 'taking the story forward' might be.

We met in a Brighton pub and she brought along a colleague, a freelance journalist called Eileen Fairweather. They suggested a deal that meant staying in the Metropole Hotel and not speaking to any other journalists about the story.

I was extremely reluctant – for a nanosecond – to give up my freezing bench for a soft, clean, safe bed and mini-bar. It may be macho and authentic to sleep under the stars, but the thought of sheets and breakfast made it no contest.

Later the three of us met at the Metropole and I immediately felt they had an understanding of the way the story was going to go. Both Amanda and Eileen had personal reasons for knowing about what alcoholism can do, so I felt relaxed about telling the whole story. At least I thought it would be the whole story.

Given our shared awareness of alcoholism, it was suggested touchingly, if rather incongruously, that we begin the interview with the Serenity Prayer – something I knew by heart from being in rehab ten years earlier. I wondered what my fellow dossers at the Babylon would think if they could see me now.

The interview lasted about four hours, and as a still 'practising' alcoholic I made good use of room service.

Next morning I was up early for the radio interviews. I'd ordered the *Daily Mail* to be delivered. The story was still running – not much else around, I figured. 'White-Collar Tramp', the paper headlined it. The piece contained two pictures – one on the bench with the blue wool hat and that picture of me with Carol Barnes and Alastair Stewart in Downing Street. 'One-time star TV reporter now living on a park bench blames the cancer of credit-card debt and says there are many more middle-class down-and-outs like him,' the piece said.

It added that I was being interviewed by John Humphrys on the *Today* programme that morning and quoted me as saying, '...so when I speak to him, he'll either have a very good laugh at my expense or take me to task, but I'm not embarrassed about what's happened to me because it could happen to anyone.'

The truth was, I was still embarrassed, but that was outweighed by the overwhelming feeling of 'nothing left to lose'.

In the BBC studios up by Brighton Station, I found myself alone in an underground 'remote' studio with just a feed of the programme in my headphones. It may have been the effects of my liquid breakfast and the fact that I had timed my visit to the toilet perfectly before going in, but I felt completely relaxed. That's the way it had always been throughout my broadcasting career – panic just before going into a studio and then calm when I was in.

The interview went well and, as usual, very quickly. Not being a politician, John gave me a fairly easy ride and just concentrated on how I'd got into the position I was in and the difficulties of getting out of it. I found out later that our chat had produced quite a response by email including several offers of a bed and a few saying come for Christmas, which was genuinely very moving.

I had another interview later on Southern Counties Radio with Gordon Astley ('If you're feeling ghastly tune in to Astley'), a very relaxed and genial presenter who knew quite a bit about the homeless in Brighton. As I left the studio he wished me Merry Christmas and gave me an envelope, saying, 'Don't open it until you're down the road.' Its contents were enough to cheer me up in the way I knew best.

As part of the *Mail on Sunday* deal, I'd agreed to be 'babysat' for the whole day so that I didn't speak to any other newspapers. That was fine by me if it meant a good lunch.

It was during that lunch with Eileen at Al Duomo, near the Royal Pavilion, that my daughter, Alex, sent me a text. She was just saying hello and mentioned that I hadn't used the word 'alcohol' in any of my interviews.

My exclusivity deal was pretty strict, and I wasn't able to talk to anyone at all, including Mandy (not to be confused with Amanda). I guess she must have spent the day having a few drinks. We both did. She turned up at the hotel that night and cross words turned into a heated argument. It was a familiar pattern fuelled by alcohol.

Only the two of us know exactly what happened and

neither of us made particularly good witnesses. She stormed off and said something to reception and the police were called. Maybe the cool night air brought back some perspective, but she rushed back to my room to warn me that the police were on their way.

Too late, the boys in blue woolly suits had already turned up, saying that someone had made a complaint about me. I thought it might be guests in the room next door.

On the grounds that a complaint had been made – and it's a matter of whoever gets in first, however fictitious their account – I was arrested and taken to my least favourite place, Hollingbury security station. It was another 15 hours in solitary, belt and shoelaces removed, mobile phone and watch confiscated and the intercom system shut down. Having read *Papillon* many years before, I spent the time exercising and pacing out the cell to measure its floor size, volume and all known mathematical permutations. I couldn't manage the press-ups.

About lunchtime the next day I was able to see the duty solicitor, who put my side of things to the duty officer. They decided on 'No Further Action'.

My rucksack and phone were returned. To their credit, the police had left my bottle of vodka untouched; the level was still at the pencil mark.

Quite a few people had been trying to get in touch with me. *GMTV* were keen to arrange a live interview for the following day on their breakfast programme. I caught a bus from Hollingbury to Hove Town Hall and polished off the remaining vodka on the way. There was a rather panicky researcher from *GMTV* down there, but everything was fixed up to meet their live-broadcast van down by the Peace Statue at 7.30am the next day.

After my night at Her Majesty's pleasure, it was a relief to be heading back to my faithful Babylon bench. On the way I bought a copy of the *Mail on Sunday*. The headline read: 'My daughter texted me: "So, Dad, you're famous again – but you forgot to mention all the drinking."'

The piece continued: 'In his first interview, the ITN man who is now homeless confesses the REAL reason he has lost everything.'

The double-page spread included two photos – the 'happy family' picture taken in Zurich and again that picture in Downing Street. So the issue had finally moved from the crippling burden of credit cards to the crippling effects of alcohol. I was relieved it was out in the open. Once again I felt I had nothing left to lose.

Police cells being, well, like a cell, I hadn't had much sleep the night before. I was completely exhausted and my bench felt like home. Before wrestling my way into my sleeping bag, I unfolded a piece of paper that had earlier been taped to my bench. It was a poem written some years ago by an *Argus* reader who thought it was now relevant in my case – which, apart from a few details, it was. I read the poem, 'Have a Heart' by Dionne Vowles, by torchlight:

As I walk down the street, I see a man
With holes in his shoes and one glove on his hand.
The clothes that he wears are tattered and torn.
He is wrapped in newspaper to keep himself warm.
As people walk by they look in disgust
At the man that a year ago was so robust.
They do not realise he once had a life with
Beautiful children, a house and a wife.
He once wore a suit and worked in the City,

But lost his job and could not stand the pity.
With the money gone and the house up for sale
His wife up and left taking children as well.
By doing this she broke his heart,
He fell into depression, his world fell apart.
So, before you walk past, and take pleasure to scorn
Please spare a thought for the life that is torn.

It was another clear night and the constellation of Orion again shone brightly. It was a familiar and comforting sight and, as always, gave me strength.

'We are all in the gutter but some of us are looking at the stars.' The author of those words, Oscar Wilde, had spent a fair amount of time in police cells. Sleeping rough can be hard, but that night the freedom to look up into the heavens felt intensely good.

9

SURREALITY
TELEVISION

The sky was still completely clear. With just six days to the
Winter Solstice, the dazzling sun had just cleared the
horizon and was rising about as far south as it would go. It
was not long before the days would be getting longer.

Packed and fuelled up, I headed for 'make-up' at the usual
lavatory. The floor, sinks and toilet bowls seemed even cleaner
than usual. It was an invigorating walk along the prom to the
Peace Statue. The morning sunlight sparkled on the frost-
covered pebbles.

I could see the *GMTV* van in the distance, its white
satellite dish standing out against the blue sky. A bit closer I
could smell the coffee and bacon rolls. I was getting close to
'normal' people.

The plan was that I should sit on the bench by the van in
my sleeping bag and look as if I had just woken up, which
wasn't that far off the truth.

The producer informed me that Andrew Castle would be
doing the interview. That morning Andrew was on the sofa
with Penny Smith. I'd worked with Penny eight years earlier

at CNBC, where she did the occasional shift when I was one of the presenters, but our paths had since diverged.

Perhaps because of the growing Christmas spirit, Andrew put his questions in a sympathetic way and I was hoping that I'd got the point across that there were many others out there, along the seafront and elsewhere, in a similar position to me. I watched a rerun of the transmission in the satellite van and was struck by how old I looked. I put it down to the cold. It wouldn't be long at this rate before I fitted the stereotypical picture of a tramp.

It was then that I was approached by a balding, grey-haired man who said, 'Ed, I've been looking for you everywhere. I've been down to your bench over the last few days. I've read about you in the papers and heard you on the radio. I can't let you sleep rough any more. Come and stay with my wife and me.' It was then that I realised I knew him from school. He had been in the third form when I was a Prefect – 38 years ago.

I was sure that the story had now run its course – there couldn't be much else to say. That morning the *Argus* was running a story headlined 'Newsreader's Alcohol Battle' which read: 'Mr Mitchell's story touched readers and offers of work, accommodation and donations poured in. Many shared stories of their debt nightmares on the *Argus* website. But it also attracted allegations that there was more to his story than just credit cards.

'He told the *Argus*, "I was a journalist and in that industry alcohol plays a role … with redundancy and divorce you think: How do I block this out? There's not a single street sleeper that I know that doesn't self-medicate and drink to help put themselves to sleep."'

Well, I wasn't sure that the original story had 'attracted allegations', particularly as the day before in the *Mail on Sunday* there had been a 2,000-word feature on my admission of alcoholism.

Somehow the subtext of these stories was that my downfall was the direct result of drinking and therefore I must have brought it on myself. Certainly it was a major factor and I wasn't blaming anyone else, but I definitely wasn't trying to cover it up. They had just never asked the question.

Now that the alcohol issue was out in the open, I couldn't think what there was left to write. But there was some even more imaginative journalism to come. The next day a headline in the *Evening Standard* screamed: 'My Drunken Bum of a Son'. According to the story by Rob Singh, Crime Reporter (why 'Crime'? I wondered), 'Ed Mitchell's world was unravelling today' (unravelling? There wasn't much in my world that was still ravelled). It went on: 'Today his mother revealed that her son, whose riches to rags story has been covered around the world, had lived with her for the summer until she tired of his drinking and asked him to leave.'

The article alleged that my mother's garage was 'packed with bin-liners containing designer shirts, cashmere jumpers and expensive coats. One neighbour, who had helped to move them out of Mrs Mitchell's house, said that she had counted 20 Savile Row suits among the collection.'

There were a few errors in this story. I don't believe that Mr Singh ever went to my mother's house, let alone into her garage. I've never owned more than six suits even though I was a television presenter; certainly not 20. Why not three times as many if it's fiction? They all came from M&S, not Savile Row. I've never owned a cashmere sweater, and never even bought a 'designer' shirt. There never were any 'expensive coats'. I didn't return regularly to wash or do my laundry. My mother has never, ever called me a 'drunken bum' and yet that was the headline. There was no sign of that 'quote' in the text. She was happy for me to use her address as a 'care of' contact point for mail, because I could not get Royal Mail to deliver letters to a park bench.

Regardless of all these 'errors', it did fill three columns for the *Standard*. They used the same old photographs. Cheap in every sense.

I knew perfectly well that journalists needed to fill space – it was a rather slack news period – but attributing words like 'my drunken bum of a son' to my mother was a bit lazy and thoughtless. At that time I couldn't give a toss, but I knew it hurt my mother, who was already in a distressed state for other, unconnected reasons.

I was pretty sure that press attention would begin to wane and that Tuesday was fairly quiet. It was then that I got a call from Dan Butcher. I'd first met Dan about ten years earlier when he was working with his brother in a highly successful foreign-exchange dealing and broking business in Windsor. I'd interviewed them both several times on CNBC and indeed at one stage briefly worked with them at their company.

We arranged to meet in the Grand Hotel's reception area. Dan explained that he had read about my story in the papers and understood my alcohol problems. He admitted that he had had an addiction to cocaine and alcohol and, a year previously, had been through rehab at the Priory in Roehampton. He was now in recovery and wanted to help others.

Dan was in the process of setting up the Recovery Network, an Internet-based interactive service aimed at helping addicts and their families. Sometime in the future there would be a video input on the website. Dan suggested that I might like to get involved on the condition that I went into rehab. In partnership with the Priory (who bought a shareholding in the Recovery Network), he offered to pay for a 28-day stay in the psychiatric hospital in Roehampton. I thought, perhaps if I went through the treatment and stayed 'clean', there might be a job presenting the television element of the network.

Naturally I was very grateful and jumped at the chance. Who, in their right mind, would turn down an offer like that? I may not have been entirely in my right mind, but I could see that it would be a way to get out of my current predicament. It was agreed that I should check into the Priory on the day after Boxing Day.

That's the way it was left. I would get sober and stay sober and, who knows, there might be a job at the end of it. Nothing was signed. Dan was taking a risk in that I could relapse but, because of the huge amount of media coverage, I'm sure he could see the commercial and promotional value of having me involved. Already on his team was Kerry Katona – someone rarely out of the headlines. His media and PR adviser was Max Clifford.

We said our goodbyes and arranged to meet again after Christmas. As I was leaving Dan very generously gave me some cash – an amount that would make the final days before Christmas that much more festive.

Purely commercially, the next phone call I received had the potential to make the arrangement with Dan, whatever it turned out to be, even more attractive for him.

It came from Emma Morgan, executive producer at an independent TV production business called Twofour. The company was very quickly putting a bid together to do an

ITV documentary on my story. The programme, if it went ahead, would be part of *Tonight with Trevor McDonald*. Asked if I'd be willing to take part, I quickly said yes, although now that I had an 'agent', Amanda Stocks, I left the arrangements to her.

So my luck was still holding. The *Argus* story five days previously had sparked widespread newspaper, radio and television interest, I had the offer of four weeks' rehab in the best psychiatric hospital in the country and now a documentary. It could mean getting out of the trap of homelessness for ever and, if I put the effort in, getting off the booze.

I found it difficult to believe all that was going on. Less than a week earlier the outlook had been relentlessly grim. Now, if I didn't self-sabotage, anything could happen. Even my cynical mind was thinking that a benign Higher Power might have had a hand in this.

I slept very soundly that night – in the hotel.

It was sheer luxury to wake up in a bed and not to have to pack a rucksack and sleeping bag. And having an en suite bathroom was a lot more convenient than a public convenience, however scrupulously clean Ma Mop was.

That morning's *Daily Mail* was a bit uncomfortable. The two-page story was by Eileen Fairweather, the woman who 'babysat' me the previous Saturday. Clearly she had been in contact with Judy with a pre-conceived idea of the story she wanted.

'Forget His Lies – I'll Tell You the Truth About My Down and Out Husband' read the headline.

I wasn't surprised that the papers had contacted Judy – it was perfectly standard journalistic practice to want to talk to 'the former wife'. But, as hard as I tried, I couldn't find the actual words used in the headline anywhere in the article itself.

Judy's quotes were actually quite fair and balanced. In fact, she was positive about the potential outcome of all the media coverage, saying that I might have the chance to deal with my alcoholism. But obviously Eileen had set out with the intention of making me look bad, even to the point of amateurishly repeating the allegation that I had '20 Savile Row suits in my mother's garage' – a garage that I firmly believe no journalist had ever visited and a 'fact' that – even if it had been true – was supremely irrelevant to my being homeless. Of course I used to have suits. I was a television presenter! But what use were suits on a park bench – whether they came from Gieves & Hawkes, Boss or Woolworths? How does owning suits make a person any less homeless?

Incidentally, my half-dozen remaining suits went to Oxfam. The lapels were too wide anyway.

Later that day it was back to the BBC studios in Brighton to do the *Jeremy Vine Show* on Radio 2. The idea was to bring in Dan Butcher so that he could mention his new website for the Recovery Network. After the programme I was contacted by the producer of the show and told there had been several offers of accommodation and invitations to have Christmas lunch. There had been an inquiry from the production company RDF about filming and, separately, a job offer to set up and run a radio newsroom in Slovakia. The position apparently came with a car and a flat in Bratislava. Things were definitely getting surreal.

Later I was told that Twofour had been given the go-ahead by ITV to make a documentary over the holiday period. For the production team, it was a very tight schedule and, apart from that, they would have to spend Christmas with an alcoholic 'down and out'. At the time I didn't give much thought to that aspect of things. For me it would be an interesting break from Hove Library, First Base, Off the Fence and my bench. They might even buy a few beers.

I met the team – David and Irene and the camera crew – in Hove and we talked through their ideas and suggestions for locations. These were the places I would normally go to, where I bought drink, where I used to live and, of course, where I slept on the seafront.

At first I was under the impression that it would be a shortish report as part of *Tonight with Trevor McDonald*, but David told me that it would take up the full half-hour. He said he wanted the whole thing to be as real and as natural as possible and that it would include interviews with Judy, Alex and Freddie.

David, Irene and the crew were warm, friendly and understanding, which I was happy about since we were going to spend the next week together. For their part, they must have been relieved that I wasn't a grunting, malodorous deadbeat with a chip on his shoulder.

They had a job to do in a limited amount of time. As a former professional I knew what had to be done and I wanted to make it as painless as possible. Conveniently, they knew that I knew. I wanted to be as honest and open as possible and tell it straight. I wasn't going to fit in with any stereotypical ideas of what an alcoholic tramp should look or sound like.

Even so, I did have some qualms about drinking openly in front of the camera, because the truth is that I'd always tried to be rather discreet about swigging from cans or bottles in public. It's degrading and illegal. But I could see that, as an image, it was important. (All dossers drink from cans of super-strength lager, don't they?) Anyway, at this stage I was willing to go along with pretty much anything.

Some of the first scenes were shot on the seafront itself, in and around the Babylon Lounge and 'my' bench. I rapidly began to get the hang of walking in a straight line, ignoring the camera and gazing out to sea.

We drove up to Portslade and to the walled garden where I used to go to get some peace, read *The Times* and drink a quarter-bottle of vodka. Despite its attractions, the garden rarely had any visitors, so it was great for solitude and thinking. This time I did some thinking out loud for the camera. David seemed to be asking all the right questions.

We also filmed at St Nicolas's Church, where I'd so enjoyed the silence, indeed fallen asleep. I wanted to talk as naturally as possible, but it must have sounded like a reporter or broadcaster – although that was me being natural. I preferred to get sentences and feelings across clearly, but I suppose that could have seemed a bit rehearsed. Then again, throwing in a few gratuitous 'ums' and 'ers' would have been acting.

As I was speaking on camera I was also aware that I had a little 'editor's voice' in my brain that wouldn't stop saying things like, 'That's a good phrase, that'll get used' or 'That was a bit clichéd. Can't you say something more original?' It was looking out for sound-bites whereas I was desperately trying to portray the raw truth. Perhaps a few more drinks would shut my internal editor up, and eventually they did.

We then went down to the Stag, where I used to drink and play chess. The regulars were welcoming but, quite understandably, not keen to be filmed. Perhaps some of them weren't supposed to be there. The compromise was a shot from the outside through the window of me downing a couple of pints. It took several takes.

Twofour had been contacting some of my former colleagues in the business to see if they would act as reporter/investigator on the documentary. The natural choice was Carol Barnes. I'd worked with her at ITN, specifically covering the Budget; had appeared with her in that well-used photograph in Downing Street, had known her socially and she lived in Brighton. Later I learned that she had jumped at the chance and did genuinely want to help me.

That night David and Irene bravely bedded down on the benches of the Babylon Lounge, partly to be ready for Carol in the morning, partly to experience what it was like to sleep rough in the open and partly to film me asleep. They didn't use any pictures of me during the night, but they certainly used the soundtrack. Unknown to me, I did a lot of moaning and crying out. A lost soul, chained to a rucksack, condemned to wander the earth for all eternity.

Even though I'd known Carol for years, I was nervous and embarrassed about meeting her. What on earth would she think about the depths I had fallen into? I definitely didn't want her to feel sorry for me.

I wanted to come across as relaxed as possible without giving the impression that I was on some jolly camping holiday. A few slugs of whisky got me into the right frame of mind. I was relieved the cameraman got the 'meeting shot' right first time, as I couldn't face conjuring up 'surprise' twice. From then on it was just like old times. Carol was genuinely interested in how I'd got into this mess and how I was surviving. We went on to film in a small cafe in Church Road famous for its lockschen and bagels. The conversation flowed easily. I felt relaxed talking about the way things had turned out and what she was up to now.

Carol was due to go on to interview Judy and the children, but before we parted I did say it would be good to meet up again after the Priory, maybe for lunch. For me it was the most natural thing in the world. It was to be the last time I saw her.

Filming the next day began with a sequence showing me buying my usual jet fuel at Londis, which made the owner's day. It wasn't a set-up for the camera because it was what I would have been doing if I'd had a bit of money – which, thanks to the media interest, I now did.

Back along the seafront, David and Irene thought it would be a good idea to film how I kept myself clean and shaved at Ma Mop's toilet on the prom.

We turned up to find another camera crew – from Switzerland – already there. Apparently the story had sparked a lot of interest across Europe, and maybe in Switzerland in particular because I'd been a television presenter there. David explained to them that I couldn't appear on camera for them because I was contracted to Twofour.

They needed something, though, so they filmed me being filmed going into the toilet. To make it even more surreal, there was a stills photographer there taking shots of a film crew filming a film crew filming a bloke going to the lavatory. I may have appeared in the frame somewhere, though probably, by that stage, I was not altogether there.

Wherever we set up the camera we were always found by Mike and his friend Mick, both of whom I knew from Emmaus. They, of course, sensed there was a bit of cash floating around for a bottle or two, but watching a camera crew in action relieved the boredom of plodding the streets. They were actually used for a couple of 'totter on' parts. They got their 15 seconds of fame.

There was a lot more filming and interviews further along the prom near the ruined West Pier. The more I drank, the more philosophical and maudlin I became. Choking back tears, I remember trying to explain how alcohol had got such a grip on me that it felt like it was eating away at my 'self'; it was destroying who I thought I was, gnawing at my soul. I just wanted to get 'myself' back again. Alcohol was killing me, but first it was driving me mad. All this time the camera was rolling.

At that point something seemed to snap inside me. I'd said all I could say. I just felt drained and exhausted by sleeping rough, by too much cider and ten days of being in the media spotlight after many months of almost no contact with the outside world. At that moment the cold, grey sea just seemed very inviting. Leaving the camera crew, I strode down the beach and knee-deep into the waves. I had no idea what my intention was, I just knew I was sick of everything. The camera kept filming.

Later that afternoon, with me still rather wet, we went up to my daughter's house in Southwick, about three miles away. My son was there as well. We did a few sequences walking and talking and standing around her Christmas tree. Alex and Freddie were interviewed separately – I'm sure they felt more relaxed about speaking without me being there. They were also interviewed by Amanda Stocks for the *Mail on Sunday*.

The resulting article, headlined 'All We Really Want Is Our Dad Back…', said, 'Ex-ITN man Ed Mitchell dramatically confessed his alcoholism in last week's *MoS*. Now in a remarkable interview, his distraught children beg him to take the first step to recovery – and to give them back the loving father drink so cruelly stole.'

Although it was otherwise a perfectly fair account, I was pretty upset to read that my children were 'distraught'. I completely understood that papers have to be sold and attention grabbed, but the children I knew, and had known intimately for more than 20 years, were not 'distraught'. They were certainly disappointed – though perhaps more embarrassed – with the way things had gone, and were fed up with my drinking, but they were sufficiently understanding to know how it had happened and realise everything that had contributed to it.

Once again I was reading about someone that I didn't really recognise. It was an unsettling feeling of being 'detached' from the person that was being described. But maybe the papers were right. Perhaps my self-image had become so warped by alcohol that I didn't know myself any more.

Christmas Eve was very cold and clear. That night it had been arranged for me to stay in one of Brighton's homeless shelters, at St Patrick's Church in Cambridge Road. Over the past few months I'd failed many times to get in for the night, but it looked as if the presence of the cameras had opened doors. I hadn't been that keen on sleeping there, given that, not long before, someone had been stabbed outside, and certainly I arrived to find a threat of violence in the air.

As it was Christmas Eve, I went out to a pub in the area with some of the other homeless men staying that night at the shelter. I reckon they thought I had cash on me because I was with a film crew. Bizarrely we spent the evening with Robert Kazinsky, who plays Sean in *EastEnders*. I was relieved to discover he was nothing like his soap character. Perhaps he was with us researching how to behave like a dosser. Judging by subsequent episodes I've watched, he'd learned a lot.

It was a disturbed and sleepless night. I actually slept in a separate office rather than in the dormitory after one of the other overnight guests threatened to 'do me over'.

I was awake very early on Christmas morning and was glad to get out of the place. Should I ever be homeless again, life on a bench in the open, however cold, would be far preferable to the troubling atmosphere in that church. If this was the season of goodwill, I would have dreaded being in there after Twelfth Night.

I didn't need Christmas as an excuse, but it seemed a good idea to head down Western Road to an off-licence which was open for early-morning drinkers – something that would have been unheard of even ten years ago. There's a good deal of lively debate about the value to the economy of mass immigration and the resulting multi-cultural society. For Mr Akhtar Kahn, manager of the 24/7 Bargain Booze Basement, it was just another working day. For the dependent alcoholic, multi-ethnicity turns out to be an absolute life-saver.

The camera crew arrived at the church and we wished one another season's greetings. They got a few shots of me looking dishevelled and muttering critical comments about the overnight stay.

The plan was to head over to the Victoria by Portslade Station, as the pub had a special Christmas Day lunch, and two friends, Dawn and Jamie, had offered to buy me and Mandy a meal. The crew would also have their festivities there. Naturally there was a good deal of drinking, most of it caught on camera.

By this time I'd become oblivious to the filming process, and probably to everything else as well. After a week's shoot it must have become second nature to me to have a camera pointing at me. I only subsequently knew this from watching the documentary, but I left the pub, zigzagged up the street and puked voluminously and loudly (almost unnaturally loudly) behind some dustbins. It was a waste of a good meal and was probably disgusting to watch on prime-time television. But that's where alcoholism had taken me.

Because there was to be more filming on Boxing Day, I was allowed an early night. The schedule required a mid-morning start at Hove Lagoon, where I did a fair bit of moody gazing at swans before having lunch with Alex and Freddie at the Blue Lagoon pub. Again the whole proceedings were on camera. It was a very enjoyable meal and good to have time with my son and daughter. But in the end none of it got used.

That night I stayed at Mandy's parents' place in Hove before the next day's train journey up to the Priory at Roehampton.

The final scenes were going to be shot at Brighton Station and on the train up to East Croydon. I'd packed a bag for the four-week stay at the Priory and was filmed approaching the station. Just before the camera started rolling, I popped into the off-licence to get my last in-flight supplies. In the last interview I talked about what I expected of rehab and speculated on what the consequences of failure might be. On the train I felt very relaxed knowing that the rather artificial process of filming was nearly over. A quarter of an hour into the journey we crossed Balcombe viaduct. I looked down at the family picnic site in the now muddy, ploughed field and had what was to be my last drink of cider.

When I reached the Priory I knew it was almost a 'wrap' except for a few thoughts on camera at the gate and my last swig from a quarter of vodka. I replaced the bottle automatically in my jacket pocket, picked up my bag and walked through the entrance to the hospital.

Inside the gates, a small group of staff welcomed me. We shook hands and then I bent down to pick up my bag. The empty vodka bottle fell out of my jacket pocket and smashed on the driveway.

It was a fittingly symbolic way to launch what I hoped would be a life of sobriety.

10

ANOTHER CRACK AT THERAPY

Like most who arrive at the Priory, I was intoxicated but felt a profound sense of relief. All that exhausting drink insanity could now be over – perhaps for good. I felt a massive burden lifting from my shoulders. Walking down the curving driveway through the tree-lined grounds and seeing the familiar wedding-cake architecture of the main entrance, I knew all too well what the next 28 days would bring.

It would be intense, emotional and unrelenting, but I was also aware that I would have a roof over my head, a warm, dry bed, safety, three meals a day and a real chance to turn my life around. I just kept thinking, I'm so bloody lucky. I just cannot believe I've escaped from that black hole. I'd be a complete lunatic to mess this one up!

I was in the right place then – a psychiatric hospital.

My room, number 59, was in West Wing, along a corridor of about 20 rooms. Comfortable and basic, it had a shower, single bed, two chairs, a desk and a small portable television, terrestrial only. Compared with a sleeping bag on a wooden bench, it was heaven. It felt odd not to have a camera filming my every move.

The room had two windows overlooking the lawns and trees facing south and south-west. At first glance they appeared to be barred, but it was just part of the mock-Gothic architecture. They certainly could not have been opened more than an inch, though. No leaping to freedom, even if you wanted to.

For the next few minutes it was just glorious peace and solitude, apart from the 747s making their approach to Heathrow, though even that sound was strangely comforting. It may have been the continuing effects of my last quarter of vodka and the welcome calm, but my first visitor was a dreamy, angelic vision. A psychiatric nurse who introduced herself as Caroline asked in a saintly voice, 'Is there anything I can do for you?'

I didn't quite know how to answer, but she added, 'Can I help you unpack?' I thought they only did that in stately homes and royal palaces.

I really didn't want her to because my kit was still pretty fetid from three months on the streets. 'Thanks, but I think I'll be OK,' I replied. Then it became clear that her offer to help me unpack wasn't really a question. What she had to do was search my bag for hidden supplies of alcohol or drugs or any other banned pharmaceuticals, mouthwash containing alcohol included.

The doctor was the next one in, this time male. He asked a series of questions, tested my blood pressure and felt around to see if my liver was hard, lumpy or enlarged. The whole process of the seven-day detox was explained. It's a way of reducing withdrawal symptoms from alcohol or drugs by using some sort of librium. Along with this you get vitamin supplements via a drip and sleeping tablets at night.

That's the core part of rehab. The agony of 'cold turkey' is numbed, you're taken away from the places and people that were feeding your addiction and it's all in a safe and supportive place that provides three nutritious meals a day. The psychotherapy probably helps as well.

Alone again, I thought I'd take a stroll across the grounds to the other part of the Priory, where the therapy sessions and workshops take place. Unlike the main building, which dates from 1811, the Lodge is a plain, two-storey, 1970s brick structure with six meeting rooms, a lounge, a kitchen and offices. Outside there's a small covered area with wooden tables and chairs where the current inmates had gathered for cigarettes and coffee. The whole block is surrounded by a red-brick wall and several fine beech and horse chestnut trees; the squirrels love it.

Like being the new kid at school, it's an uncomfortable moment introducing yourself to a group of strangers. Even though I was a relatively old hand at this therapy business, I was nervous. You just never know what sort of group you're going to get – and it's vital that you do get a good bunch because your recovery, possibly your life, depends on a friendly, welcoming and focused collection of individuals. For obvious reasons, I have changed the names of all of the people I encountered in the Priory.

'Hello, you must be new. Welcome! My name's Don. For what it's worth, I'm group leader this week. Good to see you, we need some fresh blood.'

I was very relieved. Don, who was Scottish and, as I later found out, ex-Army, seemed the sort I could relate to. It's vital to get on with people when you're going to spend 14 hours a day every day of the week with them. Even if they seem initially to be a little odd, the likelihood is that they'll turn out to be OK. They have to, as your getting well or not is, to a large extent, in their hands – and theirs in yours.

Don explained the ropes to me and it appeared that very little had changed from ten years ago. Looking at the other members of the group, a dozen or so, nothing much had changed either; it was about two-thirds male and a third female, ranging from mid-twenties to mid-forties and from a whole spread of occupations. A slow learner, I seemed to be the oldest. Everyone was at a different stage of their therapy – some nearing the end of their 28 days, some just a few days in.

Over the next month, whether I wanted to or not, I was going to get to know them perhaps even more closely than their own partners or closest friends.

Back at my room in the main building, I rang Mandy. I was extremely glad to hear that she was still determined to give up alcohol – partly to support me, but also, I reckoned, because she herself was sick of drinking and all that went with it. The prospect of abstinence didn't seem to bother her, even though being out there in the 'real world' would be much harder. The prospect of her still getting pissed would have been unsettling.

I hadn't eaten properly for months and my appetite for solids was minimal, but having three meals a day is a key part of recovery and, as I remember, a valuable part of group therapy.

There was a special, large table reserved for the addicts – the 'West Wingers'. It's not that they – or rather 'we' – were special, although we thought we were. It's because addicts have more in common than the 'glums' and the 'foodies' – those suffering from various psychiatric disorders who shared other tables and tended to sit quietly. The drunks and druggies were noisy and tended to laugh a lot, occasionally deliriously and manically.

I joined the table of about ten, introduced myself and listened to the conversation. It was the reassuring mix of moans about therapy sessions, workshops and counsellors and the sharing of 'war stories' – hilarious but frightening accounts of the depths that addiction had taken people to. There was a fair amount of talk about digestive systems, bowel movements and quality or paucity of sleep. I recalled from the last time that it was often easier to talk about personal issues around the meal table than it was to bring them up in group therapy.

I sat opposite a large, mother-earth woman called Marje, who turned out to have made several million pounds from a business venture. She lived in some style, but before she came into the Priory was relying on a bottle of Bacardi a day to stay on an even keel. She was very caring, prone to tears and, as I soon discovered, wanted to take on everyone else's problems.

At the other end of the table was Brad, an extremely loud and dominant American former soldier, who looked a whisker away from violence. I was glad I'd never met him drunk. Brad fairly swiftly informed me he was the 'Alpha male' of the group. I was relaxed to be the Omega. Next to him were two twittering young girls in their early twenties, Lulu (very apt) and Susie. One of them was on her 13th rehab.

Opposite them was Malcolm, a chap in his thirties who was shovelling in his food as if someone was about to take it from him. Apart from his healthy appetite, he looked in bad shape – a grey pallor and rivulets of sweat pouring down the sides of his face. He chewed with his mouth open and rarely missed his teeth with his fork. He was apparently addicted to tranquillisers and had never worked in his life. It was his third attempt at rehab.

Graham, who was in his late thirties, struck me at first glance to be a serial murderer. Despite his looks, he seemed a quiet and calm person. He was a professional and dedicated wine drinker. He burped a lot.

Don, that week's group leader, was there. He gave me a copy of the coming week's timetable, which showed an 8.45am start and a 9.30pm finish each day. He told me a bit about his background – night shifts, a bottle of whisky every day and the growing alienation of his family. He faced a day in court on a drink-driving charge when he left the Priory in just over ten days.

I wasn't the only one who had been admitted that day. My neighbour in room 58 was Jill, a 30-ish woman who had come in apparently feeling depressed, but subsequently faced up to her drink problem without actually thinking she was an alcoholic – at least at first. She was to turn out to be a very sensible and valuable member of the group and always seemed to be laughing which was an unexpected symptom of depression – perhaps it was to hide her depression.

Although I wasn't yet officially an inmate – there was a mountain of paperwork and questionnaires to get through the next day – I was allowed to go along to a talk that evening by an ex-patient, Eric, in the Chapel. Part of the main building, this was a wonderfully quiet and spiritual place with an ornate ceiling, large carved mantelpiece and leaded windows. Alcoholics Anonymous meetings were held there every Tuesday.

Eric immediately struck me as being relaxed and comfortable with himself. He had been in the Priory for five weeks about 18 months ago.

'It's good to be back. You're all in the right place. I hated it here to begin with. I was in a very bad way when I arrived.

I "came to" after about four days and then I joined the therapy sessions. I just didn't have a clue what they were on about. We just sat there trying to express feelings and no one said anything for ages. They all seemed barking mad. The patients didn't seem much better either. What the fuck have I let myself in for?

'That went on for more than a week, and then I thought, What the hell – my life's been a nightmare, I've spent 18,000 quid to be here and this is my last chance. I kind of got the hang of things then. I don't really know how it happened but I began to understand what the therapists were batting on about. I began to feel good – almost excited. From loathing the place, I started to really enjoy the sessions. Sobriety felt good. Towards the end I didn't want to leave. I dreaded walking out of the front gates. Could I survive in the real world, out of the cocoon of the Priory?'

Well, he clearly had survived and he struck me as serene, happy and successful. His experience was very encouraging. I wanted what he had. But what I really needed at that moment was a good night's sleep in a real bed.

The detox programme meant taking tranquillisers and sleeping pills, administered by the always genial medical staff at the nurses' station just along the corridor from my room. It also meant a visit by a nurse every 30 minutes throughout the night.

The combination of months of nervous street life, way too much vodka and cider, temazepam, sleeping pills and a nurse asking whether I was alive every half-hour produced a feverish, sweaty and hallucinatory sleep. I woke at about 5am to the thunder of Jumbos a few hundred feet above my ceiling. Hundreds of people crammed into a metal tube, stocked full of alcohol and with busy days ahead of them.

I hauled myself out of bed, stood up and collapsed; my leg had given way with excruciating cramp. The pain, chemicals and lack of vodka made me gag – an all-too-familiar start to a day.

The night-shift nurse made her last check at 7am and took my blood pressure – 212 over 150. Apparently that was dangerously high long term, but not immediately life-threatening. I just hoped it was the result of a lousy night's sleep.

As it was late December it was still dark outside. I dressed quickly and made my way outside along the long corridors and countless flights of stairs. Not a great place to be in a fire, I thought. (Early the next morning the fire alarm did go off but no one stirred from their beds – wonderful things, tranquillisers.)

By the front door there was a reception area with a coffee machine that made real coffee containing real caffeine – the only machine in the building that wasn't strictly decaff. No cross-addictions allowed. The steaming-hot drink plus the freezing air outside cleared my head slightly and began producing something that felt like an appetite.

Breakfast was served from 7.45am in the restaurant. Some got in there the moment the doors opened; others never ever made it. Despite lurking nausea, I forced in some porridge and scrambled egg. There was just a slow trickle of patients grunting their 'good mornings' and 'sleep wells?'

That day I was being 'inducted', which involved myriad and confusing (confusing to the therapist, that is) forms and questionnaires aimed at determining what state I was in physically and mentally. I ticked 'yes' to all the boxes about drinking habits and its consequences, which meant I was indeed an alcoholic. No surprise to me – I was already painfully aware that alcohol controlled my life and that I'd lost everything as a result of it.

I was relaxed about admitting being an alcoholic if by doing so I stood a better chance of recovery. Getting out of the deadly grip of alcohol was all I cared about. What I did find difficult was going along with the idea that alcoholism was a distinct disease ('dis-ease', as they put it, was easier to grasp) with possible genetic links; a disease that was progressive and often fatal. The disease model said I would always have the disorder, but I could get into a state of recovery – or was it remission?

For me it felt more like a deep-seated and habitual frame of mind formed, in my case, over several decades, that had resulted in a psychological addiction to, or dependency on, alcohol. An addiction that, despite countless attempts, didn't seem to respond to the exercise of willpower or intellect.

I was aware I was addicted, but I couldn't break the dependency, however hard I tried, whatever anyone said or whatever I lost. In the words of AA, I had a distinct physical desire to consume alcohol beyond my capacity to control it and in defiance of all the rules of common sense. I had an abnormal craving for alcohol and frequently succumbed to it at the worst possible time. I didn't know when (or how) to stop drinking. Often I didn't seem to have sense enough to know when not to begin.

Whether I understood alcoholism as a disease or not didn't really bother me too much. What I did know was that to stop drinking required a radically different attitude to alcohol and all that goes with it. I'd been voluntarily brainwashed over 40 years. I needed a thorough dry-cleaning. I needed a profoundly altered state of mind. Ultimately the revolution in attitude would have to come from within – but only with the help of others. It helped to be in a very different place.

That day I was brimming with a powerful sense of wanting

to succeed, of wanting to 'get it' this time. This heaven-sent opportunity was my last. Twenty-eight days can be seen as a long time in prospect, but I knew that in retrospect I would recall it as just a blink of time. I would hang on to every hour of every day, however often it became a pain, a bore or an irritation, which it did – frequently.

'Hello, I'm Ed and I'm an alcoholic. I'm feeling apprehensive, a bit foggy-headed, but also excited.'

'Hi, I'm Peter and I'm feeling a bit anxious and confused.'

'Hello, I'm Jill and I'm feeling depressed and I think I have a bit of a problem with alcohol.'

'Hi, I'm Craig and I'm an addict and I have no feelings.'

'Morning, I'm Mark and I'm very scared.'

And so on round the group of eight inmates and two straight-backed and expressionless therapists. This was how we 'checked in' for the morning group session seven days a week.

The 'rules of engagement' or group preamble had been read: 'We are not bad people trying to be good, but sick people trying to get well... no food, drinks or leaving the room... etc.'

Then therapist Will said, 'OK, it's your group.'

Complete silence except for the ticking of the clock.

Still silence.

My heart began to beat faster with embarrassment. Could people hear it? Who's going to say something? I thought. It's not going to be me, I'm a new boy! I'm keeping my head down and let someone else take the flak.

Silence

My mind raced. Is this some sort of battle of wills to see who breaks first? Come on, someone! I want to get well.

C'mon, this can't go on for an hour and a half! This is a waste of money – thankfully not mine.

Eventually Jill, who like me was in her first group session, broke the silence. 'Well, I don't really know how this works, but I'd just like to say that I came here voluntarily because I was feeling depressed, but having filled out a lot of questionnaires, it turns out I'm an alcoholic as well... but I don't feel like one. I mean, I may have a bottle of wine every day, but I'm still happily married, well, married, and I still have a job, even though I hate it at the moment. I haven't lost anything yet.'

The word 'yet' screamed in my head.

In a whiny, whispered voice that reminded me of an infants' school teacher, the other therapist, Bronwyn, asked, 'How does that make you feel, Jill?'

'How does what make me feel?'

'How are you feeling in this group, here, now?'

'Well, at this moment I'm feeling confused and just slightly pissed off. I reckon I'm being pressured into saying I'm an alcoholic when I'm not sure I'm ready for that label yet.'

'So you're feeling anger.' Not a question but a statement.

'Well, I thought I was just confused, but I am getting angry now.'

'Gooood, Jill. Just stay with that anger.'

Silence.

Craig, a criminal lawyer, spoke up. He was in his mid-twenties, vellum-faced, his painfully thin arms and legs tightly entwined, shivering and still in his parka despite the stuffiness of the room. He reminded me of a medieval monk who had spent his life in a dark cell – possibly even died there. He was addicted to heroin, among several other chemical exotica. It was his third attempt at rehab.

'I'm feeling like shit. I don't think they're getting my methadone right. I'm clucking badly. But I know I've got to "get it" this time. If I fail, I'm convinced I'm going to die. Over the last six months I've been to the funerals of three of my friends. I'm willing – desperate – to go along with anything that will get me off heroin before it's too late. Maybe it already is.

'At my last rehab I thought I'd done everything you're supposed to. I thought I'd got it, but the day I left I scored and, within days, I was back to square one... perhaps even worse. Please help me! Please show me how to do it!'

A high-pitched, whiny voice piped up. It was Bronwyn. She had a fixed, serene smile that suggested the exact opposite. 'Craig, you seem very angry. You may be very articulate and clever, but I think you're just talking the talk. I'm not convinced that you mean what you say. It all sounds like "therapy-speak".'

'Oh, for Christ's sake! Just because I'm not blubbing' – fists rub eyes in circular motion – 'or biting the carpet doesn't mean I don't truly feel what I'm saying. You have only known me for a few minutes and yet you say that. You ask me if I'm angry. I tell you, I'm fucking livid!'

'Goood... Feel that anger... stay with it.' Bronwyn remained serene.

A tiny speck of colour had surfaced in Craig's parchment face.

Another long and rather stunned silence. The clock seemed to have got louder. I'd positioned myself in the room so that I could look out of the window and watch the golfers on the course over Priory Lane. It may have been against the spirit of the therapy session but it helped me keep a hold on reality during the silences. Would a round of golf be more therapeutic? Probably until the 19th.

Mark, a City dealer, spoke up. 'Well, my reaction to what Craig said was that it came from the heart... I know how he feels.'

'But how do you feel, Mark?' Bronwyn asked. 'How do you feel about what Craig said? How is it for you in this group now?'

'Well, I know this is my last chance to get off booze, so I'm feeling very worried. I've been here in the Priory before. It worked for about two months and then I went back on the vodka far worse than before. I've had pancreatitis seven times now. I should be dead. If I get it again, I will be dead. I've just got to understand how to stop drinking. I'm just not sure that group therapy is the answer – but what else can I do?'

Then Bronwyn asked him, 'Are you feeling fear?'

'You bet I am... I'm scared stiff. If this doesn't work, where can I go?'

I nervously chipped in, 'I feel the same way as the others. I don't know how group therapy works but I'm willing to suspend my usual critical faculties and go with the flow. I also have an emotional blockage. I just seem to have a brick wall that won't let things out. I thought I was successful, but look where it's got me. My central aim is to stop drinking. I'll do whatever it takes to achieve that, but I know that the habit is very deeply ingrained. It feels hard-wired in my head.'

'You sound like a broadcaster, Ed,' Bronwyn told me. 'It's all very polished and professional, but where's the real you? I get the impression that you're just here to make a documentary or write a book. I'm really concerned for you that you will just go back to your same old ways – and we know what that will mean.'

'Thanks, that's useful.'

Will spoke in calm, reassuring tones. 'It's about getting back in touch with your emotions. Addicts use drink and drugs to blot out their feelings. They may have bottled – excuse the expression – bottled them up for years. It's important to get back in touch with those emotions, to understand your feelings but not to intellectualise about them. The answer lies in here,' he said, pointing to his chest, 'not in here', pointing to his head.

There was an hour and a quarter of this and I felt drained.

'Time has run out today. Thank you all. Shall we end in the usual way... with the Serenity Prayer?'

I knew this would come as a bit of a surprise to those in the group who were there for the first time. Having done rehab before, I knew what this involved. We all stood in a circle holding hands – usually sweaty from emotion – and recited the Prayer in unison. It is actually a profoundly useful nugget of philosophy – probably the most valuable piece of portable advice that anyone can take from rehab. 'God grant me the Serenity to accept the things I cannot change, the Courage to change the things I can, and the Wisdom to know the difference.'

The first-timers mumbled in embarrassment. But I knew it was something worth learning off by heart – not only because you'd have to say it many dozens of times over the next month, but also because it really does encapsulate pretty well all you need for recovery and life.

In other words, concentrate on those things in your life that you can control or change and let the rest of it go without any further thought. What you have no influence over – the weather, the past, randomness – just let it be. It has saved my peace of mind countless times since.

Cigarettes and coffee (decaffeinated) next. I needed fresh

air and time for some thought. Patients are encouraged not to 'isolate', but I reckoned thinking would come easier if I walked round behind one of the garden walls and cleared my head alone. I was already too mentally exhausted to chat. I was also the only non-smoker. I have never understood how I managed to avoid that addiction.

The next session, 15 minutes later, was an 'art therapy workshop' in room six. We all trooped in rather nervously, not knowing what to expect. In the middle of the floor was a pile of boxes in all shapes and sizes, surrounded by crayons, felt pens, coloured paper, old magazines and newspapers, sellotape, scissors, ribbons and glue. So back to nursery school then.

The therapists explained that the idea was to choose a box and use the materials in the pile to decorate the outside of the box with anything that you felt represented how you appeared to the world and what mattered to you. Then you had to put inside the box what represented your innermost feelings and emotions. Or at least I think that was the plan.

'There are no right ways or wrong ways of doing this, but the box must truly represent you. We'll give you 30 minutes and then some of you can explain their boxes.'

The therapists left the room and there was an immediate eruption of chatter and giggles and a mad scramble for all the materials.

There were some weird results, some ingenious and some just pathetic. Were they being made to fit in with what we thought the therapists wanted? Were they aimed at being technically ingenious or were they really symbols of outer and inner conflicts? One chap, Peter, produced a huge phallus made of rolled-up magazines. Not strictly a box, but it didn't need advanced psychoanalytical training to interpret it.

Well, the 75 minutes flew past. I wasn't convinced that the exercise had produced much enlightenment, but I thoroughly enjoyed it in a childish way and I was very proud of my box. (I'd drawn pictures of laughter on the outside and put dark materials on the inside.) I still have the box, but not the feeling.

Lunch back at the main building was always a rushed affair. I just had time to revisit my room, gather my thoughts, cram in some Cadbury's Dairy Milk Chocolate – my new addiction – and pick up a real coffee from reception.

The afternoon session began with everyone being told to wait in the corridor leading to room 6. We were all instructed to queue up and put on blindfolds. The therapist, Rupert, led the first person in and the rest of us followed by placing a hand on the shoulder of the person in front, rather like victims of a gas attack in the First World War.

Once we were all in the room, Rupert explained the exercise. 'You are now in a maze or labyrinth. You have to find the way out. Somewhere in here is something that will help you find your way out. Just keep looking. You cannot leave the room until you find it. Do not move any of the chairs – they have been arranged this way for a reason.

'If you find this difficult, if you are having problems or if you feel you are not getting anywhere, just stop and put your hand up. I will take this as a sign that you have asked for help. I will give you help. You can then take your blindfold off, but you must remain silent while others continue to find their way out.'

About 18 of us then began milling around the room, some feeling the walls and others feeling around the arranged chairs looking for a shape, a pattern or some clues. Some were just feeling each other. There was a lot of murmuring and giggling and this went on for at least ten minutes.

I heard Rupert beginning to say some names. 'OK, Craig, you've put your hand up and asked for help. Take your blindfold off and stand to one side. Say nothing… Right, Martin, you've asked for my help. Stop there and remove your blindfold.'

I thought, I must crack this. There must be some logic to it. I cannot find any pattern to the arrangement of the chairs, I can't find any clues and I'm not sure what I'm looking for. I'm determined to get this by myself. OK, I've searched the walls, the chairs and the floor… maybe there's something hanging from the ceiling. I raised my hand to check.

'OK, Ed, you've asked for help. Take your blindfold off.'

It was then that I saw what was happening. The chairs had been arranged randomly. There were no clues in the room and there was no way out. The only way to end the search was to ask for help. I hadn't intended to, but I'd done the right thing.

All those who had been put out of their confusion now stood to one side of the room. But one person kept going, thinking he could crack it. It was Don, the ex-soldier from Scotland. It was only when the laughter began to increase that he realised something was amiss.

'OK, Don,' Rupert said. 'I'll put you out of your agony. There was nothing to find, nothing to achieve. The exercise was to show you in a playful way that the best way to get out of being lost and directionless is to ask for help. It's the first step to recovery… admitting you cannot do it by yourself.'

'Oh, shit,' Don said. 'I think years of army training took over then. You've got to get things done by yourself and having to ask for help is a sign of weakness.'

The last session of the afternoon took place back in the main building in a large room towards the eastern end called the Barn. I think it had been one when the Priory was a private house.

It was going to be an exercise session – this time Tai Chi.

The instructor was an incredibly loud former US Marine who was built like a concrete gun emplacement. He was called Derek and had a huge, fixed, toothy grin. I'd noticed him at breakfast that morning piling up a tray with half a dozen bananas, the same number of yoghurts and several mini-boxes of All Bran. Not a man that did things in small measures. And probably not a man to share the restroom with.

'Today we're going to do something that even you weak Europeans with your stiff joints and bad teeth can achieve. It's called Tai Chi and it's a slow, graceful form of martial arts. Spread out and watch what I do.'

He switched on some relaxing sounds that involved running water and a rain forest with exotic birds and someone, probably beside a Banyan tree, playing a harp.

The moves felt wonderful and I was surprisingly uplifted. After all the emotion and brain-draining thinking of the previous six hours, it was good to end the sessions on a physical high.

After the evening meal the group members were required to attend a meeting of the local AA, in Fulham, Richmond, Kingston or at the Priory itself. For those who had gone through the seven-day detox, this meant being taken out in taxis or a minibus – the 'booze bus' or the 'druggy buggy' – to the meeting.

Being back out in the 'real world' always produced a rather adolescent, jokey, 'day out of school' atmosphere in the bus, with group members staring out of the windows at the bars, restaurant and off-licences and ironically salivating – I think ironically, anyway.

It was straight back after such meetings for a breathalyser test. I was never really sure at what point anyone could have snuck off for a drink, as the minibus driver waiting outside would have spotted them. They'd also have to have been pretty desperate.

My first meeting was the Tuesday one in the Priory Chapel, which I remember enjoying ten years ago. I had been to dozens of AA meetings before, so I knew what to expect. But for several new arrivals at the Priory, it was their first meeting and I always wondered what newcomers would make of it.

'Alcoholics Anonymous is a fellowship of men and women who share their experience, strength and hope with each other that they may solve their common problem and help others to recover from alcoholism.

'The only requirement for membership is a desire to stop drinking.'

Those are pretty straightforward aims. The AA Fellowship can't stop you drinking, but it's a proven way of staying sober once you have taken the decision to stop – its members would say the best way. What is certainly true is that meetings are extraordinarily welcoming and filled with love and understanding. Even those whose spirits have been hardened by years of drinking tend to feel the warmth almost immediately.

The meetings aren't about debating the issues; instead the time, either 75 or 90 minutes, is spent sharing common experiences. 'This is how I was, this is what happened and this is how I am now.' The format is typically a welcome by the AA's local secretary, maybe some group admin, a short silence for those out there still suffering, selected readings from the

'Big Book' – a weighty hardback tome that was first written in the 1930s by the organisation's originators, Bill Wilson and Dr Bob Smith. The secretary then normally introduces the guest who will take the chair and share their strength, hope and experience for about 15 minutes. After that the floor is open to others to get things off their chests and share their problems.

The process begins with, for example, 'Hi, I'm John, an alcoholic.' And then the assembled company will reply, 'Hi, John!' These 'shares' can be immensely varied, ranging from the repetitive, irritating and vacuous to the uplifting, inspiring and, occasionally, profoundly moving. Sometimes there is a 'professional sharer' who appears to have been polishing their 'share' at numerous meetings.

I went to one meeting where a bloke spent a good ten minutes telling everyone that his hamster had collapsed and he had devoted hours trying to give it the kiss of life. He had handled the trauma without a drink (or eating the hamster) thanks to 'the Fellowship and these rooms'.

Members, especially newcomers, are urged to find the similarities in their experience rather than the differences. I found the meetings were like panning for gold; there's a huge amount of waste material but some grains of precious metal.

Every day, all around the world, thousands of AA meetings are attended by several million people on a regular basis. Many of the meetings are held in rather dingy rooms and can initially feel depressing. In fact my first few meetings many years ago I found so dispiriting that I left and went straight to the pub.

The Chapel at the Priory was uplifting in its own right. It was packed with a cross-section of society and there were equal numbers of men and women, quite a few in their twenties and early thirties.

Coincidentally the 'chair' that evening told how his alcoholism had resulted in his becoming homeless. He had been forced to sleep rough on the seafront in Hove. I spoke to him afterwards and we compared benches and toilets.

It was a good meeting and I felt not only encouraged but also aware of the first stirrings of excitement about the future. The day was not over. The last commitment was something known as 'Reflections'. This was a time for all group members to reflect on that day, then describe their highs and lows and what was useful and what was not. It was kicked off by that week's group leader and then each group member in turn gave their thoughts. With no counsellors or therapists present, it was all very relaxed. Occasionally people were outspokenly critical of how things were going. Sometimes poetry was read out and farewell cards and presents were given to those at the end of their 28 days.

Finally, at about 10pm, the day was over. We would visit the nurses' station if we were on medication, and maybe have a snack of something left in the TV room. Our last commitment was to each fill in a short feedback questionnaire about the day's activities, feelings and progress, which the therapists would apparently read.

About a week into rehab I was sleeping well. Sheets and a mattress were still a luxury. Every single night I dreamed in vivid detail that I had relapsed and woke intensely relieved that I hadn't. Maybe my subconscious was trying to tell me something.

New Year's Eve 2007 was just another day of group therapy, workshops and meditation. During the group therapy session I'd broken down in tears and wasn't really sure why. I'd been saying that I felt an almost physical block to my emotions. I'd had to bottle them up for ages to get through things and had used alcohol to blot them out. Tears welled up in my eyes (as they are now as I think back to it) and I could barely speak. I would like to have really let rip, but embarrassment and consideration for the others prevented me. Even so, I felt better for it afterwards.

That night there had been plans to turn Reflections into some sort of New Year's Eve party, but it was never really a starter. Fifteen drink and drug addicts without their substances of choice, struggling with their demons, missing those that they loved, sipping lemonade and hugging awkwardly were not the ingredients for a knees-up. Anyway I can't dance sober. I can't dance, full stop.

I returned to my room and picked up a book that Mandy had given me – *Hard Times* by Charles Dickens. I knew from school that it was set in a place called Coketown. Clever choice. However, the title of the book should have been Hard Read and my concentration, still poor, soon waned.

Instead I made a couple of phone calls (mobiles were allowed in rooms). I thought back over 2007 which had involved living in so many different temporary places, eventual street homelessness, adjusting to divorce, coming out of probation, going bankrupt, rock bottom, the media frenzy, the strange experience of making the documentary and finally going into rehab. A year that had begun in drunken chaos was ending in hopeful calm.

Looking ahead to 2008, I had no idea what it might bring. Absolutely anything was possible. Things surely could only get better. I knew painfully what getting worse would mean.

I switched on the television and watched the New Year fireworks in the centre of London and then turned it off. Through my window I could hear the same fireworks.

On New Year's Day I woke without a hangover. I felt a surge of *Schadenfreude* towards those who had one. It was just another day at the pit-face of therapy. As a concession to the day, 'Meditations' at the Lodge was held 15 minutes later than usual. Meditations was for group members only and it was a short period of time devoted to quiet thought, though occasionally a member would use soothing words to transport us to a relaxing place. Sometimes it worked. There is a technique for ignoring extraneous noises, but I never quite developed it. The sounds of people sniffing and coughing were always distracting. I felt like giving them a good slap, albeit in a Zen-like way.

There was the usual group therapy session. No one appeared to be really 'there' – everyone was lost in their own thoughts about what the New Year might bring. It's difficult to focus complete and constant attention on group proceedings, particularly if the person attempting to unblock their emotions can't string a sentence together. I felt for their pain and maybe somehow it was doing them some good, but, since our only way of communication is through words, I did think that an endless stream of 'er', 'you know' and 'I feel nothing' was a tad self-defeating.

Always nagging in my mind was the same question. How does sitting around in a circle saying what you're feeling, or listening to someone stumble through their poorly articulated emotions, with very little input from the therapists, get you better?

Well, I never did understand how it does, but something did eventually change. Something worked. Was it a process of osmosis? Was it because, as I felt more relaxed and safe in the group, I could say whatever was on my mind? Or was it simply the passage of time in a drink-free

235

environment. Would four weeks in the Bahamas, a minder, good food, exercise and a pile of self-help books have worked just as well?

At the Priory, group therapy was the main part of the recovery process, but there were, as I mentioned earlier, other elements – workshops, art therapy, psychodrama, a few one-to-one sessions, AA and a few physical exercise sessions. Modest exercise, particularly walking, I've always found the best way to get out of temporary, mild depression, although it doesn't help much with clinical depression.

After the seven-day detox all group members were allowed (actually compelled) to join the Sunday-afternoon walk. It always took the same route (unchanged from ten years previously) down Priory Lane and into Richmond Park. It was then a sharp right, over the stream and up the slight incline to the duck pond, where most of the group lit cigarettes. There were usually about a dozen of us and the group, because of different walking speeds, stretched out in seemingly unconnected twos and threes. No one would ever know we were psychiatric patients allowed out for an hour with our therapist minders.

It was wonderful to get out, not because I felt especially trapped or claustrophobic, but it just felt good to walk, feel the wind blowing across the park, smell the pond and see what looked like 'normal' people. Depending on who you walked with, it was a great opportunity to talk things over completely freely without feeling like a patient. On each of the walks I noticed Gordon Ramsay, at that time featured hugely in gin adverts, jogging past. Amazing fucking coincidence.

I would imagine most people think that the Priory is like a health spa. It does have a gym, but that's it. It doesn't have a pool but residents, as long as they are not on medication, are able to use the one at the neighbouring Bank of England Recreation Club. This was only about 400 yards down the road, but we had to go by minibus, and of course had to be accompanied. We were usually in the water for no more than 20 minutes.

The gym was open only very sparingly and its regular use was rather discouraged to prevent exercise becoming another addiction. All that dopamine and endorphins could become moreish. I found the punchbag quite addictive.

No one was allowed out of the front gates of the Priory and, as I found, even getting close to them attracted the attention of the security guard in his little hut. There were CCTV cameras but they were more to catch tabloid journalists trying to get in.

The exception was the evening shopping run. The rule then was that you could go out only in twos or threes but one of those had to be the group leader. There were a couple of shops behind the Priory where booze could be bought. Later I learned that this was a stalking area for the paparazzi. On your return any shopping bags were searched and you were breathalysed. It wouldn't have taken much organisation to get round the precautions, but really, what would have been the point? Mind you, on one occasion when the gardeners cut back the shrubbery it was full of beer cans and small vodka bottles.

Although most patients were there voluntarily to tackle their addictions and in most cases were desperate for the therapy to succeed, there was quite naturally an undercurrent of scepticism and criticism. It was a sort of 'escape committee' mentality which was generally expressed during Reflections at the end of the day in the large, dimly lit Clarence Room. It was at one of those gatherings that a member of the group expressed her feelings about the work at the Lodge in the form of a poem:

THE LODGE (with apologies to John Masefield)
*I must go down to the Lodge again, to that bloody place over
   the grass;*
And all I ask is a stiff gin, in a frosted snow-cold glass,
*And the lime's zest and the ice-cubes and the bubbles gently
   rising,*
And a nice red and a Chardonnay or a well-chilled Riesling.

I must go down to the Lodge again for the call of Meditation;
To a clear call and a cruel call, that brooks no procrastination.
And all I ask is a bottle or two, or three, of Cloudy Bay,
And a shot or two and whisky Mac and a very nice Tokay.

*I must go down to the Lodge again to the psychodrama
   stage,*
*And the therapy and the Fellowship and patients venting
   their rage.*
And all I ask is a helping hand from a kindly fellow-rover,
*And a calm mind and a sober life when this fucking course is
   over.*

(Thanks, Jo.)

While I was at the Priory I was told that the documentary about me was going to be broadcast on 18 January and had been titled *Saving Ed Mitchell*. I was nervous about how it had been edited. I'd been told that more than 13 hours had been filmed, which gave plenty of room for different interpretations. I trusted David and Irene, but there was always the lurking threat of being stitched up. There were also parts of the filming that I simply couldn't remember. I just suspected they would be painful and embarrassing.

Five days before the scheduled broadcast, the *Mail on Sunday* published a two-page article by Carol Barnes on how she felt being the reporter on *Saving Ed Mitchell*. Headlined 'I Knew Ed Was a Briefcase Drinker – But Not How Close He'd Come to Rock Bottom', it went on: 'Carol Barnes on her bid to help former ITN colleague Ed Mitchell whose drinking has brought him to the brink of death.' The piece was generally sympathetic and balanced and I could understand – although not agree with – why Carol wrote: 'I have a nagging feeling that Ed knows he can "do" recovery. He's such an intelligent man and an accomplished performer that he'll know what he is expected to say. And when he says he has reached rock bottom at last, I'm not sure I believe him.'

Her final paragraph referred to the fact that I had suggested we have lunch, without wine, when I came out of rehab. She wrote: 'Later, I had the chilling thought that, unless his rehab is successful, Ed probably won't live to meet me for lunch at Brighton Marina. My great fear is that only then will Ed Mitchell have reached rock bottom.'

I would have loved to lunch with Carol. What I did not know then was that it would not be me who didn't live to meet at the Marina.

The timing of the documentary on a Friday evening clashed with an AA meeting at Kingston, and when our minibus got back it was already on in the TV room. As I watched it, with about half a dozen group members, I could feel my heart racing. What on earth would they think of it? There had been few emotions during group therapy that hadn't been exposed in the raw, but somehow seeing those emotions on television (and knowing millions were watching) made it seem that much more brutal.

Everyone was absolutely silent. I had to look away when the camera lingered, for what seemed an age, on me crying. I had no recollection of puking behind the wheelie bins. These were the days of my rock bottom, in all its degradation, on screen for five million people to witness. At the end of the last scene of me walking into the Priory, I wanted to shout, 'I'm doing all right! Things are going well... I'm off the booze!'

The final caption, saying that two out of every three people who come out of the Priory relapse, weighed heavily on the room. Nobody moved for some time. I could only manage to mumble, 'Well, that was painful.'

A couple of the group gave me a hug and asked if I was OK. Then I went to my room and sat alone until Reflections.

I felt embarrassed. I could hardly believe that the person I'd watched on television was really me. When the programme was being made I'd felt a bit of a spectator. Now I was an observer of that spectator. I just hoped that some good would come out of it.

If ever I took my recovery for granted, I would only have to rerun the tape.

I was coming towards the end of my 28 days. From the start I'd vowed to make the most of each day; to hang on to the moment and not wish time away. I was certainly feeling happier, calmer and more optimistic. I felt confident and lighter of spirit and, quite simply, was seeing things differently. But it was hard to fathom why. Was it simply the result of four weeks with a bed to sleep in at night, three meals a day, a chance to reflect on where things had gone wrong and the opportunity to be with other people in the same situation, in a safe place and to express thoughts and emotions that you couldn't anywhere else?

Or was it just the result of 28 days off the booze? Had more than 35 hours of group therapy, several one-to-one sessions, more than 30 varied workshops, yoga, meditation, Tai Chi, art therapy and psychodrama and a couple of dozen AA meetings really got to the heart of the matter?

Well, having delivered innumerable pieces to camera as a television journalist, I could only answer in the time-honoured, clichéd way: 'Only time will tell.'

But I was absolutely sure of one thing: if I'd still been sleeping rough, with survival the main concern and booze my only prop, I would still be on course to an early grave.

At my last group therapy session I had a good weep. I was saying goodbye to another chapter of my life and to people I'd shared a lot with. It was another one of life's 'mini-deaths'. At least my emotion ducts had been opened.

11

ALCOHOL, ALCOHOL EVERYWHERE, NOR ANY DROP TO DRINK

Twenty-eight days ago I had arrived intoxicated and relieved. Now I was leaving feeling intoxicated and relieved, but this time it was a profoundly different state of mind. I was heady with exhilaration and excitement and relieved to be going beyond the theory of abstinence and testing myself in the world 'out there'.

Was I up to it? Like most inmates who pass back out through the gates of the Priory, I had some niggling doubts, but an insistent voice in my head was also saying, Right, let's get on with the rest of my life. Never again will I walk back down this drive as an in-patient. Not that I'd ever get another chance. Failure this time and it would be curtains. No more Saving Ed Mitchells. Time to save myself.

Mandy picked me up at midday in her Smart car. She had gone through the 28 days without alcohol and looked healthier for it. She had discovered by herself that life was so much simpler, safer and cheaper without booze. And she had achieved it without the theory and expense of rehab. Some might say, 'Well, maybe she's not a real alcoholic.' My experience of being with Mandy was that she could tick every box in a questionnaire on alcoholic behaviour and symptoms, as could so many of the others that I used to drink with, and yet they might not call themselves alcoholics.

She had done it for her own reasons, but also partly to set an example for me. Mutual support – after-care, AA, keeping in touch, just having a coffee with a fellow traveller – it's all vital for staying on course. It certainly helped in my case. Long-term sobriety would have been difficult, maybe impossible, completely alone.

The media interest in my story meant it had been possible to arrange a rented flat about five miles west of where I had been sleeping on Hove seafront, in Shoreham-by-Sea. In my younger days I'd known the little town well – and its nearly 20 pubs. At one time or another I'd been to all of them, and once visited the lot during a long day's drinking.

Shoreham is cradled by the River Adur, bordered by its small airport, the sea and the Downs and dominated by the 12th-century mini-cathedral of St Mary de Haura. Now half its original size, this has magnificent flying buttresses, a beautiful graveyard and a powerful square tower that oversees the whole town. As I mentioned earlier, it was where I was married and our two children were christened.

I instantly felt the flat would be perfect; it was clean, airy and had a happy and sunny atmosphere. The balcony has a view of St Mary's, the sea and the river. The fact that it was a hundred yards from a pub I used to drink in every Sunday lunch and directly above the Beach Store, which has an off-licence, didn't bother me. There are pubs and off-licences within easy reach wherever you live. I felt no more drawn to them than I would be, as a non-smoker, to a tobacconist's.

The *Argus* was quick to pick up on the story and headlined

it 'Former Newsreader Moves into Flat Above Alcohol Store – The Off-licence Won't Be a Problem for Me'. The reporter continued: 'A former BBC newsreader whose alcohol abuse led to him sleeping rough has now left rehab and moved into a flat – above an off-licence.'

What? Is he taking the mickey? Gets out of rehab and moves straight in above a liquor store! The implication seemed to be that I had intentionally chosen to be as close as possible to my old buddy booze.

Not only was the flat very convenient for bread, milk and the papers, but it felt very safe. This sense of security was in part due to the fact that Shoreham beach is surrounded on three sides by water because of the sharp left swing that the Adur makes as it flows to the sea. In this way there's an 'island' atmosphere that attracts a certain sort of person to live down there. It was also sufficiently far away from all the old places I used to go to in Hove and Brighton – places that I now had uncomfortable, even painful, memories of.

It just felt so good to have a place of my own again after street homelessness and sleeping in at least 20 different locations over the past year or so. Money was still tight, and I still had to find a job, but the day-to-day challenge of getting food, alcohol and a safe place to bed down was over. Having a toilet and shower was quite simply a luxury.

The *Mail on Sunday* was still interested in my fate. It ran a story headlined 'Ed Mitchell Out of Rehab – and "Loving Being Sober"' which continued: 'His shaking hands now steady and his eyes clear and bright, Mitchell has made a remarkable recovery. Today his daughter Alex and son Fred will be reunited with their father and see him completely sober for the first time in their lives.'

It was a generally encouraging piece but, while I've always

happily accepted that journalists embellish, I winced at the words 'see him sober for the first time in their lives'. They knew and I knew that wasn't true. Like many other hundreds of thousands of alcoholics, I was not pissed all the time. It was a long, exhausting battle during which I would have periods when I got back some sort of control. Admittedly, in my case it was a losing battle and I had to ultimately surrender before I could reclaim my life. But it would have been impossible to keep a family together for 25 years and work for 30 years (albeit losing a couple of jobs) if I'd been drunk all the time. I fully accept that it all went horribly wrong in the end but it could have had a far more tragic outcome.

For my own peace of mind, I was never going to look back over my entire past life and see it as unbroken drunkenness. There were periods of sobriety and control – it's just that they were getting shorter. But simply dwelling on the bad times, just living with regrets, would be utterly pointless. Indeed, in AA-speak, I needed all those drinks to get where I am now.

Staying off the booze is, among other things, about constant vigilance and, in my case, reminding myself every day how bad things used to be. It's also about staying in touch with others going through the same experience. Before leaving the Priory at the end of primary care, all in-patients were encouraged to agree on an 'after-care plan' which can involve a 'halfway house', secondary treatment, weekly after-care, regular AA meetings, working the 12 Steps and getting a sponsor.

As part of my recovery I attended an after-care group at the Priory in Hove every Monday between 5.45pm and 7.15pm. Having had my primary care at the Roehampton Priory, I felt rather the outsider, at least for the first few months. It was a group that averaged around 15 in number; almost all had gone through their 28-day course at the 19-bedroom Hove hospital and seemed to have established friendships through group therapy. Most of them were in their mid- or late twenties, so I was by far the oldest. While almost all were alcoholics, a number were also cocaine and gambling addicts. A few had various addictive behaviour patterns towards food which drove them to bulimia. This meant that they would binge and then 'purge' by vomiting, using laxatives or diuretics or simply by fasting.

The value of the group was 'strength in numbers', or being able to hear about and learn from other people's thoughts, struggles, problems, progress or setbacks. It was also a useful forum for me occasionally to get a few emotions out. In a perverse sort of way, hearing about other member's relapses was among the most valuable aspects of the group. Not because I wished relapse on anyone – I know the nightmare, danger and self-loathing of failure – but because it was useful to understand how easily the demons can drag you back down. During my time with the group more than half a dozen relapsed at one stage or another.

Several in the group said they were working their way through the 12 Steps of the AA programme. The four-week course in any Priory hospital usually takes a person through the first two Steps. At that time a few group members were having problems with Step Three, which states: 'Made a decision to turn our will and our lives over to the care of God as we understood him.'

For those, like me, who do not have any perception of a personalised God who intervenes in individual lives – apart, that is, from having the rather nebulous sense that some underlying principle sustains the day-to-day existence of the universe, maintains the consistency of mathematical laws and appears to have moved towards a consciousness of itself – Step Three could leave you stuffed.

But it doesn't have to, and, more importantly for me, it would not have to if I chose to 'stay with the programme'. Since I was determined to 'go to any lengths' to stop drinking, it would mean I should attempt to understand the God concept. The AA's Big Book handily says this Step can be worked through alone, which was useful as I'd already done a great deal of solitary thinking about God and Death – for as long as I could remember, in fact. But it would be dangerous and pointless if getting stuck on Step Three jeopardised my recovery. It would be terribly counterproductive for me to say, 'I just can't quite grasp the concept of an all-powerful, loving God that is central to my sobriety. Sod it! I'll have a vodka.' To put it simply, not having a drink was far more important in the short term than 'getting' the concept of God. If I was sober and happy, the Almighty would have to bide His time.

For me the priority was breaking my dependency on alcohol and replacing that addiction with more positive behaviour. As a result there were many by-products – a return of smell and taste, clearer vision, and a better memory and concentration. Another side-effect was a 'spiritual reawakening'. I'd been out of my mind but now I was returning to my senses – above all to a sense that there was something bigger than me.

During my 28 days at the Priory at Roehampton I'd worked through the AA's Steps One and Two. The first step was to admit that I was powerless over alcohol and that life had become unmanageable – that alcohol had control over me and my life had become a mess. For many that was a difficult, painful and courageous admission. For me it would have been utterly futile to deny the glaringly obvious. The mess of my life had been made very public. I had my Step One on DVD.

If Step One was to get sober, then Step Two was about living sober. It reads: 'Came to believe that a Power greater than ourselves could restore us to sanity.'

Well, I had no problem with my need to restore sanity... my actions were clearly unbalanced. I was also increasingly aware that there was something 'out there' more powerful than me. The universe preceded my consciousness and will continue beyond my oblivion. There are constantly powers at work that are beyond my influence and control. I have learned to be more relaxed – even serene – about not being able to change the great tides of existence or accepting that sheer, blind randomness shapes the course of much of life.

I no longer feel 'separate' from the universe. I actually feel part of it (in fact, made of it) and that I should be here. If it's for a purpose, it's one I still haven't fathomed, but I am happy now to just float with the current and let events take their course – but in a very awake, aware and conscious way rather than an alcohol-induced dream.

It's tempting to think that a Higher Power did intervene benignly to get me off the park bench and probably saved my life, but, thinking rationally, that same Power could just as easily have allowed me to stumble into the path of a bus. It is only because I'm alive that, retrospectively, it seems as if my Higher Power was looking after me. Saying any outcome is 'fate' only has meaning looking back and is therefore pretty unhelpful.

But maybe it's not worth agonising about, particularly if agonising gets in the way of staying sober. The bald fact is that

I drank for 40 years, heavily over the last decade, failed many times to control it and was on the slide to an early grave. And now I don't and I'm extremely happy as a result.

So, something happened, even if I am still a bit fuzzy about what it was.

As for the remaining ten Steps, I could appreciate and understand, at the time, their value to many recovering addicts. But it was unlikely to be the course I took. I was coming round to the view that not 'working' the 12 Steps would not undermine my commitment or ability to stay sober.

To me, the Steps were helpful in the same way as an understanding of Zen Buddhism, studying world philosophies or reading a pile of self-help books. The Steps were not the be all and end all of sobriety − just another valuable source of wisdom. For me the beauty and joy of being sober was, and is, freedom from all mental constraints and that awful sense of something controlling and limiting me. Feeling the pressure (real or not) to work through the Steps and getting anxious about not 'getting' them, struck me as being counterproductive.

It was also, I think, a mistake to believe that being an alcoholic was such a distinct condition, or defined category, of human behaviour that it set the alcoholic apart from everyone else. I recall one recovering alcoholic calling non-alcoholics 'civilians' − as if they were a different and possibly lower caste.

Frequently in AA meetings I would hear the person sharing saying that they felt something, or did something, and then add, 'but I accept that *because I know that I am an alcoholic*'. And I'd think, Well, no, the thoughts and behaviour you've just shared aren't exclusive to alcoholics

– it's the way that all human beings think or act at some time or other.

Yes, there's a whole package of complex behaviours and attitudes demonstrated by those suffering from alcohol dependency – selfishness, self-centredness, deviousness, manipulation, grandiosity, childishness and so on. But it's missing the point to say that only alcoholics are like that. Alcoholics may be able to tick lots of boxes but it doesn't put them in an exclusive club. It would be a sad day if alcoholics felt so set apart that they looked down on non-alcoholics.

Putting it in another and more positive way, a large number of people who have no alcohol problems at all might find it helpful to follow the same path as recovering alcoholics – one of honesty, humility, service, acceptance and love. There should be a form of the 12 Steps for the general population, for Humans Anonymous. (Later I discovered that there is a Humans Anonymous. It's devoted to the recovery from all forms of addictions and compulsions, but I think even that may be too limited. I reckon there are so many other negative patterns of thought and behaviour that need to be 'recovered' from – selfishness, aggression, unawareness, cruelty, small-mindedness, cheating – the list is long. The world would be a much better place if everyone became a 'recovering human being'.)

What I do find difficult to understand is when alcoholics start getting competitive about their alcoholism and their recovery. It's not articulated as such, but often you can hear the sub-text of a 'chair' or a 'share' would be that their rock bottom was lower than anyone else's, their 'war stories' were more harrowing, their recovery was more miraculous than anyone else's and that their interpretation of the Big Book and the Steps was the most insightful.

At its extreme it becomes almost religious smugness, with the worst culprits quoting bits of the Big Book as if it were the Bible or the Koran. Thankfully it's rare. The humility that recovering alcoholics aspire to could well extend to an admission that no method of achieving long-lasting sobriety has a monopoly.

The love, acceptance and comradeship of the AA are very moving and valuable, but I'm just not sure about the rest of the superstructure – particularly if someone who is desperately trying to stay sober begins to believe that failure to follow the prescribed course, or scriptures, will lead to relapse.

But there are other routes that those with alcohol dependency problems can take – for example, hypnotherapy. Hypnotherapy appears to work for a wide range of behaviour and emotional problems, such as smoking, weight loss or gain, confidence, sexual issues and so on. It also appears to have benefits for alcoholics.

At the core of hypnotherapy is the idea that all these disorders are the result of holding wrong beliefs or perceptions of ourselves, the world and reality. These misperceptions, built up over time and mostly without our conscious awareness, gradually have a direct impact on us in physical and behavioural ways. It's when a person's belief system comes into conflict with the way things really are that emotional problems arise.

For example, a heavy drinker might believe that the consumption of alcohol is a necessary part of life and indeed of their own identity. Consciously trying to control drinking (and failing) can produce conflict and emotional stresses. That conflict frequently leads to increased drinking to cope with the internal turmoil.

Hypnotherapists argue that perceptions have to be changed. But it's not easy to change subconscious beliefs consciously and that's where hypnotism comes in. It's a tool to reach the huge and powerful subconscious level of the mind with the aim of changing a person's perception of themselves and reality.

Under hypnosis, or even in a trance-like state, the subconscious can be accessed and different perceptions provided without the intellect getting in the way. The system also tackles the emotions brought about by the conflict and is called in the business Emotional Freedom Techniques (EFT). This involves 'tapping', a method made well known by Paul McKenna, the author of *Change Your Life in Seven Days*.

As a result of the media coverage of my experiences I was contacted by a hypnotherapist, David Allen, who has an informative website and conducts therapy sessions from his house in Tonbridge.

David is a pleasant and convincing man who has used the techniques of hypnotherapy to change his own perceptions towards alcohol. For him, alcohol is no longer a problematic issue in his life.

I'm not a good subject for hypnotism, but I can now get myself into a sufficiently relaxed state – without alcohol – to be more receptive to new ways of perceiving things that are put across in a reassuring and repetitive way. David has made a CD that does just that. As for 'tapping', I'm not convinced. Maybe I'm doing it the wrong way.

For anyone who is really determined to tackle problem drinking, it's worth a look at hypnotherapy given its success with other addictions.

One reaction to the documentary *Saving Ed Mitchell* was: Well, did he succeed or did he relapse? Did he go back to the park bench? Did those predictions of an early death come true? The questions, and the doubts, were underlined by the caption at the end of the programme: 'Two out of every three people who leave the Priory suffer a relapse.'

To the production company that made the documentary and to ITV it seemed a natural possibility to have an update on the situation one year on. The first programme had attracted an audience of almost five million, thanks, in part, to being in between two particularly emotional episodes of *Coronation Street* dealing with the death of Vera Duckworth.

There was a good case for a follow-up programme on various grounds. Alcohol issues are never out of the headlines, particularly around Christmas and the New Year, personal debt problems were likely to get worse and homelessness never goes away.

The idea would be to follow my progress (or failure) as I attempted to put my life back together without drink. The plan was to interview my children, my mother and friends, to follow after-care, the various stages of writing a book and whatever work I got.

I was happy to go along with it because it gave me a huge incentive to succeed. Being sober feels great, but having additional carrots is a bonus. I wanted to show people that I wasn't a 'hopeless' drunk – partly as a matter of personal pride, but also as an example to others. I wanted a second documentary to show that it can be done.

Carol Barnes had done a professional and sympathetic job as reporter and presenter and her role had given the programme some shape and structure. So it seemed natural to suggest she take part in the next documentary, especially as she had had suspicions (quite rightly) that I might not make it. Life, however, took a cruel turn.

One Monday morning at my flat I was watching BBC Breakfast Television's review of the newspapers for 4 March and just caught a brief mention of that day's headlines. The *Daily Mirror's* front page was reporting that Carol had suffered a massive stroke and that doctors were saying the outlook didn't look good.

My first reaction was disbelief – surely they had got the story wrong or at least exaggerated it. I knew from meeting Carol ten weeks earlier that she was healthy and full of life. Later I learned that she had interrupted a skiing holiday to make the documentary and was due to go on holiday again soon after. She was a young 63 and when we last met she had come across as very relaxed, even serene. It just didn't seem possible that she could be so ill.

She had written an article in a local magazine, *Absolutely Brighton*, about her experience of working on the programme. The last line of the story was 'Please, Ed, don't die.' That was exactly the way I felt about her.

As the days went by, she didn't regain consciousness. It had clearly been a huge haemorrhagic stroke from which there could be no recovery. She died on Saturday, 8 March 2008.

The newspapers, radio and television reports were full of tributes and remembrances. The constant theme was that Carol was professional, unflappable and had no airs and graces. She was a level-headed person and presenter and always helpful to those new in the business, as she was to me when I first joined ITN. She was 'one of the lads' and, being committed to all aspects of the ITN ethos, liked a few beers after work. When I picture her in my mind now, she is laughing.

Her memorial service was a couple of weeks later in the Grand Hotel in Brighton. I was nervous and embarrassed about seeing old ITN colleagues again. I was determined to be there, but what on earth would they think after last seeing me as a vagrant, crying and puking on prime-time television? Given the sort of function it would be and the people who would attend, I knew the alcohol was bound to flow. It would be a rather high-profile event to relapse at.

As it turned out, I had nothing to worry about. Dermot Murnaghan, who I had known from our time in Switzerland and Channel 4's *Business Daily*, was one of the first to come up to me for a chat. We had shared many drinking sessions together over the years, but he was more professional than me in keeping alcohol separate from work. He has always enjoyed relating the stories of those alcohol-fuelled exploits – garnished with a side-order of creative Irish embellishment.

Generally people were kind and understanding, several saying something to the effect, 'There but for the Grace of God go I.' The eulogies by Jon Snow, Carol's former husband Denis MacShane MP, her son James and Sir David Nicholas were moving and pitched just right. They all, at one point or another, referred to drink and the final words from Denis were an exhortation to go straight to the free bar 'because that is the way she would have wanted it'.

I reckon he was right – that is the way she would have wanted it. And three months previously I would have needed no encouragement to be at the head of the queue for the first round. But this time the demon wasn't nagging at me. It was good to be with people again and I barely noticed the absence of alcohol. I was able to leave walking in a straight line and not having said or done anything I would regret. It was all so much simpler and relaxing being off the booze. Boredom might be a problem at some social events, but there is always the early exit. I had passed my first 'test' because, as it turned out, it hadn't felt like a test.

Filming of the planned documentary had been under way for the previous few weeks – a day here and there. Happily, the producer-director was once again David. One particularly memorable day's shoot was with my mother on Mothering Sunday. The idea was for she and I to talk as naturally as possible about how upset and worried she had been about the state I had got into and how happy she was that I'd escaped the worst outcome. The reality was exactly that. She is glad and hugely relieved that I'm off the drink and have got somewhere to live.

But would these genuine emotions come across in the rather intimidating and artificial setting of a camera crew squeezed into a small living room and a large camera thrust within two feet of her face? It can be unnerving and leave an interviewee tongue-tied. I was concerned that my mother might have a 'senior moment' and lose her train of thought.

I shouldn't have worried. It might have been the result of half a century of watching television, but she was an absolute pro. Even when there were technical hitches which interrupted the flow, she picked up the thread seamlessly. As she put it, 'I really can't see what the fuss is about being on camera, if all you are doing is telling the truth.' Maybe that's why so many politicians feel they need media training lessons.

My children, Alex and Freddie, had mixed feelings about being in another programme. They found the whole filming process interesting and enjoyed talking on camera up to a point – that point being where it just seemed artificial or repetitive. They knew what the truth was. My drink problem had got a lot worse in the later years, arguments with Judy had become more frequent and heated, and I had become detached and an embarrassment. Having a father sleeping rough was something they tended to keep quiet about. But they also knew that during their childhood they had had a loving home and two parents and lacked for nothing materially.

As Alex was quoted as saying in the *Mail on Sunday*: 'We had a perfect childhood, lovely holidays and Dad was on TV. Things were great. Dad was very much a family man. We had lovely Christmases and he always helped us with our homework.' The introduction to the same article began: 'His distraught children beg him to take the first step to recovery and give them back the loving father drink so cruelly stole.' And Freddie was quoted as saying: 'Dad is intelligent, but not intelligent enough to stop drinking.'

All this was true. They just found themselves a bit torn. They'd had a good childhood, so they didn't want to slag off their dad, but they also knew that I had to get myself sorted out. Their problem was, how many different ways can you say this and still sound spontaneous and natural without acting?

In the months since coming out of the Priory I've seen quite a bit of Alex and Freddie, who both live within a couple of miles of my flat. Inevitably they have a certain amount of scepticism about my recovery. Much reduced by a year of sobriety. They don't dwell on the possibility I might relapse because they know what will be will be and they've got their own lives to lead. Naturally I'd like to think that my drinking hasn't damaged them. Certainly they seem to have turned out to be well-balanced personalities, with sharp wits and a good deal of realism. Except in extreme cases, it's my view that parents rather overestimate the contribution they make to the way their children develop. My experience is that it's about providing a stable and loving foundation and then encouraging them to fulfil their potential whatever that turns out to be. It's a light touch on the tiller rather than endless nagging.

It's also about always being there for them. By that criterion, I failed in their later teenage years, and I regret that. Dying early through my own actions would have been an even greater failure. Being alive and sober has given me the chance to make amends. With any luck, I've got the next 30 years to do that.

As a journalist I know what elements make up a good story. When you are that story it can produce contradictory emotions. My prime aim was to go to any lengths to stay sober, but I was also perfectly happy to be the subject of a film. Who knows what might result from it? The slight downside was that it put me in a position that reignited old, habitual thoughts.

One day of filming, with Irene of Twofour as production director, was done on Brighton seafront near the Fortune of War pub. It was hot and windy, with the sun glaring down from a cloudless midsummer sky. The prom was absolutely heaving with crowds of drinkers at the dozens of open-air bars enjoying the weekend weather. After a few set-up shots of me walking through the bibulous throng, we did an interview at one of the beach-side bars.

Thirsty and surrounded by hordes of people noisily knocking back pints of beer, I was asked how it felt, six months out of rehab, to be in the sun in the middle of a crowd of young, attractive people who were drinking alcohol, laughing and clearly enjoying themselves.

The camera was rolling. Amid the hubbub I felt detached. How could I comment objectively on a subject that I have deep feelings about that are difficult to articulate because I'm still in the early stages of understanding them? Part of me screamed out to be young and normal again and knock back several guilt-free pints of ice-cold lager. The old 'sun-fun-beer' connection was still in there somewhere. But so was the reality of 40 years' experience. I was feeling old.

The camera kept rolling… Finally I began to say, 'Well, there was a time when it would have been perfectly natural and pleasurable for me to sit here and drink happily and thoughtlessly. Part of me would love to now and probably one pint wouldn't matter. But I know it wouldn't be just one pint. I'm certainly not craving alcohol because there is currently none of the chemical in my system. Picking up a drink for me is simply not possible and I have learned to accept that. For all these people it's good, normal fun and they're clearly enjoying themselves. Later tonight in the middle of Brighton, it'll probably turn ugly and maybe for some in this bar, in later life, it could also turn personally ugly. I just know it's a slippery slope and everyone should be made aware of just how slippery it is. It's fun now, but is frequently foul later.'

My answers rambled on and I was aware I was thinking aloud on camera. It was time to move on to the next bit of the shoot. I'd left word with Off the Fence that I wanted to meet up with Mike, who I had been with at Emmaus and on the bench. We drove west a couple of miles along the seafront to the Babylon Lounge, and there, on 'my' bench, was Mike with three other rough sleepers. There's something about the presence of a camera crew that attracts people and makes them behave differently.

It was good to see Mike again. While I was at the Priory he had managed to make contact to say he was in another Emmaus in Scotland and that he was off the drink. Judging by the way he looked, he was back on it in a big way. His eyes were watery and unfocused, his face weather-beaten. He'd lost a lot of weight. It struck me that maybe that's how I would have been if chance hadn't separated our paths in life. Overcoming any moral qualms, I slipped him a tenner, knowing he was skint and remembering the torture of not having alcohol. Mind you, all four of them were already drinking cider from mineral water bottles.

Mike was with Mac, a Scot, who had been in the Army for 12 years. He'd been shot in the leg and was keen to show me the wound. Mac had been invalided out and, now at 55, found it impossible to get work. His small pension made survival only just possible, but, having been a soldier, he said he could hack it.

Among the four men on the bench was a young woman – unusual in the homeless world. Kate looked in her mid-twenties, was reasonably dressed and coherent. But there was something about her that suggested there might be psychiatric factors involved in her homelessness. Her sparkling pink eye make-up may have reflected her desire to keep up appearances or she had recently been to a party arranged by some 'care in the community' agency.

The other man looked of North African origin, appeared to speak little English and was very reluctant to be on camera.

Mike enjoyed being interviewed and soon got into his stride. He spoke movingly of his alcohol problems. He said he had tried hard to give up and get out of the hole he was in, but, as he put it, 'It's like bashing your head up against a brick wall. I'm crying out for help, but nobody listens. I'll tell you, Ed, I've recently been thinking of suicide. When I look back at what I had and what I've lost through booze…' Then he turned to the camera. 'Did I ever tell you I lived in Eilat in Israel? I speak fluent Hebrew, you know…'

Shalom, Mike.

Off the Fence told me they are trying to get Mike into rehab. I got the feeling, though, that maybe, just maybe, he actually enjoys the freedom of homelessness because it allows him to drink.

Or did I believe that because I once thought it myself?

The light began to fade, making any more filming impossible. Although it was just after Midsummer's Day, a chill wind was blowing in over the sea from the south-west. Mike and the others had gone to the off-licence to spend their appearance fee.

As the camera crew packed up the kit, I sat alone on 'my' bench in the growing darkness. The now fully functioning blue neon sign reading 'Babylon Lounge' was glowing bright. The palm trees and rose bushes by the bench looked luxuriant. I can only put it down to my frequent midnight watering during the winter months. They clearly thrive on recycled cider.

Sitting there, it was impossible not to think that, without chance intervention, this was the place and the time that I would have been settling down for another fitful night's sleep with the help of alcohol. I would have been feeling a lot different to the way I felt at that moment.

It also crossed my mind that the last time I was here, six months before, I was being interviewed by Carol.

The documentary involved filming the various stages of writing this book – discussing ideas, contents, visiting the publishers and the build-up to publication. It resulted in the bizarre and rather confusing situation of being filmed writing a book about being filmed and being a recovering alcoholic while writing a book about alcoholic recovery, at the same time as being filmed with the writer being the subject of the book and the film but also trying to recover. It was important to have a clear head.

Being homeless did have some advantages. One of them was that it kept my weight down. I was often walking about 20 miles a day with a fairly weighty rucksack. I'd never found alcohol fattening, mainly because a drink tended to take my appetite away and anyway alcohol calories are 'different', aren't they? The result was my weight fell just below 12 stone (I'm slightly over five feet ten). I have occasionally wondered just how skinny I would have become if I'd remained a rough sleeper.

Now that I've got a roof over my head, don't need to pound the streets and am a lot more relaxed, my weight has shot up nearly three stone. Not drinking has had the opposite effect to what the generally accepted theory says. In the end, though, it could simply be that serenity makes you fat. Just look at the Buddha.

I've bought a bicycle in an attempt to burn off the flab and with any luck this bike will stay in my possession longer than my previous four. Mandy (who has, incidentally, lost a stone as a result of not drinking) and I have also taken up tennis. Could be a case of *Serving Ed Mitchell* rather than *Saving...*

When I was in the Priory I thought that, if I stayed clear of alcohol and did not relapse, there could be a job presenting video packages and live input on the web-based Recovery Network. Naturally I was, and always will be, grateful for the chance to go through rehab and I would have been happy to work with fellow recovering alcoholics through the Network. In the meantime, I would mention the work of the Network in any interviews I did. Dan had already got a great deal of free exposure through the many newspaper articles and the documentary – coverage that would otherwise have cost him many tens of thousands of pounds.

An invitation came through for me to be interviewed by Natasha Kaplinsky on *Channel 5 News*, which had also invited Dan along to talk about his website. I would have been very happy to do the interview (and meet Natasha), but my contract with Twofour for the second documentary precluded my doing any other television work, so I wasn't able to accept. I'm not sure why, but I subsequently heard that the offer of work on the Recovery Network had been withdrawn. I wish Dan well with his recovery and with the Network, which could play an important part in helping recovering addicts around the world.

As for getting work, I'm now in a much better position than when I was living out of a rucksack, sleeping on a bench and dependent on alcohol. When you're in the quicksand of homelessness it's extremely difficult to shine at job interviews.

I have fully regained my confidence and love of life, thanks to sobriety, and I have 35 years of professional experience under my (slightly extended) belt. I'd also like to think that I'm in a position to use my experience to help others – if they are at that stage when they know in their own minds they need it. Really wanting to is the most important step to sobriety.

Almost all the mistakes I've made in my life have been the result of alcohol. I reached a hard and public rock bottom, so I had no excuses left for denial. The sheer horror of a return to that life is my single strongest incentive for abstinence. Being in contact with other recovering alcoholics is a constant reminder of what happens to those who relapse.

I don't live in fear of that, though. Life is just so good sober that I want other sufferers to know it and enjoy it themselves. Everyone has to reach that point by their own route – but it's a well-trodden path and no one should feel alone.

Millions around the world right now are on that path. Many more are desperate to find it.

12

A PERFECT
MOMENT SOBER

I am writing this sitting alone in an old wooden and canvas deckchair set on pure white sand at the edge of a sparkling, turquoise and deep blue sea. A North African sun is beating down out of a clear sky; the air is being cooled by a gentle, steady breeze blowing in off the Mediterranean. The beach is virtually deserted. The only sound is the gentle, rhythmic lapping of the waves. I'm not hungry, I'm not thirsty, I have no worries and there are no insects.

It's a perfect moment. Nothing is missing and I don't want to be anywhere else. Why would I need anything more? For so many years my immediate, unthinking reaction was to have a drink – it would make a perfect moment even more so. Even now I can still feel a vestige of that old, firmly established connection. It was formed with my very first drink and strengthened by tens of thousands of connections over 40 years. It was a slow, alluvial build-up and, before I was aware of it, the river of my life had changed course.

It had always appeared natural that the best of times could be made even better with a drink and the pain of the worst of times could be anaesthetised the same way. The most boring of situations and people could be made to seem more interesting after a glass or two of wine. My own fear of being boring could be dealt with in the same way.

That thought does still lurk somewhere in my head. I'm aware of a distant, small, repetitive voice calling me to the nearby, palm-thatched bar along the beach. So what's changed? Why don't I get up and stroll along the sand and have a cocktail? Why stop at just one?

Several reasons: the most important is that I now know in sobriety that the 'drink thought' is exactly that – just a thought, and a thought can easily be changed.

Of course, when I was totally, chemically in the grip of alcohol, it quite simply was not a 'thought that could easily be changed'. It was a nightmarish, obsessive, all-consuming compulsion that screamed, shouted and raged until alcohol temporarily shut it up. It was a physical, mental and insane drive to have more of the substance that had created it in the first place. It was a profound need that would not, and could not, respond to common sense, intellectualising, logic or endless nagging.

'Look, Ed, if alcohol is causing you such problems, why don't you just stop drinking?'

'Yeah… If it was that easy, do you really think I'd choose to be in this agony? Would hundreds of thousands of others choose this torture?'

That's why that all-consuming iron grip has to be broken at all costs before anyone can deal with the real business of staying off alcohol – before there can be a 'spiritual awakening'. That vice-like grip can rarely be broken by the drinker alone. The sufferer must surrender and be, in effect, locked away – if necessary, in a padded cell. The agony can be lessened by a programme of detoxification. Only then can the business begin of learning to be, and loving being, sober. And there are many ways of tackling that. When the alcohol has left the body (after about 72 hours) the rest should be relatively easy – but it's still not simple. The campaign has to be fought on many fronts. But the best way to do that is actually not to regard it as a 'battle'. For me it has been a positive, enjoyable, day-by-day reconstruction of my world view through tiny changes in repetitive behaviour.

In some ways it's like tackling some forms of cancer. The tumour must be cut out as a first step before other therapies can be brought to bear. Similarly the chronic alcoholic must be cut off from the way of life, as well as the substance, that supported it, however agonising that first step might be. Really wanting to change is by far the most important factor. With cancer, really wanting to beat it is important, but, in most cases, sadly, not enough. With alcoholism, to have the true desire to beat it is to be already halfway along the road to victory.

Sitting in this deckchair with the breeze and sun on my face, feeling completely serene and able to happily ignore old, tiny voices somewhere in the background, it's difficult and rather uncomfortable to think back to the panicky, terrified, shivering, shuddering and puking state I used to get into.

And that's another thing that's changed. The old, powerful, immutable relationship between alcohol and 'good times' does seem to have been well and truly broken. I now associate alcohol with feeling like hell, with being out of control, with self-loathing and disgust.

It's a kind of Pavlovian thing, but without the bell or saliva. I was that dog conditioned (albeit willingly) to associate drink with fun. Years of fouling up have reconditioned me to associate drink with pain. I can look at a quarter of Smirnoff on the shelf in the shop and my stomach heaves at the memories.

I never want to go back to that bleak, desolate place ever again. Whenever I hear that niggling internal voice, it gets short shrift and I quickly think of something else. It can't sneak up on me and surreptitiously make me have a drink, because I know it's there, I recognise its voice and I know all too well its inevitable outcome. Sleep-walking through life leads to relapse. And to return to old habits of behaviour and thought is fatal.

I don't live in constant fear of a relapse. Living permanently in fear is no life at all. But I am constantly aware of its possibility – just attending after-care meetings regularly demonstrates how it can entrap the unaware. Every single day, at the beginning and end, I remind myself how bad things were and how good things are now and how easy it is to stay that way – just don't pick up a drink. For the rest of the day I put it out of my mind. I've made my decision. I'm not going to go over it again and again. I'm going to just let it go – and relax, one day at a time. All I ever wanted was serenity and peace of mind. I am reminded of that thought, '*If we have not quiet in our minds, outward comfort will do no more for us than a golden slipper on a gouty foot.*'

But I can only do and say that now because that distorting poison, that devious molecule, that powerful, cunning and baffling chemical, is out of my system. When it's not in my system I can clearly see the big con for what it is – just that, a con. It's a confidence trick that has been perpetrated over many centuries and in most (but not all) societies. The delusion is that you can only have fun if there's alcohol involved, you can only relax if you have a drink, it tastes good, it makes you happy, it's good for you, it's sexy, it's macho, it gives you confidence, it gives you courage, it controls your nerves, it makes you more interesting, articulate and attractive – but, of course, only to the person who's had the drink.

This drink/happiness connection is so deeply ingrained in the fabric of society that it seems as natural as water to a fish. It's everywhere, it's always been there, it'll always be there and life is inconceivable without it. I won't push the metaphor too far – we don't know how much fish think – but certainly alcohol is everywhere, always has been and always will be. It's advertised in all available spaces; it's sold cheaply; it's associated in films, soap operas, magazines and books with social gatherings, important life events, relaxation and laughter. Tinkering with alcohol taxes and opening times to influence consumption misses the point.

If alcohol were to be invented now, it would be immediately classified as a Class A drug. But it is here already and Prohibition would never work. It would just be driven underground and lead to widespread crime. Alcohol is here to stay. Humans will always love it and its effects.

From the age of 16 I accepted drinking as perfectly normal and acceptable without much analysis, in the same way that I accepted without question so much else growing up in Western society in the 1950s and 1960s.

My view was: It's obvious alcohol is fun, it feels great... everyone agrees. All the good guys drink. Teetotallers are weird. What's the point of having a party or a holiday without a drink?

It's a form of brainwashing where those having their brains washed are perfectly happy for it to happen. In truth, most don't know it's happening for quite some time. Very rarely did alcohol make me feel bad in the early years. If it did, I'd cut it out for a while, increase the exercise regime, improve my diet and take more vitamins. If it was affecting my work I'd try harder. If I made mistakes or upset someone I'd apologise and promise not to do it again. If I injured myself I'd take it on the chin. What's the problem? I'm successful!

The threads of habit became chains. I was looking at me, but the 'I' that was doing the looking was being deluded by the poison. It's a psychiatric disorder that tells you that you haven't got it. Then I arrived at the point where I couldn't cut the chains without help and a fundamental break in the pattern of my life.

Carrying on doing the same things over and over again, expecting a different outcome, is just insanity. But that's exactly what alcoholism is.

Of course, just being constantly aware of the dangers of relapse isn't really going to work by itself. In my case, thinking about alcohol, patterns of behaviour associated with getting alcohol and attempting to cover it up had taken up too much of my life. It was an exhausting waste of brain power that had gradually made my life very small. Not only that, the secrecy was making me sick.

Giving up the entire mad edifice was a huge relief. But it also leaves a vacuum, a 'hole in the soul' that has got to be filled. For many hundreds of thousands of recovering alcoholics this hunger is satisfied to a large extent by the fellowship of Alcoholics Anonymous. Indeed it's recommended by AA that a newly recovering alcoholic should attend 90 meetings in 90 days to firmly establish new habits of thinking and behaviour, and to thoroughly fill that emptiness.

I was happy to try AA, and I felt comfortable at meetings.

It was good to know I was not alone, but it was unlikely to be a lifelong, full-time commitment.

I can understand the value of AA and it clearly helps a large number of recovering alcoholics. I can also see the value for some of having a 'sponsor' and helping at the meetings, or 'doing service'. But I will always find it very difficult to ask another individual to sponsor me and for that person always to be willing to listen to my problems and difficulties. My recovery might be important to me, but I just couldn't face wittering on about it all the time to someone on the phone or over a coffee. Both of us being recovering addicts, the sponsor's advice and suggestions could just as easily be as flawed as my own.

This, of course, is heresy. The AA orthodoxy suggests that those who don't go to meetings, get a sponsor, do service and work the Steps are likely to relapse. In many cases that does happen, but there might be other reasons for relapse not related to non-attendance. Going to meetings is certainly no guarantee of sustained sobriety. Many regulars fall by the wayside, as the statistics clearly show. Those who relapsed at my Priory after-care meetings seemed to be the most vocal about the need to attend meetings. Many who have stopped going to meetings continue to live sober lives. (Entire countries live sober.)

The AA and Priory model states that alcohol is a progressive disease that is often fatal; that there is no cure but there is recovery through abstinence; that a relapse will inevitably lead to a swift return to out-of-control drinking which will be worse than it ever was; that the alcoholic demon sits on your shoulder, waiting for you to make a mistake, and will pounce more strongly because it has been exercising its powers during your abstinence.

That's a pretty bleak and frightening picture. I don't want to spend my life afraid of anything. I also don't really want to spend my last quarter-century thinking, obsessing and talking about alcohol except in the pursuit of helping others to deal with alcoholism – if they ask for that help.

Quite simply, despite the fact that alcohol is so deeply ingrained in society, I want to make it an irrelevance in my life. Currently I have no more difficulty walking past shelves of beer, wine and spirits than I do walking past the tobacco counter.

Naturally I'm aware that I devoted a large part of my life to alcohol; the past few years obsessively so. For a long time I felt in control of my drinking and held down a number of responsible and high-profile jobs, was married for 25 years and raised two children who have turned out to be good, balanced, happy and humorous members of society. But I did lose control of alcohol and it began to control me. That to me is not a disease in the same way we know smallpox, Aids or MRSA. How can it be a disease that only gets worse and has no apparent cure when the definition of the disease is so vague and there remains a lot of debate about whether an individual is suffering from it, but there exists the possibility of recovery? There is no cure but there is recovery. No wonder the average GP is confused about what to do – even if the resources were there.

To me alcoholism is a psychiatric disorder resulting usually from a long period of wrong thinking and associations that could have underlying, often unidentified emotional factors and that leads to a powerful habit and ultimately a full-blown chemical dependency. The way I see it is that in the beginning there is no direct, causal link between the chemical and the –ism. Otherwise everyone who has a drink would become an alcoholic. It may be that some people have a predisposition to becoming an alcoholic, but it's not likely to develop without the thought pattern, the belief system and the environment that together make it possible. And that's the good news. Those thought patterns, belief systems and the environment can be changed.

So, getting out of the trap of dependency needs a change of thinking and a change of behaviour. By change of behaviour I simply mean a person has got to do things differently, go to different places, possibly see different people, and that means thinking through how old behaviour patterns led to certain outcomes. Just to emphasise, in my case I could not carry on doing the same things and expect a different outcome.

The time spent drinking can, and must, be replaced by far more pleasurable, positive and profitable activities.

The core of the issue is always being *aware*. I know that I must be aware of certain states of mind and body that can trigger the old thought patterns. AA uses the mnemonic acronym HALT. It stands for *H*unger, *A*nger, *L*oneliness and *T*iredness – all of which can reignite the thought that alcohol can solve the problem. There is no problem so great that alcohol cannot make it worse. But HOW do you stay sober? Through *H*onesty, *O*pen-mindedness and *W*illingness.

I'd like to add my own acronym. Watch out for when life becomes a BITCH. It stands for *B*oredom, *I*rritation, *T*hirst, *C*onfusion and *H*assle.

I always knew that being *B*ored or being in a boring situation could be made to seem more entertaining with a drink. I would get easily *I*rritated by slow-moving queues, incompetence or bullies in uniforms and my first thought was a drink. *T*hirst, I thought, could best be treated by a pint of ice-cold cider or lager; water just didn't do the job. If I ever felt *C*onfused, I knew that alcohol would clarify the situation. (Yes, that's the madness of drink.) Also, I couldn't stand being *H*assled by anyone or anything. Being hassled for any length of time would lead to drinking.

Of course, life is still full of all those things, but, as Shakespeare wrote, 'There is nothing either good or bad, but thinking makes it so.' Boredom, irritation (or impatience), confusion and being hassled are all states of mind – just thoughts. Thirst is a physical condition and, without any doubt, water is the best remedy, whereas alcohol makes you even thirstier.

Nothing can get to me unless I let it, but to be completely on the safe side I try to make sure, as far as I can, not to get into those situations in the first place. 'Grant me the Serenity to accept the things I cannot change, Courage to change the things I can, and the Wisdom to know the difference.'

As someone told me one freezing night on the bench, 'If a cold east wind blows, put on an overcoat, don't complain about the wind.' You can't change the weather, but you can change your response to it – physically and mentally.

I'm still in the deckchair by the water's edge. A gentle, warm wind is now coming off gardens filled with the scent of orange blossom and jasmine. The sun is beginning to redden over the vast empty interior of the Sahara.

I am grateful to be ending another day without having had a drink, knowing that even in the smallest of activities I have done my best and that I will wake up in the morning with a clear head and thankful to have another day.

But my days are not now defined by 'not drinking' any more than the days of someone who is on a diet are defined by 'not eating'.

'Not drinking' is for me the outcome, the by-product, of doing other more positive things: reading, walking, writing, cycling, talking and probably more importantly listening. There's a lot to be said for just sitting and meditating.

The whole point is to put down, layer after layer, day after day, new patterns of behaviour and thinking.

In Buddhist writings it says, 'You sow a thought, you reap an action. Reap an action, you sow a habit. Sow a habit and you reap a character. Sow a character, you reap your Destiny.'

The thought sown in my mind all those years ago was that alcohol made things better. The action was I kept drinking. The constant drinking sowed the habit of drinking whether I really wanted it or not. That habit led to dependency and the gradual change in my character to the point where I had lost all my possessions, position and respect. I was losing my 'self'. My destiny seemed to be the loss of absolutely everything, including life itself.

It so nearly was.

The sun has set over the desert. There's a chill in the air as I write these words. As I look out towards the black sea, the randomly scattered stars glisten sharply. But I don't see the randomness. I see shapes and patterns which thousands of years of civilisation have given meaning to.

Looking along the beach into the northern sky, I can see the shape of the Plough now turned on its end. It has always been a plough and always will be; I cannot see it any other way. The last time I looked at that constellation I was lying on an old mattress in the rubbish tip outside Emmaus. At the time, focusing on the Pole Star, I felt I had lost my bearings and sense of direction. It scared me.

Now, I still haven't much idea where I'm going, but, far

from being frightened, I feel excited. I may not be able to control the future, but I am now back in control of myself, rather than being a slave to alcohol. There's nothing to worry about because I can make rational choices rather than lazy, befuddled ones. The stars may not lead me in any preordained direction, but their light shows me where I have been and where I am now.

The word 'destiny' suggests that life is predetermined, and follows an inevitable course of events. But it looks fixed only in retrospect. There only seems to be a set pattern, because that's the result of the desperate need to see shape and meaning, just as we do looking into a chaotic night sky (or a roulette wheel).

Anyone's future, however short, is a blank sheet; no one has written the script. Only a novelist can determine the ending of a life's story, and there is no Divine Author.

Einstein famously said, 'God does not play dice.' But that's because God does not play anything. He also does not plan anything. The roll of the dice is random, but, given sufficient rolls, meaningful statements can be made about them in retrospect. A trillion dice may be thrown, but the next roll is always unpredictable, thank God.

If what happens tomorrow is preordained, there's nothing I can do about it, so I shall relax and enjoy this moment. If what happens tomorrow is the result of randomness, there's nothing I can do about it, so I shall relax and enjoy this moment. It is supremely futile to agonise about the origin or cause of the next moment. I am just glad there is one. In AA-speak, 'Life on life's terms. Let it be.'

All that any human being has is the ability to consciously choose how to react to the way the dice fall and, if necessary, change that reaction. Neither of those possibilities (choice and change) is relevant to what has already occurred. No one can change the past or choose a different history, but through experience (mostly mistakes) you can react in a better way to second chances.

Choice and change in response to chance – the very core of what consciousness and free will are about.

Through millions of barely conscious choices, I made my own (very uncomfortable) bed and had to lie in it. Through the spin of life's roulette wheel I was given the chance to change. I shall for ever be grateful that I was still physically and mentally able to seize that opportunity. Not much longer and I wouldn't have been capable.

Standing on the sand with my feet cooled by the shallow water, I look out over the vast ocean and once again focus on the scattering of stars now reflected in the calm black sea. I know their distribution is chaotic but I can only see friendly pictures. Over there in the west is the familiar and reassuring constellation of Orion beginning to sink majestically below the horizon, followed loyally by the brilliant Sirius.

How fondly I loved those stars when I was fearful of the night on that unforgiving park bench close to a very different beach.

EPILOGUE

I F

If I hadn't had a career in the media, I would have been invisible and almost certainly stayed on that bench on the seafront like the others who are still there.

If one of the overnight charity volunteers hadn't also worked for the local newspaper, I would have remained anonymous.

If the main topic in the press at the time hadn't been the personal credit crisis, my financial problems wouldn't have made headlines. Having big debts and being bankrupt fitted the 'riches-to-rags' story.

If it hadn't been a few days before Christmas, during a quiet news period, the story wouldn't have been allowed so much space. Revelations about my alcoholism kept the story going.

If there hadn't been so much coverage, I wouldn't have been given a place in rehab and broken my dependency on alcohol and there would not have been a television documentary.

If there had not been a documentary, it would have been

impossible to get private accommodation. I would still be 'non-priority' and sleeping rough.

Without this miraculous sequence of events that resulted in a roof over my head and sobriety, I could never have written this book. If my homelessness and alcoholism had continued for much longer, I wouldn't have been able to write at all – or do much else.

Knowing and appreciating all this makes life so much sweeter. In a way it has had the same impact on me as a near-death experience. I am simply grateful to wake up in the morning and to feel that anything is possible – indeed just to wake up at all.

I am fortunate to have been given another chance and I intend to build on it. A rock bottom is a very firm foundation for a new construction. Having lost everything and with no apparent way of getting anything back, it's the small things that now seem so precious. I had nothing left to lose and that experience has removed any fear of losing anything again. It is a profound release to fear absolutely nothing at all.

Divorce, bankruptcy, joblessness, loss of all possessions, homelessness and alcoholism stripped me of everything I had. I got to that position through countless, tiny, subconscious choices – but maybe, just maybe, that's where I subconsciously wanted to be. It most certainly wasn't a plan, but it was the outcome of self-sabotage and the subconscious desire to get rid of the suffocating and frustrating baggage of life.

The only baggage that remained I carried on my back. It was the only real sign that I was homeless, but, given long enough sleeping rough, I would have begun to fit the typical image of a tramp – shuffling, dirty and leather-skinned. I would have been completely ignored by the world.

IF

I had slid into destitution thoughtlessly, but had always lived with the hope that there would be some way out. The escape would be through reversing all those thousands of subconscious choices – chipping away at the thick prison walls of bad thinking.

'Hope', 'chipping away', 'escape'. It reminded me of one of my all-time favourite films, *The Shawshank Redemption*. The central figure in the story, Andy Dufresne (Tim Robbins), is convicted of a double murder. He's innocent, but his behaviour convinced the jury that he had actually committed the crime and he is sentenced to life in Shawshank Prison. After a while he teams up with 'Red' (Morgan Freeman) and he speaks of his dream of being free and running a small fishing business on the coast of Mexico. 'Hope is good. Hope may even be great.'

Andy is interested in geology and acquires a small rock hammer from Red. In complete secrecy he slowly scrapes out a large hole in his cell wall which is then covered by a poster. Over the years, secretly chipping away, he creates an escape tunnel which connects to the prison sewer.

The near-final scene is set during a dramatic electrical storm. Andy makes his escape by crawling through half a mile of shit in the sewer. He emerges into the cleansing rain and, illuminated by the flashing lightning, he stretches his arms out wide in an almost religious pose. He is free at last. He is cleansed, reborn, resurrected. He is redeemed. 'Get busy living or get busy dying.'

He finally lives his dream in freedom on the Mexican coast and is eventually joined by Red.

Rather less dramatically, I felt the same way. Homelessness was that tunnel filled with excrement (literally so, one night). I desperately hoped that I would escape the trap of destitution

283

and the prison of alcoholism, but I wasn't sure that it was possible through my efforts alone. A miracle got me out of that dark place and into the glorious sunshine. I had been given a second chance. It was my Seafront Redemption.

The word 'redemption' is apt. It means to recover, to restore, to regain, to reinstate and, perhaps most importantly, to repay.

And that can only be achieved in freedom. Freedom from the slavery of alcoholism. Freedom from the shackles of penury and fear. Free to choose, free to change and free to make the most of the chances that life randomly deals us.

Free will and self-awareness are what make us truly human. To drown that free will in addiction and unawareness is to have no life at all.

I wanted to live more than I needed to drink.

Not just to exist, but to relish the intense, ineffable wonder of consciousness in every treasured moment.

In the end, it is all we will ever have. It's probably all there is.